Hiking the Big South Fork

Hiking the Big South Fork

Second Edition

Brenda D. Coleman and Jo Anna Smith

The University of Tennessee Press KNOXVILLE

The paper in this book meets the minimum requirements of the American
National Standard for Permanence of Paper for Printed Library Materials.
∞
The binding materials have been chosen for strength and durability.

♻ This book is printed on recycled paper.

Frontispiece: Autumn in the Big South Fork (National Park Service)

Library of Congress Cataloging in Publication Data

Coleman, Brenda D., 1947–
        Hiking the Big South Fork / Brenda D. Coleman and Jo Anna Smith.
        —2nd ed.
                p.   cm.
        Includes bibliographical references and index.
        ISBN 0-87049-795-2 (pbk.: alk. paper)
        1. Hiking—Big South Fork National River and Recreation Area
(Tenn. and Ky.)—Guidebooks. 2. Trails—Big South Fork National
River and Recreation Area (Tenn. and Ky.)—Guidebooks. 3. Big South
Fork National River and Recreation Area (Tenn. and Ky.)—Guidebooks.
I. Smith, Jo Anna, 1944–   . II. Title.
GV199.42B55C65   1993
917.68'71—dc20   92-37468
                                        CIP

This guide is dedicated to our understanding and supportive

husbands and sons who "made do" while we took to the trail:

Tom and Steve;

David, Jason, Stephen, Reif, and Forrest.

Contents

Preface   xiii

Introduction to the Big South Fork Area   1
   Rivers   1
   Geology   2
   Forest   3
   Wildlife   5
   Weather   6
   The People of the Big South Fork and Their History   7

The Big South Fork National River and Recreation Area   11
   Creation of the Park   11
   Directions   11
   Camping and Accommodations   13
   Rafting and Canoeing   15
   Hunting and Fishing   15
   The Trail System   16
      Horse Trails, Mountain Bike Trails,
      Hiking Trails, Trail Rating System
   Safety   18
   Backcountry Regulations   20

Using the Trail Guide   23

Tennessee Trails   25

1. **Bandy Creek Campground Trailhead**   25
   Bandy Creek Campground Loop   27
   Grand Gap Loop   27
   John Litton/General Slaven Farm Loop   34
   Oscar Blevins Farm Loop   38

2. **Jacks Ridge Trailhead**   44
Laurel Fork Loop   46

3. **West Entrance Trailhead**   52
Bandy Creek Campground   52
Jacks Ridge via Laurel Fork Creek   54

4. **Middle Creek Trail**   56
Middle Creek Loop   56
West Entrance Trailhead via Laurel Fork Creek   59

5. **Sawmill Trailhead**   63
Slave Falls Loop   63
Charit Creek Lodge via Slave Falls   66

6. **Twin Arches Trailhead**   70
Twin Arches   70
Twin Arches Loop   73

7. **Rock Creek Loop Trailhead**   80
Rock Creek Loop   80

8. **Leatherwood Ford Trailhead**   85
O & W Bridge   87
Leatherwood Loop   89
Angel Falls   91
Station Camp Crossing   93
Angel Falls Overlook via Fall Branch   95

9. **East Rim Overlook and Leatherwood Loop Trailheads**   98
East Rim Overlook   98
Leatherwood Loop Overlook   100
Sunset Overlook   101

10. **Burnt Mill Bridge Trailhead**   102
Burnt Mill Bridge Loop   102
John Muir Spur Trail   106

11. **Honey Creek Loop Trailhead**   107
Honey Creek Loop   107

12. **Historic Rugby**   117
    Gentlemens Swimming Hole and the Meeting of the Waters   117

13. **The John Muir Trail**   121

Kentucky Trails   145

14. **Bear Creek Scenic Area**   146
    Bear Creek Overlook   146
    Split Bow Arch Loop   147

15. **Blue Heron**   149
    Blue Heron Loop   149
    Catawba Overlook and Big Spring Falls   156

16. **Yahoo Falls Scenic Area**   159

17. **Yamacraw–Yahoo Loop**   163

18. **The Kentucky Trail**   171

19. **Kentucky–John Muir Connector**   184

20. **The Sheltowee Trace**   186

Appendices
    1. Trail Chart   213
    2. Backpacking Combinations   217
    3. Addresses and Telephone Numbers   222
    4. Check List: Mammals of the Big South Fork   225
    5. Check List: Birds of the Big South Fork   227
    6. Check List: Wildflowers of the Big South Fork   232

References   235

Index   239

Illustrations

Maps

Vicinity Map. The Big South Fork National River
and Recreation Area   10

General Location Map. The Big South Fork Area   22

Trail Map 1. Bandy Creek Campground Trailhead   26

Trail Map 2. Jacks Ridge Trailhead   45

Trail Map 3. West Entrance Trailhead   53

Trail Map 4. Middle Creek Trailhead   57

Trail Map 5. Sawmill Trailhead   64

Trail Map 6. Twin Arches Trailhead   71

Trail Map 7. Rock Creek Loop Trailhead   81

Trail Map 8. Leatherwood Ford Trailhead   86

Trail Map 9. East Rim Overlook and Leatherwood Loop Trailheads   99

Trail Map 10. Burnt Mill Bridge Trailhead   103

Trail Map 11. Honey Creek Loop Trailhead   108

Trail Map 12. Historic Rugby   116

Trail Map 13. The John Muir Trail

  a. O & W Bridge to Station Camp Creek   122

  b. Station Camp Creek to Divide Road   128

  c. Divide Road to Pickett State Park   139

Trail Map 14. Bear Creek Scenic Area   147

Trail Map 15. Blue Heron   151

Trail Map 16. Yahoo Falls Scenic Area   160

Trail Map 17. Yamacraw–Yahoo Loop   164

Trail Map 18. The Kentucky Trail

    a. Peters Mountain Trailhead to Ledbetter Trailhead   172

    b. Ledbetter Trailhead to Yamacraw Bridge   178

Trail Map 19. Kentucky–John Muir Connector   185

Trail Map 20. The Sheltowee Trace

    a. Pickett State Park to Hemlock Grove Picnic Area   188

    b. Hemlock Grove Picnic Area to Laurel Ridge Road   193

    c. Laurel Ridge Road to Yamacraw Bridge   200

    d. Yamacraw Bridge to Flat Rock, Kentucky   204

    e. Flat Rock, Kentucky, to Cumberland Falls State Park   207

Photographs

Autumn in the Big South Fork   *frontispiece*

Massive boulders and rapids on the Big South Fork   2

English-style barn built by John Litton   35

Log house on the Blevins Farm   39

Twin Arches: North Arch   73

Twin Arches: South Arch   74

The O & W Bridge   88

Bluff view of the Big South Fork gorge, with the O & W Bridge   120

The John Litton Cabin   131

Devils Jump   150

Blue Heron Coal Tipple   155

Yahoo Falls, with rock shelter   162

Preface

Whether you are a hiker seeking an easy morning stroll or a backpacker looking for a wilderness challenge, an opportunity awaits you in the Big South Fork National River and Recreation Area. While this area to the northwest of Knoxville, Tennessee, is hardly so well known as the Great Smoky Mountains National Park (the most-visited park in the National Park system) to the southeast, the Big South Fork is equal in the natural beauty and the diversity of experience it offers the hiker. The big difference between the two areas is in the number of people visiting the parks each year. The Big South Fork offers a seemingly untouched wilderness where you can scale a bluff and look for miles across the river and plateau without another person in sight. It is an area ripe for exploration and discovery. We hope that this guide will help you begin your Big South Fork adventure.

Acknowledgments

Several individuals gave more than generously of their time and knowledge in assisting us to put this guide together. We would especially like to thank Howard Ray Duncan, Interpreter, National Park Service, who is a lifelong resident of the Big South Fork area. Howard Ray is an avid history buff and naturalist who has hiked the width and breadth of the park. His knowledge of the area seems limitless. Dan Bickford, former Chief of Maintenance at the Big South Fork National River and Recreation Area, is another hiker and birder who always kept us abreast of park developments. Dan and his wife, Myra, gave us a list of their bird sightings. Jack Collier, former Resource Management Specialist at the park, assisted us with information on wildlife and geology.

The entire staff of the Big South Fork National River and Recreation Area gave us enthusiastic support from the very first mile. We thank you all. We value the friendship of the new staff members, treasure the old, and miss all of those have moved on to other parks or have retired.

When we began the Kentucky section of the park, we turned to Jim Thorsen, former District Ranger of the Stearns Ranger District, U.S. Forest Service. Since most of the park in Kentucky had originally been a part of the Daniel Boone National Forest, he was most helpful in obtaining information about the area. Also, thanks to Floyd Clark of the Tennessee Department of Conservation for explaining to us the activities of the Scott State Forest.

We were lucky to obtain firsthand insight into life along the Big South Fork from a descendant of one of the area's original longhunters. Oscar Blevins and his wife, Ermon, were gracious enough to share their memories with us. Since Mr. Blevins passed away in 1988, his interviews are now all the more precious. Herbert Smith, son of Alfred Smith, was also kind enough to share the story of his family. Local historian John Mason assisted us with several place names. Judge Robert S. Brandt, editor of the Sierra Club's *Tennessee Hiking Guide*, provided information on the struggle to establish the park. Charles P. Nicholson, Jr., a wildlife biologist with TVA, furnished us with the checklist of birds that he has compiled for the Big South Fork area.

Mary Ann Padget, an English instructor at Tennessee Tech who is also a personal friend, has given us invaluable help in editing the text. Lamont Ingalls, a former manager of Charit Creek Hostel, who has also had extensive editing experience, assisted.

Thanks to our many friends, old and new, who made this guide possible.

Hiking the Big South Fork

Introduction to the Big South Fork Area

The Big South Fork is located atop the beautiful Cumberland Plateau. The Cumberland Plateau is the southern part of the Appalachian Plateau that extends from New York to northern Alabama. It is bounded on the east by the Appalachian Valley and Ridge Province and on the west by the Central Lowlands.

Rivers

Cutting through the Cumberland Plateau of East Tennessee, the Clear Fork and New rivers combine to form the Big South Fork River. In a relatively short time—geologically speaking—the rivers have carved deep, sandstone-rimmed gorges. Tributaries of these rivers have etched deep valleys in the plateau. Semicircular sandstone bluffs with 100-foot waterfalls cap the upper reaches of many of the valleys within the Big South Fork Area.

As the Big South Fork River and its two major tributaries cut their way northward across the Cumberland Plateau, the relief of the land varies greatly. The most rugged terrain is in the southern headwaters, where cliffs along the river rise to 500 feet. Northward, where the Big South Fork River nears Lake Cumberland, the terrain is less rugged, and, instead of steep cliffs, low, rolling hills border the river. The main channels of New River and Clear Fork River descend approximately 11 feet per mile. The main channel of the Big South Fork River falls approximately 4 feet per mile. As water rushes downstream, it continually cuts away at the streambed. In numerous places along the river, resistant rock in the channel has slowed the erosion, making an uneven pattern in the streambed and causing shoals and rapids. Obstructions formed by rocks fallen from adjacent cliffs and steep hillsides, as well as large boulders that have gradually eased their way downhill, have also caused rapids (U.S. Army Corps of Engineers 1976: 21). The swiftness of the river and the many rapids along its course have made it popular among whitewater enthusiasts.

Massive boulders and rapids on the Big South Fork (National Park Service)

Geology

The base rock of the Cumberland Plateau is sandstone. Sandstone was
formed from layers of sediment deposited millions of years ago during the
Pennsylvanian Era, the geological time when small reptiles were first
emerging. A large inland sea covered much of the Ohio River Valley during
the period; the area around what is now the Big South Fork was comprised of
lagoons and low-lying marshlands. In addition to the layers of sand that
resulted in sandstone, layers of silt were compressed to form shale. Organic

deposits formed the seams of coal streaking the hillsides. The steep cliffs that rim the gorge are of Rockcastle Conglomerate, a composition of sandstone, conglomerate, and siltstone, highly resistant to erosion (U.S. Army Corps of Engineers 1976: 21).

Water has been the most prominent sculptor of the Big South Fork's landscape. It not only created the gorge and valleys but also eroded cliffs to form rockhouses, overhangs, and arches. As streams flow over a ledge of resistant rock, backsplash from the falls erodes the less-resistant rock at the base of the cliff, creating overhangs. At the same time, water is working in the cracks and crevices of the more-resistant rock cap above. Freezing and thawing enlarge cracks in the roof of the overhang. Eventually, large boulders and layers of rock break away and fall, creating protective shelters. Frequently used as temporary housing by Indians and early settlers, they became known as rock shelters or rockhouses. Arches are often formed when the back of a rock shelter erodes to the point that it actually separates from the bluff. The large arches at Twin Arches were formed when a narrow ridge eroded from the base on both sides of the ridge (Corgan and Parks 1979: 75).

The pothole is a smaller but often seen landscape feature. Formed where a pocket of silt has eroded away more quickly than the surrounding sandstone, potholes appear as hollow indentions in otherwise smooth rock surfaces.

The massive boulders that fill the Big South Fork River and its many tributaries were once part of the thick rock layers capping the plateau. Through weatherization, they too separated from the bluff wall. Moving gradually downhill as the soil beneath them eroded away, they have come to rest in the rivers and streams. This process, known as soil creep, continues to shape the landscape (U.S. Army Corps of Engineers 1976: 22).

Intricate patterns of reddish bands occur on exposed rock walls throughout the Big South Fork Area. These bands are caused by iron leached from the surrounding sandstone and accumulated in the crevices created by weatherization. Since iron is more resistant to erosion, the surrounding sandstone has retreated, leaving the iron ridges protruding from the rock wall. Sometimes yellow streaks caused by sulfur color the rock wall. The presence of sulfur indicates coal deposits. (Steve Smith 1986)

Forest

As you follow the trails along the relatively flat plateau and in and out of the many valleys and gorges interlacing it, you can see that the forest of the Big South Fork varies. Along the ridgetops you'll find a mixed-hardwood forest of oaks, both white and scarlet, and tulip poplars. In areas where the soil is thin, especially along weathered bluffs and in recently cleared areas, Virginia pine predominates. The forest of the Big South Fork is all at least second growth because the area was heavily logged from the 1880s to the 1950s (U.S. Army Corps of Engineers 1985: 8–10).

As you leave the ridgetops and descend into the valleys, you seem to enter another world. In the steep-sided valleys, the hemlocks with their graceful, spreading branches provide year-round beauty. Huge hemlock trees still grow here because the loggers thought they had no commercial value. The light gray beech tree, easily identified by its smooth bark, also escaped the logger's ax; it was considered too knotty and easily splintered. Although the large hemlock and beech trees dotting the hillside are magnificent, rhododendron is the plant most characteristic of the Big South Fork valleys. This glossy-leaved evergreen, along with its close relative, the mountain laurel, flourishes as the dominant understory plant of the valleys and gorge. A self-guided brochure available at the Bandy Creek Visitor Center assists hikers in identifying the many species of trees found along the Angel Falls Trail.

The forest is still in the process of change called succession. After the plateau and hillsides were logged, the first plants to move into the area were grasses and weeds. Sun-loving shrubs and bushes such as blackberries and sumac followed. Next, pines sprang up. As the pines grew, they created sufficient shade for hardwoods to thrive. Most of the forest on the plateau has reached the stage where twenty- to thirty-year-old hardwoods have begun to crowd out the pines and understory plants. Hardwoods predominate in a mature forest. As you hike the Big South Fork, you witness different stages of forest succession.

In areas where mining has destroyed the soil as well as the vegetation by dumping slag from coal mines down the hillsides, the Park Service is now aiding the process of succession. Reclaiming slag sites involves first covering the site with lime, then spreading grass seed, straw mulch, and a net. Later, Virginia pine and Black locust seedlings will be planted. It takes fifteen to twenty years to fully reclaim a site. (Cornelius 1987)

A wide variety of beautiful wildflowers can be found growing in the Big South Fork area. The trails along the river at Leatherwood Ford are especially good for enjoying a leisurely wildflower walk. In Kentucky, Catawba Overlook was named for its profusion of Catawba Rhododendron and the Split Bow Arch Loop is another favorite wildflower trail. Included as Appendix 5 you will find a partial listing of the more commonly seen wildflowers and their approximate blooming periods. Weather conditions as well as topographic locations may alter these blooming times. Typically, in the Big South Fork area, the Mountain Laurel and Catawba Rhododendron peak in late May while the Rosebay Rhododendron may not flower until July. Please remember that all species of plants are protected in the park and picking, digging, or collecting them is prohibited.

Wildlife

The Big South Fork Area is rich in wildlife because of its diversity of habitat and numerous springs, ponds, and streams. The sounds and signs of wildlife are common, but actual sightings are less frequent.

You may hear the crash of underbrush and see the flash of a white tail as a deer bounds away. Although the legislation establishing the park authorized hunting, and deer are hunted intensively, their population remains high. In the summer they feed on the berries and honeysuckle growing in cleared areas, while in the winter they eat acorns and nuts in the hardwood forest. You are likely to see deer along the roadside or in any of the cleared fields most of the year, except during hunting season.

Wild hogs roam the Big South Fork River area. You will often see evidence of their rooting and resultant habitat destruction along many of the trails. These hogs are not native but are descendants of Russian wild boar released in the Charit Creek area when it was a privately owned hunting camp in the 1950s and 1960s. Even though hogs are still hunted during big game season in an effort to control their population, their numbers have increased until they compete with deer for habitat.

In addition, a number of smaller animals live within the Big South Fork. Gray squirrels are returning as the hardwood forest matures. The Eastern chipmunk inhabits most wooded areas. While skunks are a common sighting, you won't see as many raccoons; not only are they nocturnal, they also have been overhunted. Your best evidence of their presence will be an occasional pawprint near a stream. You may be lucky enough to see the red foxes, gray foxes, and bobcats that feed on the rabbits, mice, and voles living in the open areas. Some areas within the park are leased to farmers in an effort to maintain open area for wildlife habitat (U.S. Army Corps of Engineers 1985: 21).

A diversity of animal habitat is also maintained through controlled burns. You may from time to time see evidence of a prescribed fire. They are carefully planned, set and confined to a designated area to provide new growth and browse for deer and other wildlife. Early settlers often burned large areas on the plateau to provide grassland for their livestock.

For years the black bear has not been able to call the Big South Fork area home. Logging and mining eliminated the mature forests and the isolation necessary for the female to raise her cubs. Reintroduction studies have been done, and if they are successfully completed, the black bear will again roam the forests of the Big South Fork. In fact, a few bears have been checking out portions of the park on their own!

(See Appendix 4 for a checklist of mammals of the Big South Fork supplied by the park, with notes on their habitats compiled by Jack Collier.)

The Big South Fork Area is wonderful for birdwatchers. Some birds are hard to miss, while others may escape the attention of all but the most serious birders. If you hike for very long, you are almost certain to be startled at least once by a sound like a jet engine taking off in low flight through the trees. Hidden by the underbrush, the ruffled grouse is usually not seen until it takes to the air. The loud hammering that you sometimes hear may be a pileated woodpecker vigorously attacking a tree. Backpacking or camping at night, you will find the screech owl's mournful call a spine-chilling sound. Because death as well as life is a part of the forest story, large, carrion-eating birds such as the turkey vulture often soar over the major drainage valleys. The remote overlooks are the best places to view their aerial displays.

Dan Bickford and his wife, Myra, seasoned birders and hikers, have catalogued 132 bird species within the Big South Fork Area. Although they have hiked every trail within the park, their most productive sightings have been around old home sites and the surrounding roads, fencerows and fields. (Their sightings have been added to the checklist compiled by Charles P. Nicholson, Jr., a wildlife biologist with TVA. Serious birdwatchers will be interested in this list, Appendix 5.)

Weather

The Cumberland Plateau is characterized by mild winters and moist, warm summers. The average temperature on the plateau is 55°F. The highest temperatures occur in July (86°F average), and the lowest in January (47.5°F average). However, winter temperatures may drop below zero and not rise above freezing for several days at a time. Temperatures within the park are generally 5 degrees lower than those in Knoxville, Tennessee. In addition, temperatures from the bottom of the gorge to the plateau may vary as much as 5 degrees. Nights are usually cool, even in the summertime.

Average annual precipitation is 51 inches. Heavy rains and flooding are most likely to occur between December and March, although summer thunderstorms may cause some flash flooding. The plateau averages 17 inches of snowfall a year (U.S. Army Corps of Engineers 1976: 155). Snow and ice sometimes force the closing of TN 297 through the river gorge. You should be prepared for sudden, extreme changes in the weather, especially in the spring and fall.

Each season offers its own inviting reason to hike the trails of the Big South Fork. The panorama of fall colors as seen from the bluffs above the river, the more revealing view of the landscape during the winter months, the abundance of wildflowers in spring, and the lush, green coolness of summer in the laurel-filled ravines—each invites you to enjoy its particular beauty.

The People of the Big South Fork and Their History

Although today you can hike for miles without seeing another person, people have been living in the Big South Fork area for more than 13,000 years. Paleo-Indians entered the area during the last ice age, around 12,000 BC. The archaeological evidence points to primarily seasonal occupation, mainly by hunting parties. The abundant mast from the forest's chestnut, oak and beech trees supported healthy populations of white-tail deer. Black bear, elk and wild turkey were other important game species. Hickory nuts, huckleberries, and persimmons were among the edible wild plants available for harvest. Native Americans would probably travel to the Big South Fork country to hunt and process these forest species for a few months in the fall, then return to more permanent camps or villages in the rich Tennessee and Cumberland River basins.

Most evidence of prehistoric Indian occupation is found in the thousands of rockshelter sites along the blufflines of the Big South Fork River and its tributaries. These rockshelters provided dry, protected, convenient campsites for our early ancestors. Rockshelters near springs or creeks and those with a southern exposure were the most heavily occupied. Today the rockshelters are protected by law since they contain evidence of the food animals, fruits, and nuts that these prehistoric hunters and gatherers ate, as well as the tools that they manufactured and used to process their food resources. (Des Jean 1992) As other Indian cultures appeared and declined, climaxing with the Cherokee culture, the Big South Fork remained a hunting ground. Despite abundant game, the lack of broad, fertile river valleys discouraged permanent settlement.

In the late 1700s longhunters came into the area. Historians have two theories about the name: it may derive from the long rifles they carried or else from the length of their hunting trips. In October groups of hunters would leave their homes in North Carolina and Virginia and travel to base camps in what is now Tennessee and Kentucky. From these base camps they would depart in groups of two or three, returning to the camp to deposit skins and pelts. There are several places in the Big South Fork area that were used as base or station camps. After a winter of hunting and trapping, they would load their pack animals and head home (Blevins and Blevins 1982: 22).

As hunting grounds moved westward, people from the seaboard states began to follow the major migration routes west. Some of these longhunters returned to settle in the isolated valleys of the Big South Fork although the Big South Fork area was bypassed by the two major routes west. Diverging at Cumberland Gap, one route went north of the area toward Lexington, Kentucky, and the other went south toward Nashville, Tennessee. Both routes followed old, established animal paths and then Indian routes to more fertile, rolling grasslands. The few longhunters and their descendants were the sole inhabitants of the area for almost 100 years (Howell 1981: 25).

Although the original longhunters continued to hunt the ridges and valleys, their descendants cleared the narrow bottomlands to plant corn, wheat, and flax. They were subsistence farmers who were able to supply most of their needs through farming, large gardens, and hunting. As they accumulated livestock, they fenced their fields and left the cows, sheep, and hogs to roam the hillsides in search of food. Because the mature forest covering the hillsides and ridgetops lacked the undergrowth of today, the animals could fatten on nuts, grass and cane. The farmers kept track of their livestock by notching their ears; Tennessee had an open range policy until the 1950s (Howell 1981: 34).

The communities that developed along the Big South Fork's tributaries remained isolated. Because the river's many rapids made it unnavigable, the people's contact with the outside world was limited to infrequent trips out of the gorges and valleys over long, steep, twisting, wagon roads. Most social contact was between families in neighboring valleys.

This way of life was only briefly interrupted by the Civil War. Some young men left the area to join the Union Army, while others remained and joined the Home Guard to protect against guerrilla raids by Confederate sympathizers from Fentress and Pickett counties. But in the Big South Fork area the Civil War was a minor occurrence compared with the changes wrought by the industrial revolution that followed. The demand for timber and coal led to the building of the Southern Railway between Cincinnati, Ohio, and Chattanooga, Tennessee, in the 1870s. The building of the railroad in turn created a demand for ties and gave an initial boost to the logging industry. Logging continued until the 1950s, by which time the area was almost deforested. Several shortline railroads were built to haul timber and coal to the Southern Railroad (U.S. Army Corps of Engineers 1982: 12). In the early years of the twentieth century, several large coal companies and numerous independent miners worked the seams of coal exposed along the ridges. The largest company, and the one with the greatest economic and social impact, was the Stearns Coal and Lumber Company, which owned over 200,000 acres in the Big South Fork area.

Mining camps sprang up on almost every major tributary in Kentucky. In Tennessee, mining was concentrated along North White Oak Creek, with some small mining operations along the Big South Fork River. The mining camps brought an influx of outsiders—both skilled and unskilled workers, as well as company managers. The Blue Heron Mine site and the town of Stearns, Kentucky, are reminders of this phase of history along the Big South Fork. Mining peaked in the 1920s. As the coal and timber resources became depleted and the Great Depression brought labor unrest, the coal and timber industries began a decline that was halted only briefly during World War II and culminated in the cessation of most operations by the 1950s.

In 1937 the Stearns Coal and Lumber Company sold vast quantities of land in Tennessee to the state. Pickett State Park and much of Pickett State Forest were created from these lands. (U.S. Dept. of Interior 1986: panels v-14, v-16). Additional lands were added to the state forest as the state acquired land from bankrupt farmers. (H. Duncan 1986) Stearns also sold vast holdings in Kentucky to the federal government, much of which is now part of the Big South Fork National River and Recreation Area. World War II briefly energized the economy, but its most lasting impact was the outmigration of people to work in the defense plants of the north. Although to an outsider subsistence farming may seem an idyllic way of life, in actuality it is a sunup-to-sundown, seven-days-a-week, back-breaking job. Thus, it is no wonder that the set work week of the defense plants with their high wages attracted many people out of their isolated valleys to towns such as Muncie, Indiana (Howell 1981: 28).

As mining camps closed, only scattered timber operations remained. A few families stayed, but on the whole the area entered a dormant period, waiting for the next influx of people and ideas.

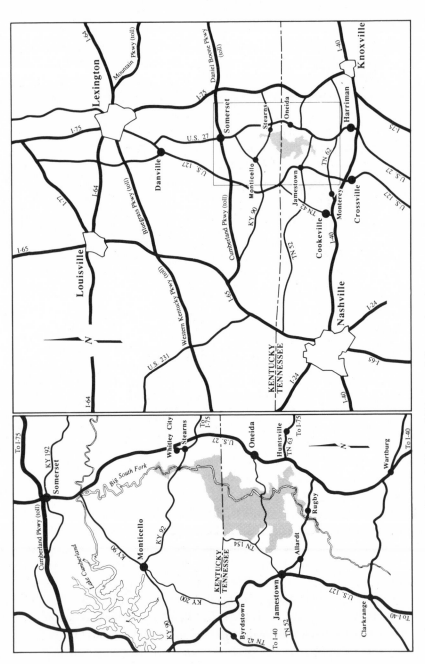

Vicinity Map. The Big South Fork National River and Recreation Area

The Big South Fork National River and Recreation Area

Creation of the Park

The idea of using the Big South Fork River for hydroelectric power was considered as early as 1930. A proposed dam near Devils Jump in Kentucky would have flooded the entire gorge. For thirty years conservationists and river enthusiasts led the battle to preserve the natural beauty of this wild river. Both groups proposed that the area be used for recreation. (Brandt 1986)

In 1974, Congress passed the bill creating the Big South Fork National River and Recreation Area. Its beginnings were unusual in that the Army Corps of Engineers planned and developed the park, then turned it over to the National Park Service to manage. Of the 125,000 acres authorized by Congress, over 106,000 acres have been purchased. Since the park is now under the jurisdiction and management of the National Park Service, that agency is responsible for further land purchases and development. As one of our country's newest National Rivers, the Big South Fork is truly a park for all reasons, a park for all seasons. (Wiggins 1992)

Directions

The Big South Fork National River and Recreation Area is situated on the Cumberland Plateau, which lies west of the Appalachian Mountains in Tennessee and Kentucky.

It is a ninety-minute drive northwest of Knoxville, three hours northeast of Nashville and only four hours from Chattanooga, Tennessee. It is also only seven hours from Cincinnati, Ohio or Louisville, Kentucky.

Travelers on I-40 west bound from Knoxville have several options. You may take the Jamestown-Crossville exit onto U.S. 127. Take U.S. 127 north thirty-six miles into Jamestown. North of Jamestown, take TN Hwy. 154 north to the intersection of TN Hwy. 297. Follow 297 into the park. Before you reach the river you will see the two-mile spur road that leads to the Bandy Creek Campground and Visitor Center. It will be approximately 24 miles from Jamestown.

While the above route eliminates the 13% grade through the river gorge, other routes from west Knoxville are shorter. You may opt for the Oak Ridge exit and take TN Hwy. 62 to its intersection with U.S. 27 in Wartburg. Follow U.S. 27 north to Oneida and then turn left onto TN Hwy. 297 west to enter the park. (U.S. 27 can also be picked up at the Harriman exit off I-40.)

Coming from the Nashville area, I-40 east bound travelers will find it shorter to take the Jamestown-Monterey exit over to TN Hwy. 62 and follow TN 62 for sixteen miles to the intersection of U. S. 127. Turn left and follow U.S. 127 for approximately 18 miles to Jamestown. From Jamestown, continue on to the park by following the directions above.

For travelers north bound on I-75 wanting to come into the Tennessee portion of the park, take the Huntsville-Oneida exit onto TN. Hwy 63. Follow TN 63, the Howard Baker Memorial Highway for 21 miles through Baker's hometown of Huntsville to U.S. 27. Turn right on U.S. 27 and drive north 7 miles to Oneida. At the first traffic light, turn left or west onto TN Hwy. 297 and follow the signs for approximately 15 miles to the park.

Travelers headed to the Blue Heron Campground in Kentucky should remain north on U.S. 27 through Oneida and turn onto KY Hwy. 92 west near Stearns. Out of Stearns, take 1651 to Revelo where you will turn onto KY Hwy. 742 and follow it to the campground.

South bound travelers on I-75 also have several options. You may exit at Mt. Vernon and take KY Hwy. 461 to KY Hwy. 80. Follow KY Hwy. 80 into Somerset and then take U.S. 27 south. For the Kentucky portion of the park you will want to take KY Hwy. 92 west to Stearns and follow the directions above. For the Tennessee portion of the park, continue south to Oneida and then take TN Hwy. 297 west.

Other I-75 south bound exits are as follows: Take U.S. 25W at Corbin, Kentucky, to KY Hwy. 90. Follow KY 90 through Cumberland Falls State Park and on to U.S. 27 south. For Blue Heron, turn west on KY 92 but for Bandy Creek, continue on to TN 297 west in Oneida. A scenic, but curvy route across KY Hwy. 92 from Williamsburg also leads to U.S. 27.

WARNING: When you enter the Big South Fork from the east on TN Hwy. 297 you must negotiate 13% grades and hairpin turns both up and downhill as you cross the river gorge to reach the Bandy Creek Campground and Visitor Center. Large RVs or vehicles pulling heavy trailers may want to consider entering the park from the west.

ATTENTION: Please note that the Eastern/Central time line divides the Big South Fork. The park operates on Eastern time.

Camping and Accommodations

Two large developed campgrounds are located within the boundaries of the Big South Fork. Bandy Creek Campground in Tennessee is located off TN 297 (the Leatherwood Ford Road). A large sign on TN 297 west of the river gorge directs you to the 2-mile-long road leading to the campground. The Blue Heron Campground is located west of Revelo on KY 742 in the Kentucky portion of the park.

Adjacent to the Visitor Center, the Bandy Creek Campground provides 100 developed sites with hookups for RVs, 50 improved sites for tent camping, and two large group sites with cooking shelters. Conveniently located throughout the campground are bathhouses with hot water showers. The large pool with nearby volleyball court and playground attracts swimmers. With the 1991 completion of the Park Headquarters building on the east side of the river, the reopening of a camp store at Bandy Creek may soon be a reality. The Bandy Creek Campground is open year round. The Visitor Center is closed only on Christmas Day; however, operating hours are usually shortened during the winter months.

Blue Heron, a smaller campground, offers 45 campsites with water and a bathhouse. Future plans include electricity at each site. The campground is within walking distance of the Blue Heron Visitor Complex, which houses exhibits, a snack bar, and a terminus for the Big South Fork Scenic Railway. All campsites within the Big South Fork Area, except for the group sites, are on a first-come first-served basis. A campground fee is charged at Bandy Creek and Blue Heron.

A small camping area at Alum Ford on KY 700 offers sites with tables, grills, and pit toilets. This area was originally a Forest Service Campground but is now maintained and administered by the Big South Fork National River and Recreation Area. Alum Ford also has a boat launching ramp.

Great Meadow Campground, a well-maintained U.S. Forest Service campground with improved campsites and pit toilets, is located on the north bank of Rock Creek. You can drive to it from the east by following the signs from the Yamacraw Bridge on KY 92. From the west you drive past Pickett State Park on TN 154. Just past the Kentucky state line a road to the right leads into the Daniel Boone National Forest. Follow the signs past the Hemlock Grove Picnic Area to the campground. When hiking, you must ford Rock Creek to reach Great Meadow Campground from the Sheltowee Trace.

Primitive camping is allowed throughout the Big South Fork Area except in areas designated as non-camping and within the yellow safety zones surrounding Bandy Creek and Blue Heron campgrounds. See page 20 for backcountry camping regulations.

Charit Creek Lodge, operated by a National Park Service concessionaire, provides year around lodging for hikers as well as horseback and mountain bike riders. The renovated lodge has bunk space for twelve in each of two large rooms as well as two separate cabins that also sleep twelve. Full meal service is optional, along with limited use of a fully equipped kitchen. Full service is not available during the winter months. Check with the Charit Creek Reservation Office at (615) 429-5704 for current information and reservations. The closest vehicle access to Charit Creek Lodge is the hiking trailhead on Fork Ridge Road. To reach this trailhead, take TN 297 west to TN 154. Go north 1.8 miles on TN 154. Turn right onto Divide Road. From here it will be 6 miles to the trailhead. Follow Divide Road past Middle Creek Trailhead. Turn right onto Fork Ridge Road and follow it past Sawmill Trailhead. Immediately past Sawmill Trailhead go left at the fork, obviously the main road, and continue for 3.8 miles. One-quarter mile before reaching the hiking trailhead you will pass the horse trailhead. A steep 0.8-mile trail leads down to Charit Creek Lodge. WARNING: Expect to get your feet wet crossing Station Camp Creek during periods of higher water. Do not attempt a crossing if the creek is high and running fast. A dryer and more popular route to the lodge is by way of the Twin Arches. See the Twin Arches Trailhead on page 70 for directions.

Pickett State Park, west of the Big South Fork Area on TN 154, offers beautiful campsites, a bathhouse, a recreation building, a swimming area, a playground, and tennis courts. At Pickett State Park you may also rent cabins and chalets.

The historic community of Rugby, on TN 52 at the southern end of the Big South Fork area, offers accommodations in a restored Victorian inn and cottage. Single or double rooms and accommodations for families or small groups are available year-round. You can dine in a Victorian setting at the Harrow Road Cafe.

Cumberland Falls State Park, on KY 92 at Corbin, Kentucky, is at the northern end of the portion of the Sheltowee Trace we describe in this guide. Established in 1930, this resort park offers a lodge, dining room, campground, grocery store, swimming pool, game room, tennis court, and museum.

The Bandy Creek Visitor can provide you with current information on private campgrounds, motels and restaurants near the Big South Fork area. Addresses and telephone numbers for the above accommodations can be found in Appendix 3 on page 222.

Rafting and Canoeing

Whitewater rafting is a popular activity on the Big South Fork. Several outfitters are licensed by the National Park Service to provide guided raft trips on the river. Many trips are planned for the gorge area between Burnt Mill Bridge and Leatherwood Ford, taking rafters through Class III and IV rapids with names such as Double Falls, Washing Machine, and the "E11." According to the American Red Cross, rapids rated as Class III and IV have very turbulent water, require precise maneuvering, and require scouting from the shore. Less difficult trips may be adapted to the varying skills of particular groups. Some outfitters also offer canoe and tube rentals, shuttle service, mountain bike rentals, and rock climbing.

A current listing of outfitters having commercial use license for the Big South Fork and their services may be obtained from the Bandy Creek Visitor Center. (See Appendix 3 for the 1992 listing.)

Please check with the Visitor Center or a Park Ranger before paddling the Big South Fork. They can advise you on current water levels (CFS) and sections suitable for your skill level. A*lways* wear a PFD or life jacket on *all sections* of the river (this includes tubing!), and a helmet is strongly advised for the more difficult runs. Since the Big South Fork is a free-flowing river, rafting and canoeing is limited to appropriate water levels.

Hunting and Fishing

A national recreation area offers a wide variety of outdoor activity, including hunting and fishing. Regulations within the park follow the guidelines set by the states of Tennessee and Kentucky. For a current copy of these regulations and hunting seasons, write or call the Tennessee Wildlife Resources Agency, and the Kentucky Department of Fish and Wildlife Resources. See Appendix 3.

A valid state license is required when hunting or fishing in each respective state. Tennessee and Kentucky do not have reciprocal agreements. While the Visitor Center does not sell licenses, they may be obtained from various establishments outside the park.

Additional regulations enforced by the National Park Service include the following:

1. No carrying of firearms unless actively engaged in hunting.
2. No discharging of firearms except in the taking of game; for example, no target practice is allowed.

3. Observe the no-hunting zones around park developments as designated by yellow bands on the trees.
4. Use portable tree stands only; no permanent structures may be attached to trees.
5. When transporting firearms by vehicle, boat, or horse, keep the gun inaccessible, unloaded, and rendered temporarily inoperable.
6. Observing wildlife by using artificial lighting, such as car lights, is prohibited even for non-hunters. Conditioning the animals not to fear the lights makes them unfair game. Poaching hurts hunting for everyone.

Please report any hunting violations. In Tennessee, call 1-800-255-TWRA to report violations. In Kentucky, call 1-800-25 ALERT.

Fishermen should follow respective state regulations. The gathering and collecting of mussels is prohibited as some are on the endangered species list.

You may obtain a complete list of National Park Service regulations including safety zones at the Bandy Creek or Blue Heron Visitor Center, or write to the Big South Fork National River and Recreation Area, Rt. 3, Box 401, Oneida, TN 37841.

Be warned: Laws regarding vehicular traffic, firearms, and alcoholic beverages are strictly enforced.

The Trail System

Horse Trails

Horseback riding is a popular activity in the Big South Fork Area. There are over 130 miles of blazed horse trails within the park.

The Bandy Creek Stables, a park concessionaire, not only provides short term stall rental and a tack shop, they also offer horse rentals with guided trips ranging from one hour to two or three day trips. Charit Creek Lodge also offers stabling facilities. (See Appendix 3 for addresses and telephone numbers.) Horse trailheads with large parking areas to accommodate vehicles and trailers are located throughout the park. All riders bringing horses into the park must have proof of a current Coggins test. Horse trails are blazed with a yellow horsehead on white and horses may not ride cross-country.

Mountain Bike Trails

Ever increasing in popularity are the newly developed mountain bike trails. Maps of these trails are available from the Bandy Creek Visitor Center. Bikers may use the horse trails, with first consideration given to horseback riders. Mountain bikers and hikers encountering horses should stand in the open where they can be easily seen and speak out to the passing riders since horses are used to human voices. (Linder 1992) Bikers may also ride the hundreds of miles of old logging roads. The O&W Railroad grade is very popular with mountain bikers. Bicycles are *NOT* allowed on the hiking trails which are blazed with the red arrowhead or the blue silhouette of John Muir. (Exceptions are noted when specific portions of trail are blazed or marked as dual purpose, e.g. Collier Ridge Loop.)

Hiking Trails

From a short, easy walk through the woods to a strenuous backpacking trip, the Big South Fork Area has a trail that is right for you.

Over 200 miles of hiking trails have been cleared and blazed within the park. The John Muir Trail, a Tennessee Scenic Trail, covers 40 miles within the Big South Fork National River and Recreation Area before entering Pickett State Forest. It is blazed with a blue silhouette on white. The 254-mile Sheltowee Trace originates in Pickett State Park and passes through both the Big South Fork National River and Recreation Area and the Daniel Boone National Forest. Our book covers the Sheltowee Trace from Pickett State Park in Tennessee to Cumberland Falls State Park in Kentucky. The Sheltowee Trace is blazed with either a white turtle or white diamond. All other trails within the Big South Fork Area are blazed with a red arrowhead on white. (Some spur trails may use a different colored arrowhead to distinguish them from the main trail.)

Trail Rating System

We have personally hiked and measured each trail included in this guide, describing and rating it to the best of our knowledge. Of course, our ratings are of necessity somewhat arbitrary: A person in excellent physical condition may consider the ratings too stringent, while another, less fit, individual may feel that they underestimate the difficulty of the trails. Using the following guidelines, we have tried to aim our ratings at the hypothetical average person. Easy trails are fairly level; moderate trails vary more in elevation. Both easy and moderate trails may have steps or stairs. For these trails all hikers should wear good foot protection, such as tennis shoes. For difficult trails, which may involve steep climbs and descents, boulder scrambling, and the use of hands and knees, we recommend hiking boots.

Due to the nature of the plateau and its steep-sided gorges, the trails covered in this guide vary greatly in their degree of difficulty. Remember that a majority of the trails include steep descents into valleys and long climbs back to the ridge. Many of the trails also involve fording streams that are greatly affected by weather conditions. The best way for you to select a trail that suits your ability is to read in its entirety the section of the guide on the trail you wish to take. We also suggest that you consult the National Park Service rangers at the Bandy Creek Visitor Center or the U.S. Forest Service rangers at the Stearns District Office for the most up-to-date information about trail conditions. Improvements are continually being made to the trail system, but sometimes nature adds unexpected hazards.

The Big South Fork National River and Recreation Area is still a very new park. When the Roads and Trails Management Plan is completed and a final disposition for all roads and trails has been determined, you may find some changes in the system. The availability of funds will determine when and what improvements are made.

Safety

Ensure your enjoyment of the trails in the Big South Fork Area by observing safety precautions. Evaluate each venture and plan with the following items in mind.

Registration at the Park Visitor Center is recommended. Backcountry permits are free of charge. Don't hike alone; accidents can happen. Always tell someone where you plan to hike and what time you anticipate returning. You may reach rangers after office hours by calling the county sheriffs' offices in Fentress and Scott counties in Tennessee and McCreary County in Kentucky. (See Appendix 3.)

Hypothermia, or the chilling of the body's inner core, can be fatal. Temperatures do not have to be below freezing for hypothermia to occur. According to the American Red Cross, most hypothermia cases occur in temperatures between 30° and 50° F. The symptoms of hypothermia are shivering, slurred speech, impaired judgment, weakness, and drowsiness.

Hypothermia is a real concern for hikers in the Big South Fork Area because of the numerous stream fordings required on many of the trails. **Proper clothing**, including appropriate footwear such as tennis shoes, is essential. You need hiking boots for the trails rated difficult. Because many trails are narrow and some are overgrown, long pants are desirable. For extended trips, include a poncho. Be prepared for a wide range of temperatures.

Supplies should always include food, water, a first-aid kit (don't forget moleskin for blisters), a knife, a compass, maps, and matches. Especially on longer hikes, take along flashlights and extra batteries. We highly recommend insect repellent for warm-weather hiking. You should also be aware that ticks, which can carry Lyme disease or Rocky Mountain spotted fever, are a potential problem where there is a high deer population.

Water in the park area may contain harmful parasites (such as giardia, which causes severe intestinal infection), making it unfit for drinking unless properly treated. Boil the water for 2 minutes or use water purification tablets. Use flowing water from small streams or springs if possible and *always* treat it before drinking.

Hunting, with proper licensing, is permitted in the Big South Fork National River and Recreation Area. We don't recommend hiking during big game hunting season, but if you do, wear blaze orange. The season generally runs from mid-November to mid-December but varies between states. Check with park rangers. Most trails quickly leave the safety zones.

Water levels may vary greatly. Remember that conditions for fording branches, streams, creeks, and the Big South Fork River can change quickly. *Never attempt to ford in high water or against a strong current.* Naturally, the closer any stream comes to the river the deeper and more difficult to cross it will be. Also, remember that the rocky bottoms of many streams are moss-covered and extremely slick. Note the water levels and weather conditions before beginning your hike. Check maps for alternate routes you can use if necessary. Flooding is most likely from December through March but can occur at any time. Although many local people and visitors swim in the Big South Fork River, be warned: *The river can be extremely dangerous.* Hidden rocks can entrap feet and legs. Strong undercurrents can exist in places where the water appears calm. We recommend that all swimmers wear life jackets.

Nighttime can be dangerous even on clearly blazed trails. Prepare to camp out if you see that you will be unable to reach your destination before dark. The prevalence of steep cliffs makes wandering around in the dark extremely dangerous.

Wildlife of all forms is protected. Observe and enjoy but never disturb. Wild boar live within the park, but they are dangerous only if you corner them or approach their young.

Copperheads and Timber Rattlers are the only two poisonous snakes indigenous to the area. Use ordinary precautions. Wear shoes and *always* carry a flashlight after dusk.

Open mine shafts, abandoned strip mines, and tunnels are deadly hazards. They may have oxygen-deficient air, loose rock and unstable ground, explosive atmospheres, and poor roof conditions. *Never enter an old mine tunnel.*

Cliff tops and bluffs offer spectacular views of the gorge and its valleys. Remember that rock at the edges may be unstable and slippery when wet. Do not allow children to run ahead on the trail. *Use extreme caution at overlooks*: Most overlooks are unprotected, and some sections of trail closely follow the edges of cliffs with 100-foot drops.

Ice and snow can create footing hazards. In addition, some trails pass directly beneath the drip line of the bluffs. Large icicles often form along them, crashing to the trail below when they fall.

Campfires are permitted, but you should build your fire on cleared soil and burn only dead and down wood. Be certain that your fire is completely out before leaving it.

Unattended vehicles, even locked ones, are never really secure. Leave anything unnecessary at home, and mark all of the equipment you bring. Store items out of view if they are to be left in your vehicle. If you're planning an extended trip, check with the rangers about the security of individual trailheads.

Children should be kept close at hand when hiking trails within the Big South Fork Area. Swift-running streams and steep cliffs are two major hazards for children. Also, trails are often hard to follow. A child could easily wander from the designated trail. Teach your child to stop, remain in one place, and "hug a tree" when lost (a good thing for everyone to remember).

Backcountry Regulations

While backcountry permits are not required at this time, it is always a good idea to either phone or stop by the Bandy Creek Visitor Center or the Blue Heron complex and fill one out. In addition to registering your vehicle, it assists Rangers in finding you in case of an emergency call from home.

1. Camping is not permitted within 100 feet of the center line of the Bandy Creek Access Road, TN Hwy. 297, Blue Heron Access Road, and the Blue Heron Overlook Road.
2. No camping at developed parking areas. Camping is allowed nearby if the campsite is at least 200 feet from the parking area and is not visible from the parking area.
3. No camping within 25 feet of any cave, cemetery, grave site, historic site or structure, rock shelter, the rim of the gorge, trail, roadway, or any other location designated with a no camping sign. The river floodplain is open to camping at this time.
4. At Bandy Creek, Blue Heron, and Alum Ford campgrounds, camping is allowed only at designated sites or by special use permits within the designated safety zone.
5. Human waste must be buried at least 6 inches deep and 100 feet from any water source, campsite, or within sight of a trail.
6. Only dead and down wood may be used for campfires. Chain saws cannot be used to cut firewood.
7. No animals, plants, minerals, or cultural artifacts may be removed from the park, with the exception of game in compliance with hunting regulations and edible fruits and nuts gathered for personal consumption.
8. All archeological sites and cemeteries are protected by federal and state laws. Therefore, digging beneath rock shelters is prohibited.
9. Pack out what you have packed in.
10. Horses, bicycles, motorcycles, and ATVs are not permitted on hiking trails.
11. Do not shortcut trails. Severe erosion problems develop as a result.
12. Store all food so that it is inaccessible to wildlife.
13. When in doubt, contact a ranger.

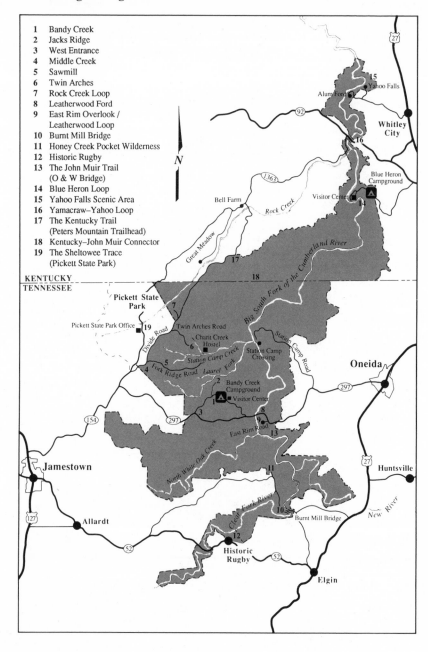

1   Bandy Creek
2   Jacks Ridge
3   West Entrance
4   Middle Creek
5   Sawmill
6   Twin Arches
7   Rock Creek Loop
8   Leatherwood Ford
9   East Rim Overlook /
    Leatherwood Loop
10 Burnt Mill Bridge
11 Honey Creek Pocket Wilderness
12 Historic Rugby
13 The John Muir Trail
    (O & W Bridge)
14 Blue Heron Loop
15 Yahoo Falls Scenic Area
16 Yamacraw–Yahoo Loop
17 The Kentucky Trail
    (Peters Mountain Trailhead)
18 Kentucky–John Muir Connector
19 The Sheltowee Trace
    (Pickett State Park)

General Location Map. The Big South Fork Area

Using the Trail Guide

Using the major headings of Tennessee Trails and Kentucky Trails, we have separated the hiking trails according to their general location. Trails have been further divided into sections according to their trailheads. A description of each trailhead, with the specific location, prefaces each section. Trails originating from each trailhead have been described individually, including mileage, rating, blaze, special considerations, accommodations, and suggested hiking time. The suggested times allow for a comfortable, leisurely pace, rest stops, and sightseeing. (Most people hike at a rate of about 3 miles per hour on moderate trails.) Distances are given in miles, rounded off to the nearest tenth in most cases. In some instances, where portions of a trail cover the same terrain, you are referred to another section of the guide for more information.

The John Muir Trail, the Kentucky Trail, and the Sheltowee Trace are long-distance trails. The introduction includes necessary information, such as access or resupply points. Although the headnotes alert you to special considerations, it is particularly important in making advance plans for the longer trails for you to read about the entire trail before starting out. Doing so will help you to determine how far you can travel each day and where possible campsites are located.

Maps have been included in the guide. The overall map on page 22 shows the general location of each trailhead. Before each trailhead description, a map shows the general location of all the trails originating at that particular trailhead. The following symbols are used frequently on the trail maps:

🏃	Beginning of trail, mile 0.0 in description		
🅣	Trailheads	– – – –	Trails
🅗	Historic sites	••••••••••	Horse trails
●	Points of interest	▬▬▬▬	Roads
■	Buildings, visitor centers	≷	Rapids, waterfalls
IIII	Steps	◉	Overlooks
STT	Sheltowee Trace Trail	★	mileage in between
JMT	John Muir Trail		

The long-distance trails have several maps, each covering a portion of the trail. The maps are intended only to orient you and to give a general impression of the trail's directions. They cannot possibly show all the turns, switchbacks and old road, horse and mountain bike intersections encountered along the trail. Instead, the text and its mileages provide detailed information. For backpackers we recommend that you purchase the trail map sold at the Visitor Center. Some information on the history and culture of the Big South Fork area, as well as its natural history, is included in the introduction. Other information has been saved for on-site reading to enhance your hiking experience. Take your time, imagine yourself back in history, and enjoy the Big South Fork area.

For a quick, easy reference in selecting a trail, we have included as Appendix 1 a chart giving ratings, mileages, and some of the features of each trail. You may also want to select portions of the longer trails and plan your own hikes. We have made some suggestions for possible backpacking loops. See Appendix 2. In addition, we have provided as Appendix 3 a list of addresses for contacting the various sources and agencies mentioned in our guide.

Tennessee Trails

Approximately two-thirds of the Big South Fork National and River Recreation Area lies within the state of Tennessee. There are twelve trailheads and one long-distance trail, offering a variety of hiking experiences.

Located near the center of the park, on or near TN 297, you will find Bandy Creek Campground, Jacks Ridge, West Entrance, Leatherwood Ford, East Rim, and Leatherwood Loop Trailheads. Along the western boundary you'll come to Middle Creek, Sawmill, Twin Arches, and Rock Creek Loop Trailheads. Scattered at the southern end of the park are Burnt Mill Bridge, Honey Creek and Historic Rugby. The John Muir Scenic Trail travels northward along the Big South Fork river. Just before reaching Kentucky, it turns westward, ending in Pickett State Forest.

1. Bandy Creek Campground Trailhead

Bandy Creek Campground is one of the two major campground developments within the Big South Fork National River and Recreation Area. Oral tradition has it that "Bandy" came from the word "abandoned" and once referred to an abandoned home site along the creek (H. Duncan 1986). A large sign on TN 297 west of the gorge directs you to the 2-mile-long paved road leading to Bandy Creek Campground.

A Visitor Center, staffed by park rangers, is located opposite the campground entrance. At the Visitor Center you may obtain information regarding the park and other area attractions, including the York Grist Mill (Sgt. Alvin C. York of World War I fame), Historic Rugby, and the Big South Fork Scenic Railway.

One short hiking trail leaves the Visitor Center parking lot. All the remaining trails originate at the Bandy Creek Campground Trailhead 0.2 mile down the paved road past the Visitor Center and campground. The parking area for the trailhead is on the left. Restroom facilities are available at the trailhead.

You can also reach the Bandy Creek Campground Trailhead by following the walkway to the amphitheater. The blazed trail to the right will lead to the trailhead in 0.2 mile.

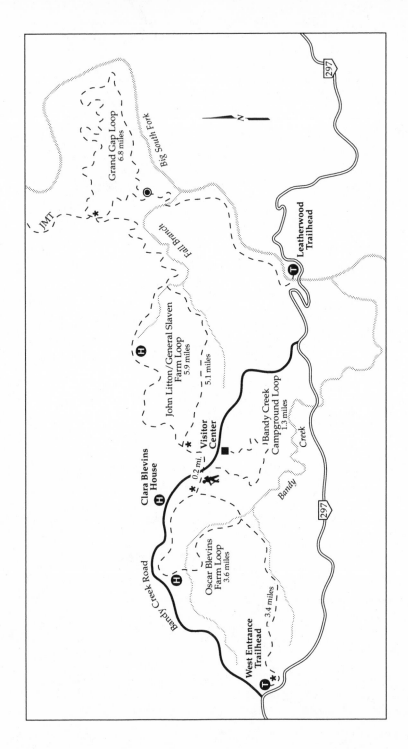

Trail Map 1. Bandy Creek Campground Trailhead.

Bandy Creek Campground Loop

Distance: 1.3 miles
Rating: Easy
Suggested time: 30 to 40 minutes
Blaze: Red arrowhead
Accommodations: Bandy Creek Campground/Visitor Center
Special consideration: Good jogging path

This very easy loop is a level gravel path. It is suitable for those who want a quiet walk in the woods but are not up to the physical strains of the other trails. It would make an excellent jogging path. Since there are no outstanding scenic features or distinctive landmarks, the mileage will be marked by the wooden footbridges.

Mileage Description

0.0 The trail begins at the west end of the Visitor Center parking lot on the paved walkway leading to the amphitheater. The trail goes off to the left past the pond, and will circle back of the stables. Deer are frequently seen along this trail.

0.06 Cross the horse trail.

0.4 Footbridge.

0.7 Footbridge.

0.9 Footbridge next to an open field.

1.00 Long footbridge.

1.3 The trail ends at the Visitor Center. This trail may be easily reversed.

Grand Gap Loop

Ratings: Moderate to difficult
Suggested time: All-day hikes
Accommodations: Leatherwood Ford Trailhead (telephones), Bandy Creek Campground/Visitor Center
Special consideration: Trail name misleading, alternate beginning

Option 1: To Grand Gap Loop

Distance: 10.2 miles round trip
Blaze: Red arrowhead
Special consideration: Ladders

Option 2: Around Grand Gap Loop

   Distance: 17 miles round trip
   Blaze: Red arrowhead/JMT
   Special considerations: Sheer bluffs, no source of water on loop

Option 3: To River Overlooks

   Distance: 13.2 miles round trip
   Blaze: Red arrowhead/JMT
   Special considerations: Sheer bluffs, no source of water on loop

Option 4: To Leatherwood Ford

   Distance: 9.0 miles one way
   Blaze: Red arrowhead/JMT
   Special considerations: Ladders, sheer bluffs, narrow rock ledge, steep
      descent, possible high water over bridge

The trail to Grand Gap Loop begins at the Bandy Creek Campground Trailhead. It follows Fall Branch as the stream descends to the Big South Fork
River and ends at Grand Gap Loop, which is at least 3 miles from any
trailhead. The name refers to the large natural gap that provides access to the
river from the east side of the loop. Horses frequently use this low water ford,
crossing the Big South Fork River near Bill Branch. Please note: The sign in
the Bandy Creek Campground for the Grand Gap Loop can be misleading.
After hiking 5.1 miles you will only have reached the beginning of the Grand
Gap Loop. Once you reach the loop, you have several options: (1) Return to
the campground; (2) Hike the 6.8-mile Grand Gap Loop, making a 17-mile
round trip back to Bandy Creek Campground; (3) Go straight ahead on the
loop for about 1.5 miles to scenic overlooks of the river gorge, including the
Angel Falls Overlook. Retracing the route from the Angel Falls Overlook will
make a 13.2-mile round trip back to the campground; (4) Continue straight
ahead as you enter the loop for 1.3 miles until a sign directs you to the Leatherwood Ford Trailhead. Exiting at Leatherwood Ford makes the trip approximately 9.0 miles one way. Prior to your hike you will need to make arrangements for transportation back to Bandy Creek Campground.

   The trail is blazed with the red arrowhead on white; however, the loop is a
portion of the John Muir Trail, and the blaze changes to the John Muir Trail
blue blaze upon reaching the Grand Gap Loop.

Mileage Description

0.0   From the trailhead the trail goes to the right, crosses the Bandy Creek road, leads past the campground, crosses the Duncan Hollow road within the campground, and enters the woods.

0.2   Alternate beginning: Across from the swimming pool on Duncan Hollow Road.

0.6   After a short walk in the woods, you climb down a 6-foot ladder to a lower ledge. Continue along the ledge until you descend another ladder into a lush hollow filled with mountain laurel, rhododendron, and fern. The tributaries within this hollow form Fall Branch.

0.7   Follow the trail past a long, sandstone-capped overhang and rockhouse.

1.05   Scott State Forest boundary.

1.7   Notice the rocky bottom of this large tributary of Fall Branch. Because the soil is thin, many streams quickly reach rock level. Camping alongside the stream is made difficult by the thick, twisted undergrowth of mountain laurel.

2.14   The trail passes between the rock ledge and the creek.

2.2   Fall Branch Falls. The creek falls about 6 feet from a deeply undercut rock shelf. A footpath goes down to the falls, where a natural dam forms a small pool. As you continue on the trail, notice that although your path has remained relatively level, the valley floor and stream have dropped away sharply.

2.8   After crossing over another small tributary and switchback, to your right you can see the rockhouse over whose top you have just hiked. In summer the rockhouse is hidden by thick vegetation.

3.1   The wooden bridge spans the north fork of Fall Branch. The branch is lined with hemlock and rhododendron. Just past the branch, a sign gives directions to the old John Litton/General Slaven Farm. The portion of the trail that you have just hiked is also a part of that loop.

3.2   You can leave the trail immediately to your right and find a small waterfall. The trail follows a rock path leading past a large, deep rockhouse.

3.3   The trail leads uphill past an overhang. Two sharp switchbacks follow some stone steps.

3.6   Scott State Forest boundary. The trail seems to be following an old roadbed now. The old road goes off to the left as the trail continues on to the right.

3.8   You can see the remains of an old log ramp uphill to your left. Timbermen rolled logs downhill and loaded them onto trucks, using this ramp. The trail continues across the old logging road.

3.9   *A sign warns of high cliffs ahead.* The sheer cliffs can be deadly, but by being careful you can hike the trails safely.

4.1   Footbridge

4.2   Looking down the Fall Branch watershed, you can see across to the hills beyond the Big South Fork River. The exposed white cliff with the single pine up to the left of Fall Branch is the popular Angel Falls Overlook.

4.7   Cross the bridge over the stream.

5.1   Grand Gap Loop. The trail, previously marked with the red arrowhead, is now blazed with the JMT blue blaze. The trail that comes in from your left goes around the north side of the loop. The trail to your right goes around the south side of the loop past the junction with the Leatherwood Ford Trail.

Option 1

Retrace your route to Bandy Creek Campground Trailhead, making a round-trip hike of 10.2 miles.

Option 2

Complete the Grand Gap Loop and return to Bandy Creek Campground.

Mileage Description

0.0   Enter the Grand Gap Loop. The following directions will guide you counterclockwise (right) around the loop, bringing you back to this point on the trail in 6.8 miles.

0.1   Cross the old roadbed.

0.7   The small gravestone on the left side of the trail is in remembrance of Archie Smith, the infant son of Alfred Smith. Archie died of pneumonia in 1932. Herbert Smith of Oneida, Tennessee, related the story of his family. His parents, Alfred and Elva Smith, raised nine children at their nearby home site. His mother grew a large garden to feed the family and fetched water from a nearby spring. Alfred Smith, who worked as a logger for the Stearns Coal and Lumber Company, was gone from home during the week, moving from place to place with the lumber camps and returning home on weekends. When the Stearns Company ceased their logging operations in the 1940s, the family was forced to leave the ridge and seek employment elsewhere. Alfred Smith went to work for the "secret" government plant in Oak Ridge, Tennessee.

1.2   A large exposed sandstone ledge offers a view up the Fall Branch drainage as well as a view of the Big South Fork as it makes an S-shaped curve and flows towards Angel Falls.

1.3   A sign directs you to continue straight ahead to the Angel Falls Overlook.

1.5   The almost bare cliff to the right is Angel Falls Overlook. *Always exercise extreme caution when viewing the river from high cliffs such as this one.* Angel Falls is directly below the overlook. From here you can see the Falls only when the trees are bare, but you will come to a better view of the Falls farther downstream as you follow the bluff line. (You can discover how Angel Falls got its name on page 93.)

1.7   After leaving the river for a short distance, the trail passes by what appears to be a small rockhouse. Look carefully for the small natural arch. This type of arch was formed by the widening of a joint in the back of a rock shelter.

1.8   The trail passes below the bluff line between the sandstone bluff on the left and large boulders on the right. These boulders have split from the bluff and are gradually moving downhill.

2.5   A sharp switchback gives you the impression you are heading back upriver, but your trail soon turns and continues downriver.

2.56   The trail returns to the bluff line. Look back upriver for the best view of Angel Falls.

2.67   The trail returns below the bluff line to an area where large boulders have separated from cliffs above.

2.7   Notice the rock shelter to your left.

3.2   You can see a dark, cool stand of hemlock ahead. Downhill to your right offers a good view of large boulders just beginning to split away from the underlying sandstone base.

3.3   Past the small drainage branch, an old logging road crosses the trail. Signs give the distances to Leatherwood Ford and Station Camp Creek. This road, sometimes used by horseback riders, descends through the "Grand Gap" to reach the Big South Fork River.

3.8   There are several possible campsites in this area, but there are no year-round sources of water on the loop. To camp on the Grand Gap Loop, you must pack in water.

4.5   The trail very briefly travels along a roadbed and then turns to the left.

5.0   The trail emerges onto an overlook with such steep cliffs that it is hard to see the river below; however, you have an excellent view of the cliffs across the river. Notice the large rockhouse in one of the cliffs. The large gap in the plateau across the river is where Rough Shoals Branch enters the Big South Fork.

5.2   Additional views of the river.

5.45   Cross the old logging road. Along this section, the trail parallels an old road on your left. This road, one of many old logging roads that crisscross the park, leads eventually to Bandy Creek Campground. You should remain on the trail.

6.71   Intersection with the northbound John Muir Trail. If you take the trail directly ahead, you will come out at Station Camp Creek. Hiking the trail to the left will continue the loop.

6.76   Cross the road that the trail has previously paralleled.

6.8   You have now completed the Grand Gap Loop. The trail to your right is the trail back to Bandy Creek Campground. This trail is 5.1 miles in length, making your round trip 17 miles.

Option 3

View Angel Falls Overlook and return to Bandy Creek Campground.
Follow directions for Option 2 until you reach Angel Falls Overlook. Retrace your route. Be careful to notice where you entered the loop. It will be 1.5 miles back to that point. The trail back to Bandy Creek Campground is to your left. The trail straight ahead begins the clockwise pattern around Grand Gap Loop. The round trip to Angel Falls Overlook is 13.2 miles.

Option 4

Exit by way of Fall Branch and Leatherwood Ford Trailhead.
Follow Option 2 until you come to the sign along the trail (1.3 miles) that directs you to Leatherwood Ford. Continuing the mileage from the Bandy Creek Campground:

Mileage Description

6.4   A sign directs you downhill through a series of quick switchbacks. Climb down the short ladder to the next ledge.

6.47   The trail seems to disappear as it crosses a narrow, rocky ledge. Although the ledge is quite narrow, the drop-off is not great. The trail bears to the left at the bottom of this ledge.

6.5   The trail passes beneath a large overhang. Opposite the overhang you will find a footpath leading to a bluff with a beautiful view of the Fall Branch watershed. *Be careful when walking out to the overlook.*

6.6   Continue hiking the trail around the base of a sheer rock cliff.

6.8   You pass a huge, tilting boulder with numerous potholes.

7.0   At the bottom of the stone steps, the switchback leads you upstream along Fall Branch. The trail will not be as steep now. The well-used but unmarked trail to your left will take you to several possible campsites along Fall Branch and near the Big South Fork River.

7.1   Fall Branch drains much of the area between Bandy Creek Campground and the river. From the footbridge over Fall Branch you have a beautiful view both up- and downstream of the overhanging rhododendron, large boulders, and small falls and pools.

7.2   Follow Fall Branch as it flows toward the river.

7.5   The trail parallels the river.

8.8   Walking beside a sheer rock face, you pass some of the rapids that make canoeing so popular on the Big South Fork.

9.0   The trail ends at the wooden steps just above the old bridge over the Big South Fork River at Leatherwood Ford. Cross the bridge to the Leatherwood Ford Trailhead on the east side of the river.

John Litton/General Slaven Farm Loop

Distance: 6.3 miles
Rating: Moderate
Suggested time: Half-day hike
Blaze: Red arrowhead
Accommodations: Bandy Creek Campground/Visitor Center
Special considerations: Steps, ladders, alternate beginning

The John Litton/General Slaven Farm Loop crosses the ridgetop and descends to a valley where the John Litton historic farmhouse and outbuildings give a glimpse of the lifestyle of Big South Fork families during the first half of the twentieth century, a lifestyle that continued for the Slaven family until October 1979. The trail then follows the north fork of Fall Branch to its confluence with Fall Branch. Nearby is a large rockhouse. The last portion of the loop returns to the campground by way of the Fall Branch drainage.

Mileage Description

0.0   The loop trail to the Litton/Slaven Farm begins at the Bandy Creek Campground Trailhead. Follow the path to the right as it crosses Bandy Creek Road and then enters the campground.

0.2   Alternate beginning: across from the pool on the Duncan Hollow road. A sign directs you to either the right or the left to begin the loop. Our book directs you clockwise (left) around the loop. Although this trail is rated moderate, there are stairs and two short ladders on it. Follow the dirt road on your left.

0.44   Scott State Forest boundary. From your left a horse trail enters the roadbed.

0.6   The stands of white pine on the left are part of the Scott State Forest field laboratory. Clippings from the tops of superior-ranked pine

English-style barn built by John Litton (National Park Service)

trees within the Scott State Forest have been grafted onto superior root systems that came from laboratories at the University of Tennessee. Seeds from these trees are then sold around the world. Scott State Forest was created in 1929 after Scott County deeded the land to the state. Scott County had accumulated this land as landowners were unable to pay their taxes. (Clark 1986)

0.9   Leave Scott State Forest.

1.1   The trail passes through the power-line cut. The road forks. The horse trail follows the Duncan Hollow road straight out to the end of the ridge. The Duncan Hollow 5.3-mile bike loop goes left. Take the road on the far right. This gated road is a steeper but shorter access to the farmhouse. The trail again crosses the state forest boundary.

1.4   The road enters an area of open fields.

1.5   The trail leaves the road and crosses the ditchline on a wooden bridge. Rerouted from the middle of the agricultural lease field, the trail skirts the field next to the woods and follows an old U-shaped wagon road.

1.6   Cross a footbridge.

1.8   The trail reenters the woods and soon begins to descend into a hollow.

2.1   Descend the wooden stairway.

2.3   The trail crosses the bridge over a small creek.

2.4   Now you can see the old John Litton/General Slaven Farm. John, whose grandfather, James Litton, was an early settler and the first teacher in Scott County, moved to this valley with his bride, Elvira Doss, and raised five children here.

Like the early settlers who moved into the Big South Fork area, John Litton selected a site along a creek where there would be water for the family and the livestock. Drinking water came from springs on the hillside. On the flat land immediately surrounding the creek, he planted corn, wheat, and flax. On the hillside surrounding the farm, his hogs ran freely. The crops were fenced to protect them from livestock.

The English-style barn, with stalls on either side of a central driveway, was built by John Litton around 1900. The original portion of the house, which is constructed of hewn hemlock logs, was also built by John Litton at that time. The rooms to the south and west, as well as the porch, were added at a later date. Adding on to existing structures was a common practice in this area. Notice the newspaper "wallpaper" inside the house. This was a common means of covering inner walls. The other log structure still standing may have once been closer to the house and served as a separate kitchen (U.S. Army Corps of Engineers 1986: 19–20).

According to Dorothy Gable's *James Litton, The Wayfaring Stranger*, the John Litton family was almost totally self-sufficient. He farmed, hunted, and kept beehives; his wife maintained a large garden. John Litton even made his children's toys, including their marbles, using rocks, a grinder, and a makeshift water mill (1981: 29).

At the John Litton farm you can feel the isolation of the early settlers who inhabited the hollows and creek valleys of the Big South Fork. The farmer and his family would make the long wagon trip up the steep roads out of the gorge as infrequently as twice a year. General Slaven was the last private owner of this property. After many moves following logging work in the area, General Slaven bought the old Litton place in for $200 and moved his family into the remote site with the assistance of Estell Payne's old G.I. truck. His family remained, farming the land for more than thirty years in much the same manner as the John Litton family had before him. (Malanka 1992)

2.5   The loop trail continues past the barn and to the east of the farmhouse.

3.1   As the trail descends along North Fall Branch, you notice a change in vegetation from the hardwoods on the ridgetops to the hemlocks, white pines, and laurel found along the creek banks. Although the trail is continually descending, it is very gradual and easy to walk.

3.3   The trail passes a rock wall with red bands streaking the sandstone face. In approximately 50 yards the trail intersects the Grand Gap Loop Trail. To continue the Litton/Slaven Farm Loop, turn right. If you detour about 50 yards to the left at this intersection, you will find a large rockhouse that is well worth seeing.

      After viewing the rockhouse, retrace your steps to the intersection with the Grand Gap Loop Trail and begin the gradual ascent to the campground up the Fall Branch drainage.

3.5   After passing a large hemlock on your left, you'll see a rockhouse in the hillside on the left, but you must look carefully if you're hiking during the summer. You can see it best approximately 50 yards before the sharp switchback to the left.

4.0   The trail passes beside a small rock overhang.

4.2   You will hear Fall Branch Falls before you see it. A small sign marks the turnoff to the falls on the left side of the trail. At Fall Branch Falls the creek drops approximately 6 feet from a deeply undercut rock shelf. A natural dam across the stream forms a small pool beneath the falls.

4.25   The trail passes below a rock overhang.

4.3   On the left bank between the trail and the creek you'll find some possible campsites. On the far side of the clear, rock-bottomed creek is a rock wall.

4.5   The trail passes between a rock overhang and the creek.

5.3   Scott State Forest boundary.

5.5   To this point the ascent has been gradual; however, at the rock out-crop the trail begins to steepen.

5.6   The large sandstone overhang has littered the trail below it with rock.

5.7   Duck as you pass beneath the low overhang.

5.75   You will have to climb two ladders to reach the ridgetop.

5.9   The trail now levels out.

6.1   The trail reenters the campground, passing by the trail to the camp-fire circle.

6.3   Bandy Creek Campground Trailhead.

Oscar Blevins Farm Loop

Distance: 3.6 miles round trip
Rating: Easy
Suggested time: 2 hours
Blaze: Red arrowhead
Accommodations: Bandy Creek Campground/Visitor Center
Special consideration: Stairs, mountain bikes share a portion of this trail

Including both cultural and natural history of the Big South Fork area, this trail is well cleared and easy to follow.

A brochure for a self-guided walk (S. Duncan 1992) accompanies the numbered posts found along the trail and is available near the trailhead or at the Bandy Creek Visitor Center; however, our guide was written in the opposite direction, perhaps saving the best for last.

Mileage Description

0.0   As the Oscar Blevins trail begins you will travel through a Virgina pine thicket that only twenty-five to thirty years ago served as cleared farm land. In July you may even want to stop and enjoy

Log house on the Blevins Farm (Audney Lloyd)

some blackberries found in abundance here and at several other locations along this loop. Cross the horse trail and begin to follow a tributary branch of Bandy Creek.

0.25 The trail forks, and a sign states that you can reach the Blevins Farm in 1.4 miles by taking the trail to the right and in 1.8 miles by taking the trail to the left. (If you don't have time for the entire loop, a short 0.5-mile hike to the left will bring you to a beautiful, wet-weather waterfall and sandstone bluffs with iron ridges transecting them.) Our book will direct you to the right, counterclockwise around the loop. Until you reach the Blevins Farm, you will hike along a fairly level trail surrounded by a new forest composed of pines and young hardwood trees. Occasional glimpses of an old fence will remind you of how recently this land on top of the plateau was farmed. For much of this section you are traveling parallel to the old Leatherwood Ford Road, now called the Bandy Creek Road.

0.35   The trail enters a more open-floored wooded area. You will soon notice where more sunlight filters through, small pines are beginning to emerge.

0.53   The trail skirts a hollow.

0.75   After crossing a small drainage, the trail passes a low rock wall.

0.93   The exact cause of the large depression to your left is not known but following local tradition, this unusable land was turned into a garbage dump for early settlers who had to dispose of their trash in the best manner that they knew how. A spur trail to the right offers a side trip to the Clara Sue Blevins Homesite and the Katie Blevins Cemetery, both located along the Bandy Creek Road.

1.16   The hiking trail continues straight ahead as it crosses a mountain bike trail.

1.36   The trail travels briefly uphill and into a hemlock grove.

1.44   Cross the footbridge. In season, the low box huckleberries may provide a tasty snack.

1.57   A larger bridge crosses a drainage.

1.6   At this signed intersection in front of the Oscar Blevins Homesite, the road to your right comes off of the Bandy Creek Road and continues in front of the house. The trail continues left along this old roadbed which was once the road leading to Leatherwood Ford.

Oscar Blevins Farm. The Blevins family has lived within the Big South Fork area since the late 1700s when the longhunter Jonathan Blevins came into the area. Jonathan was Oscar Blevins' great-great-grandfather.

According to the U.S. Army Corps of Engineers' *Structural Treatment Plan* (1982: 24) and our interviews with the late Oscar Blevins, this farm, located above the headwaters of Bandy Creek, is comprised of structures representative of the area's late-nineteenth-to mid-twentieth-century farms. Passing through the handhewn picket fence, you come to the frame house built about 1950 and occupied by Oscar and Ermon Blevins at the time the land was purchased for the park.

Behind the frame house is the old story-and-a-half log house built soon after his marriage by the Rev. John Blevins, a cousin of Oscar Blevins' father, in the 1890s. He was a Baptist preacher and a noted singer as well as a farmer. The east end of the house, built of hand-hewn oak, pine, and poplar logs, was the original section of the house. Although built over a century later, it is similar to the simple cabins constructed by pre-Revolutionary Kentucky settlers. This land was purchased from Rev. Blevins by the Stearns Coal and Lumber Company, which in turn leased the land to a succession of families, including Oscar Blevins' parents from 1908 until 1920. Oscar was born in the one-room log house in 1915.

The west end of the house was added in the 1920s after Oscar's family had moved to Charit Creek. It was constructed of sawn timbers by Rev. John Blevins' brother, Jacob, who then occupied the land. To the right of the log house is a corn crib constructed on the property during Oscar Blevins' father's time. It is made of hewn logs joined by half-dovetail notching. The shed to the west of the crib was added at a much later date.

The Stearns Coal and Lumber Company owned a majority of the land within the Big South Fork area during the first half of the twentieth century. They leased the land, rent free, in order to prevent individuals from homesteading. This system was advantageous to both the company and the leasee, as the company's right to the land was protected and the individual farmer lived on the land rent and tax free.

By the 1940s the Stearns Company had logged most of the prime timber on the plateau and had disposed of some of their land holdings. Previously, in 1935, they had sold all of the land currently within Pickett State Park to the State of Tennessee. They then began to sell to private individuals.

In 1940, Oscar Blevins purchased the farm where he had been born. He built the large barn on the property in 1963. The Blevinses were subsistence farmers who grew corn, planted an orchard, maintained a large garden, and hunted in the surrounding woods.

The wayside exhibit to the right of the house will enhance your wanderings around the old farmsite. Return to the trail and continue to your right down the old roadbed. The trail follows the road that was used as a route to Leatherwood Ford even earlier than was the old Leatherwood Ford or Bandy Creek Road.

1.7   Notice the structure to your right. Lacking electricity, root cellars or springhouses were frequently the early settler's answer to keeping food cool. The trail travels beside a split-rail fence. In the field you may see sorghum growing during the summer months. The National Park Service leases this land to local farmers, who grow traditional crops on the land to keep the area open and representative of subsistence farms and to provide wildlife habitat. Sorghum was a staple of the subsistence farmers, who made sorghum molasses for sweetening foods and used the mash to feed their livestock.

2.0   The trail crosses Bandy Creek on a wooden bridge.

2.2   An old roadbed comes in from your left. Watch for mountain bikers. This is one exception where bikers and hikers must share a short portion of trail. Several springs keep this section of road wet. Walking along the old roadbed you will see fields being allowed to return to their natural state. The order in which plants return to a cleared area is called natural succession. First grasses, then shrubs such as blackberries, next pines, and finally hardwoods reclaim the abandoned fields. At the next trail intersection, the hiking trail goes left and parallels the creek. Bikers may be coming downhill from the trail on your right.

2.6   The old building and cleared fields in this area belonged to neighbors of the Blevinses. All subsistence farmers in the Big South Fork area lived near creeks, branches, or springs because they couldn't dig wells in the sparse soil and underlying sandstone.

2.7   After crossing a bare rock surface, the hiking trail turns left while the bike trail continues straight ahead on the old road bed.Within a short distance, the loop trail intersects a 2.4-mile trail to the West Entrance Trailhead. The loop trail back to Bandy Creek Campground continues straight ahead and crosses the wooden bridge over Bandy Creek.

3.0   Cross the footbridge. This next section of trail is magnificent when the rhododendron is in bloom. The spur trail to your left leads up to Muleshoe Rockshelter, so named because of the muleshoes that were found there. Historical uses of rockshelters in the Big South Fork Area varied from animal pens to moonshine hide-outs, from prehistoric homes to schools and Sunday meeting places. Dirt piles are now sad reminders of vandalized shelters that once held the secrets of our past.

3.15   The trail passes through several rockshelters. Enjoy the spring seeps, the wet-weather waterfall, and the interesting patterns created by the iron ridges emerging from the sandstone bluffs.

3.3   Scott State Forest boundary. Climb the stairs beside the wet-weather waterfall and follow the branch uphill toward Bandy Creek Campground.

3.4   You have completed the loop. Take the trail to the right.

3.6   Bandy Creek Campground Trailhead.

2. Jacks Ridge Trailhead

Jacks Ridge Trailhead is actually a parking area for a horse trail. However, you can hike one of the more scenic loops within the park from this point, so we have listed it with the hiking trails. You may either hike to the trailhead from the Bandy Creek Campground Trailhead or drive to it in a 4-wheel-drive vehicle or high-centered truck.

To drive to Jacks Ridge, take the Bandy Creek Road through the campground. Pass the entrance to the campground and Visitor Center as well as the entrance to the Bandy Creek Campground Trailhead parking area. The paved road changes to gravel and dirt. From the point where you begin the dirt road, travel 1 mile to a dirt road that cuts sharply back to the right. It is just beyond the county line marker and is the first road past the Clara Blevins Farm and the Katie Blevins Cemetery. Follow this road 0.8 mile to the Jacks Ridge Trailhead. Bear to your left at every fork in the road. You'll find a sign at the trailhead.

To hike to Jacks Ridge, begin at the Bandy Creek Campground Trailhead. Take the gravel path directly behind the trailhead sign. After approximately 30 yards, the trail intersects a horse trail blazed with the yellow horsehead. Go right on the horse trail 15 yards, and you will intersect the Bandy Creek Road. Upon reaching the road, you may either continue along the horse trail to Jacks Ridge Trailhead or follow the driving directions above.

The Clara Blevins house is typical of local architecture in that it was built in stages. The east end of the house was the first completed. It was built by George Blevins (Oscar Blevins said that it was Lora Blevins) in 1929 out of hewn, yellow-pine logs. When the west end of the house was completed, the house contained a parlor and guest room downstairs and sleeping rooms upstairs. Cooking and dining were done in an attached shed that has since been removed. The chimney was originally of sandstone.

The log barn was also constructed by George (or Lora) Blevins in 1929. The shed additions across the front and back were added later. The smaller, single-pen, log barn served as a corn crib (U.S. Army Corps of Engineers 1986: 24, 28).

Like Oscar Blevins, Lora Blevins, born in 1869, was descended from the

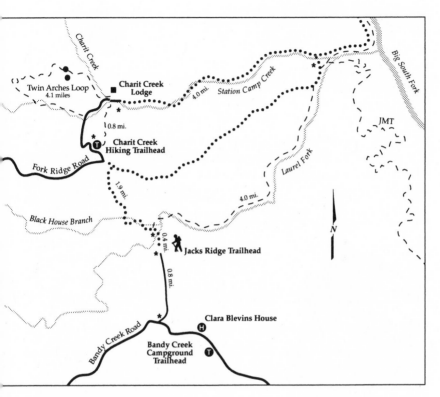

rail Map 2. Jacks Ridge Trailhead

longhunter Jonathan Blevins. Clara is the daughter-in-law of Lora Blevins (Blevins 1987).

Past the farm yard is the Katie Blevins Cemetery. The first burial was the son of Jonathan Blevins: Jacob Blevins, 1811–1869. The cemetery is named after Jacob's wife, Katie. Jacob's son, Jake, and his wife, Viannah, who lived at Jakes Place near Charit Creek are also buried here, as are John and Elvira Litton, whose old farmstead may be seen along the John Litton Farm Loop.

Recommendations have been made to bring a spur trail off of the Oscar Blevins Farm Loop that would cross the Bandy Creek Road and go down to Laurel Fork. A look at Trail Map 3 shows the closeness of the two trails. Even if this trail does not become a reality, you still might opt to follow the Blevins Farm Loop to the mountain bike crossing at 1.16 miles. Turn right and follow the bike trail a brief distance to the Bandy Creek Road. Turn left on the road and follow it for 0.3 mile to the county line marker.

Laurel Fork Loop

Distance: 11.1 miles
Rating: Difficult
Suggested time: All-day hike or 2-day backpacking trip
Blaze: Red arrowhead/Yellow horsehead
Accommodations: Charit Creek Lodge
Special considerations: Trailhead location, road (vehicular traffic), horse
trails, confusing signs, stairs, steep climbs, rocky terrain, frequent
fordings (possible high water)

The trail along the Laurel Fork of Station Camp Creek is one of the most
beautiful trails in the Big South Fork Area. It is a portion of a longer trail that
begins at the Middle Creek Trailhead and leads to Station Camp Creek. Because of the length of the entire trail and the particular beauty of this one
section, we have separated it from the rest, using horse trails as well as hiking
trails to make a scenic loop.

Although the first section of the loop is only 4.4 miles in length, the hike
is slow, as the rocky trail winds up and down the hillside and between rock
outcrops. At 2.6 miles you can see an impressive waterfall on Laurel Fork. If
you want a short hike, this is a good turnaround point.

If you continue the loop, you'll have numerous streams to ford as well as a
steep climb out of the valley to the top of Fork Ridge. You should prepare for
at least an 8-hour hike. You'll need hiking boots, as much of this trail is
rocky. There are several good campsites along the route.

Mileage

Description

0.0   From Jacks Ridge Trailhead, take the road to the left. The blaze for
this section of the trail is the yellow horsehead. The road is soon
blocked by a gate. The road is rocky, and the decline is steep.

0.08   Notice the sandstone overhang to the right of the trail. The thick
layer of sand eroded away from the overhang displays the reverse
process from the sedimentation that originally compressed sand into
stone millions of years ago.

0.2   To the left of the trail you can see large potholes indenting the
smooth surface of a massive boulder.

0.4   As you approach Laurel Fork, you can find a good campsite on the left of the trail. Ford Laurel Fork Creek. Although generally shallow, it is approximately 15 feet wide. The signs may seem confusing as some distances listed are for horse trails and some are for hiking trails. The two are not distinguished on the signs, so you may see two signs right next to each other giving different mileages to the same location. Continue straight ahead on the roadway. (The trail joining the roadway on your left originated at the Middle Creek Trailhead, 9 miles to the west.) The yellow blaze is now joined by the red arrowhead blaze as the horse and hiking trails combine for 0.1 mile.

0.5 The hiking trail diverges to the right through tall grass. The sign gives 4.7 miles to Station Camp Crossing, a low-water ford on the Big South Fork.

0.6 Cross Laurel Fork. Good stepping-stones usually make a dry fording possible. To the left of the trail is an excellent camping site. Recross the creek. This is the last fording on this section of the trail, but there are many more if you hike the entire loop. The trail now follows the north bank of Laurel Fork through large beech and hemlock trees. Also, white pine, hemlock, mountain laurel, and rhododendron grow closer to the creek and in its moist drainages. This very rocky trail winds up and down the hillside, giving you occasional glimpses of boulder-filled Laurel Fork Creek.

1.1 After following the rock steps downward, you may think you've lost the trail, but it actually turns sharply left and inconspicuously crosses a rocky area.

1.3 To the right of the trail, notice the smooth rock wall resembling a fortress.

1.4 The trail descends to a small, year-round branch. Across Laurel Fork Creek you can see a large stand of hemlocks with a clear understory that would make a good camping location. Another branch also flows into Laurel Fork from the opposite side.

2.0 Four medium-sized trees growing from one trunk mark the beginning of a couple of switchbacks you may not readily see. The red arrowhead blaze on the tree points downhill.

2.3 The large hemlock to the immediate right of the trail is 11 feet in circumference. This tree is an example of how the forest appeared

before logging became big business in the Big South Fork Area at
the beginning of this century.

2.6   Just off the trail you can find an impressive waterfall created by
water cascading over large boulders in the creekbed. There are no
singular landmarks to identify the spot. Leave the trail at the medium-sized boulder with the small footpath along the far side of it
and walk downhill toward the creek for a view of the falls. Listen for
the sound of rushing water to help locate the spot. To the left of the
trail is a well-used campsite. This is a good turnaround point for
anyone not wishing to make the entire loop. The round trip at this
point would be 5.2 miles. However, shortly beyond the falls the trail
merges with an old roadbed, making hiking much easier.

3.2   The trail returns to the creek bank. The creek is more tranquil here,
and you no longer see large numbers of boulders. The trail soon
takes a sharp left turn to go uphill. Be alert: This trail is very easy to
miss even though it is blazed. But if you do miss this section of the
trail, you can rejoin it further downstream by continuing on the
roadbed to the open floodplain. Where the road appears to enter the
creek, do not cross the creek. Instead, about 20 feet before the road
ends at the creek, turn left and go uphill over the small bank and
then bear right. You can see the trail ahead of you. The floodplain
has a good camping spot.

3.6   The trail joins an old roadbed.

3.8   The trail passes briefly through a dark hemlock forest and then sud-
denly emerges into some old fields newly grown over. You are near-
ing Station Camp, formerly a thriving community.

Jonathan Blevins was the first longhunter to settle permanently in
the Station Camp Creek area. Although he continued to hunt for a
livelihood, his children became subsistence farmers as they cleared
the bottomland for crops. Benita Howell (Associate Professor, Anthropology Dept., University of Tennessee) has found that by 1850
there were 126 people living along Station Camp Creek (1981: 26).
By 1900 the population had increased considerably, as families
farmed all the way up Station Camp Creek, and by the 1930s there
were enough families to warrant a post office. Today all that remains
of this community are the cleared fields that are slowly being reclaimed by nature.

4.2 A horse trail joins the trail from the left. The Big South Fork River is on the far side of the high ridge to your right.

4.4 You are in the narrow valley created by Laurel Fork Creek on the south and Station Camp Creek on the north. Between the two creeks rises Fork Ridge. The bridge to the right across Laurel Fork Creek is part of the John Muir Trail. It follows the ridgetops south above the Big South Fork River to Leatherwood Ford. Do not cross the bridge but continue straight ahead. The Charit Creek trail goes to the left, marked by the sign, "Charit Creek Hostel: 3.6 miles." It will be blazed by a yellow horsehead on white.

4.5 Ford Station Camp Creek.

4.65 The trail dead-ends into an old road. Although the sign at the intersection does not mention Charit Creek, go left on the road. The yellow horsehead blaze marks the trail. The trail will rise gradually as it follows Station Camp Creek up the valley to the Charit Creek Lodge. The recently graveled roadbed makes hiking this horse trail a little easier.

6.15 The trail emerges from the forest near an old homesite. You can see the bluffs of Hatfield Ridge to the right. If you wish, take the side path to the north of the trail approximately 40 paces prior to the clearing and walk down to the Blevins Cemetery, where Jonathan Blevins and his two wives are buried. The graveyard is another 40 paces down the side path. In addition to the modern gravestone erected by the descendants of Jonathan Blevins, you can find numerous fieldstone markers predating the Civil War. (Spradlin 1992)

6.3 Ford Station Camp Creek.

6.4 The trail enters the creekbed and follows it approximately 25 feet upstream, where it rejoins the old road on the south side of the creek.

6.5 You will find a good campsite on the right between the trail and the creek.

6.55 Cross back to the north side of the creek. Although there are some large boulders in this portion of the creek, there are fewer than on the Laurel Fork of Station Camp Creek.

6.6 Ford the creek.

6.65   Ford the creek for the last time before reaching Charit Creek Lodge. Notice the single, large, sandstone boulder on the north bank. The trail will now remain to the north of Station Camp Creek.

6.8   The trail forks. Go right.

6.85   You'll see an old fence to the left of the trail.

6.88   Cross the small drainage branch.

7.2   Two dilapidated gateposts stand on each side of the trail.

8.0   Charit Creek Lodge. According to local legend, the name "Charit" is in memory of a young girl named Charity who drowned in this creek during a flash flood. (H. Duncan 1986) (To learn more about the Charit Creek area, read pages 76–78.)

The trail back to Laurel Fork Creek begins in front of the Charit Creek Lodge. You will see a sign for the trail and red arrowhead blazes on the trees. The first 0.8 mile is a steep trail leading from the valley surrounding Charit Creek Lodge to the ridgetop. An old road, now used as a horse trail, also leads to the ridge, but it is longer and steeper.

Rock hop across the stepping-stones in Station Camp Creek and continue over the floodplain. The trail now parallels a drainage branch.

8.1   After ascending a long series of steps, you will leave the branch and turn to the left, hiking between two large boulders.

8.4   Continuing to climb the steep hillside through a series of switch-backs, you once again return to the drainage branch.

8.6   Notice the huge tree trunk slowly decaying, enriching the soil for the benefit of other plants. Several small trees are already growing from its trunk.

8.7   The trail reaches the bluff line where stairs ascend the bluff. To the right of the stairs, the semicircular bluff becomes a waterfall in wet weather. From the top of the bluff you have a good view of Hatfield Ridge on the opposite side of Station Camp Creek.

8.8   The trail passes a rock shelter, crosses a small footbridge, and emerges on top of the ridge at the parking area for Charit Creek Lodge. You can reach the Lodge by horse or hiking trails only. The gated road that goes down the ridge to your right is the horse trail and administrative access to Charit Creek. From the Charit Creek Hiking Trailhead, travel straight ahead along the road.

9.0   The trail leaves the road to the left. From here you can see where the road joins Fork Ridge Road. You should follow the trail to Fork Ridge Road and continue straight downhill on the horse trail.

9.2   The trail forks. Both trails are marked with the yellow horsehead blaze. You should turn to the right.

9.4   The trail crosses a large power-line clearing.

9.6   There is a gate across the trail. When the Big South Fork National River and Recreation Area was established, the enabling legislation stated that certain areas of the park, mainly the river gorge and the valleys of its main tributaries, be off limits to vehicular traffic. That is why you come to so many gates across old roads as you enter valleys within the park.

9.7   Cross the cleared power-line area. The trail begins a long, occasionally steep, descent to Black House Branch.

10.2   Ford Black House Branch.

10.35   Crossing Black House Branch again, you will walk a short distance up a portion of the creekbed.

10.4   Ford the branch once more. Notice on the right the rock ledge hanging over the creek.

10.6   Junction with the Laurel Fork Trail. Continue to the right, following the red arrow blazes.

10.7   Trail junction at Laurel Fork Creek. The trail to the right going upstream leads to the Middle Creek Trailhead. Follow the trail that crosses the creek and leads up to Jacks Ridge Trailhead. You'll climb the steep, rocky roadbed to the top of the ridge.

11.1   Jacks Ridge Trailhead.

3. West Entrance Trailhead

The West Entrance Trailhead is located near the western boundary of the park on TN 297. It is about 4 miles west of the paved road to Bandy Creek Campground.

Bandy Creek Campground

Distance: 3.4 miles one way
Rating: Easy
Suggested time: 1.5 hours
Blaze: Red arrowhead
Accommodations: Bandy Creek Campground/Visitor Center
Special considerations: Stairs, footbridges

Mileage Description

0.0   The trail to Bandy Creek Campground leaves from the east end of the West Entrance Trailhead parking lot. The trail begins as a small, overgrown path not easily seen from the parking area. Look for the red arrowhead blaze.

0.4   The trail enters an eroded area, crosses an old roadbed, and begins to follow an old logging road. Entering from TN 297, mountain bikers share this section of hiking trail.

0.7   Mountain bikers go left; hikers go right.

0.9   The trail leaves the logging road to the right. The trail has been fairly level, but it now begins to descend.

1.5   Five split-log bridges cross a small branch and low-lying area near Bandy Creek. During rainy weather these may be under water. After crossing the bridges, the trail follows a level route through hemlock, laurel, and ferns. Because of the thick undergrowth, you probably can't camp here.

      During the 1920s and 1930s, Poley Payne ran traplines up and down this section of Bandy Creek. The numerous pelts he recovered kept his pockets flush with cash even during the leanest days of the Depression. (Malanka 1992)

1.7   Scott State Forest boundary.

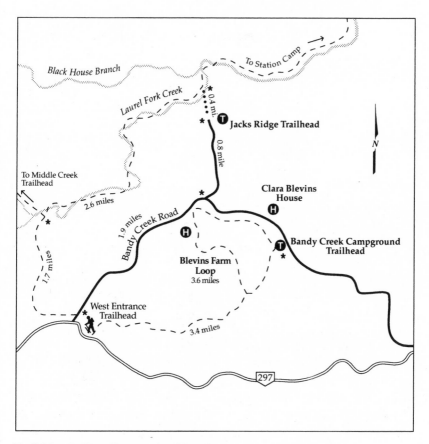

Trail Map 3. West Entrance Trailhead

1.9   Notice the number of large white pines, identified by the swirl of
       five needles around each node, along the creekbed.

2.2   Cross the logging road that serves as a bike trail and continue
       straight ahead.

2.4   The trail intersects with the Oscar Blevins Farm Loop. The trail to
       the left will lead in 1.2 miles to the Oscar Blevins Farm. Follow the
       trail to the right and cross the bridge over Bandy Creek.

2.6   The branch flowing alongside the high rock wall is lined with rhodo-
       dendron. After passing an overhanging ledge, you begin to climb
       back to the ridgetop. For the next 0.3 mile, you can see sandstone
       bluffs with ridges of exposed iron bordering the trail.

3.0   Scott State Forest boundary. Climb the stairs beside the wet-weather waterfall and follow the branch uphill toward Bandy Creek Campground.

3.2   Leaving this portion of the Blevins Farm Loop, take the trail to the right. Within a few yards it crosses a horse trail and then passes through an area of young pines.

3.4   Bandy Creek Campground Trailhead.

Jacks Ridge via Laurel Fork Creek

Distance: 4.7 miles one way
Rating: Difficult
Suggested time: Half-day to all-day hike
Blaze: Red arrowhead
Special considerations: Road (vehicular traffic), steep climbs, rocky terrain, frequent fordings (possible high water)

This trail begins at the West Entrance Trailhead. It leaves the ridge and goes down 1.7 miles to Laurel Fork Creek, and becomes a portion of the trail that follows Laurel Fork from the Middle Creek Trailhead on the western boundary of the park to Station Camp on the Big South Fork River.

Laurel Fork is a clear stream rushing over a rock-filled creekbed and descending rock ledges on its way to the Big South Fork River. Rhododendron and mountain laurel cover its banks, and large beech and hemlock trees dot the hillsides. Don't try to hike this trail during high-water periods because you must ford Laurel Fork ten times. The Park Service hopes to reroute portions of this trail to eliminate some of the creek fordings.

Mileage Description

0.0   From the parking area follow the trail leading west across the Bandy Creek Road. The trail first parallels TN 297. It soon follows an old roadbed and descends gradually.

1.3   You come to an area of exposed sandstone where the thin layer of topsoil has eroded away. Beyond this point the trail begins a 0.4-mile steep descent.

1.5   The trail leaves the roadbed to the right, returning to the same roadbed approximately 100 yards downhill.

1.7   Intersection with the trail along Laurel Fork Creek. The trail to the left goes to the Middle Creek Trailhead. The trail to the right will eventually take you to Station Camp. Our description here includes only the portion of Laurel Fork up to the junction with the trail to Jacks Ridge Trailhead. Go to the right.

1.75   Ford the creek.

1.9   Ford the creek.

1.95   Ford the creek.

2.4   Ford the creek. Notice the rock ledge above the left bank.

2.5   Ford the creek. You will find a number of good campsites between this spot and the next creek fording.

2.7   Ford the creek.

2.85   Although the trail appears to fork as an old road goes down to the creek, continue to the right.

3.0   Ford the creek.

3.5   Ford the creek. The trail follows the creek downstream a short distance before coming out on the right bank. Just beyond the creek, the trail forks. Take the left trail along the creek bank.

3.6   Ford the creek. You can find good campsites now.

3.8   Steep cliffs line the opposite bank.

4.25   Notice the large boulders in the creekbed.

4.3   Laurel Fork Creek crossing. The trail to the left continues along Laurel Fork Creek to Station Camp. Ford the creek and follow the steep, rocky roadbed 0.4 mile up the hillside.

4.7   Jacks Ridge Trailhead.

To hike back to the West Entrance Trailhead by way of the Bandy Creek Road, go south from Jacks Ridge Trailhead along the dirt road. Keep to the right at every fork. This section is level, easy walking. In 0.8 mile the road intersects the Bandy Creek Road. Turn right. A 1.9-mile walk along this road will bring you back to the West Entrance Trailhead and a total loop hike of 7.4 miles.

A more scenic, but somewhat longer alternative is to hike 0.3-mile along the Bandy Creek Road and then turn left walking down the old roadbed and joining the Oscar Blevins Farm Loop in front of the old homesite. Follow the old roadbed in front of the house approximately 1 mile to the junction of the West Entrance to Bandy Creek Campground trail. Turn right and follow the 2.4 mile trail back to the West Entrance Trailhead. This alternate route makes a pleasant 9.1 mile loop trail.

4. Middle Creek Trailhead

The Middle Creek Trailhead is located on the west side of the Big South Fork National River and Recreation Area. From Bandy Creek Campground, take TN 297 west to the intersection with TN 154. Go right (north) on TN 154 for 1.8 miles. Turn right and follow Divide Road 0.7 mile to reach the Middle Creek Trailhead.

Middle Creek Loop

Distance: 3.5 miles round trip
Rating: Moderate
Suggested time: Half-day hike
Blaze: Red arrowhead

The Middle Creek Loop begins at the Middle Creek Trailhead. It follows the top of the ridge through a hardwood forest before descending below the bluff line, where large rock overhangs, rockhouses, and high cliffs dominate the trail.

Mileage Description

0.0   Beginning on an old roadbed, in about 150 feet the trail splits to form the Middle Creek Loop Trail. We will take the trail to the left, following the loop clockwise. The trail passes along the ridgetop through an area of hickory, maple, and oaks. This part of the trail is level and easy to walk.

0.25   Yes, that carpet of green is Poison Ivy.

0.4   Notice the large gall caused by insects on the tree to your right.

0.6   The trail enters a hemlock grove. Fork Ridge Road can be seen to the left.

0.9   The trail begins to descend from the ridgetop.

1.0   The trail forks. The trail to the left will lead to Laurel Fork Creek and eventually across the width of the Big South Fork Area to Station Camp. Take the trail straight ahead to continue the Middle Creek Loop Trail.

       The trail crosses a small branch on a foot bridge. Some of the Red Oaks that you see are being attacked by the same blight that

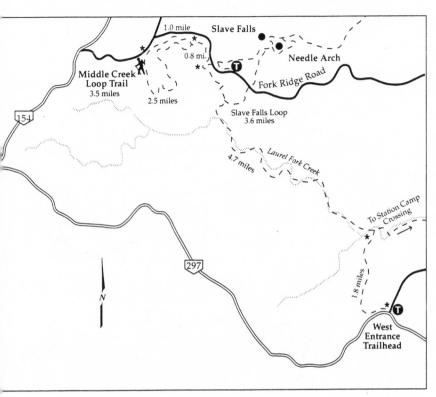

Trail Map 4. Middle Creek Trailhead

wiped out the American Chestnut. You can see several large stumps along this trail, all that remains of those magnificent trees.

1.1 You are now headed west below the bluffs over which the trail previously crossed. At this sandstone overhang there is a hemlock with a large, exposed root system growing on top of a boulder. In most places on the plateau, the soil is thin, and trees have extensive, horizontal root systems.

1.2 At this large rockhouse you may notice the constant seepage of water through the ledge above. This slow seep gradually dissolves the rock, and freezing water further cracks it. These natural processes have separated the large boulders found at the base of the overhangs and rock walls. Through its slow, constant action, water is one of the main creators of the Big South Fork landscape. Beyond the rockhouse you take a sharp switchback.

1.25   You pass a large bluff.

1.3   The large bluff and overhanging ledge continue for 500 feet. Once at the bottom of an inland sea, the layers of sand were compressed over a long period of time into the thick ledges and bluffs of sandstone. Water has continued to erode the sandstone, causing the many fissures in the bluffs. Notice that the different layers of sedimentation vary in density. Some erode easily because the sand and other particles that make up the sandstone are not as tightly compacted. The cracks generally occur between layers, and large, rectangular chunks of sandstone will separate and fall.

1.36   Many of the rockshelters on this loop are home to the threatened Lucy Braun's Snakeroot. Take care not to walk among the plants and compact the loose sandy soil in which they thrive.

1.41   Destruction of early history is evidenced by the dirt piles from uncontrolled digs in this rockshelter. Notice the small arches formed in the base of the bluff.

1.64   While exploring this large rockshelter notice the blacked ceiling caused by earlier campfires and the water pouring from a small pipe emerging near the base of the bluff.

1.7   Hemlock roots surround a boulder in their reach for the earth. Water from a wet weather waterfall drops over two ledges of this rock shelter. Rainwater filtering through the rocks begins to seep out at the base of a bluff. Streams or small rivulets may extend their channels in the headward direction and begin undercutting the bluff. Further erosion by freezing, thawing, wetting, and drying eventually results in further erosion and the development of rock shelters and semicircular bluffs, such as the one you see here (Corgan and Parks 1979: 9). Notice the red stain and the small veins of red in the rock walls, caused by iron leached out of the sandstone.

2.0   The trail passes below the bluff line. The soft sand within the rockhouse is a good place to look for animal tracks.

2.08   The trail passes a pool to your left and a deep rockshelter to your right. The pattern of iron ridges in the sandstone bluff resembles the veins of a giant butterfly.

2.12   The trail goes up the rock steps.

2.2   Cross the small footbridge over the stream.

2.4   Follow the trail down the rock steps and under the bluff. Notice the lichens and mosses growing from the rock wall. In their struggle to gain a foothold, the roots break away tiny particles of sandstone. They also hold windblown dirt and sand in place. In this way, lichens and mosses build soil in which other plants, such as ferns, soon take hold. This rock wall allows a close-up view of the many plants that call such barren places their home.

2.55 Cross the drainage on the footbridge.

2.85 Huge boulders have fallen from the bluff. Go down and back up stone steps.

2.92 Notice the gap in the bluffline.

2.98 This is the last rockshelter that you will pass as you gradually climb to the ridgetop.

3.18 Turn right onto the road and follow it back to the trailhead.

3.5   Middle Creek Trailhead.

West Entrance Trailhead via Laurel Fork Creek

Distance: 8.3 miles one way
Rating: Difficult
Suggested time: All-day hike
Blaze: Red arrowhead
Special considerations: Poorly signed trail, steps, steep climbs, rocky terrain, numerous creek fordings

The trail from Middle Creek Trailhead to West Entrance Trailhead begins on a ridge, passes a large rockhouse, and descends to Laurel Fork. You must ford the creek eighteen times before your final, steep ascent back to the ridgetop at West Entrance Trailhead. The trail along the creek is very scenic and worth the extra effort involved in the creek fordings; however, avoid this trail when the creek is high.

Mileage Description

0.0   Begin the trail by walking down the old roadbed. In about 50 yards, the trail goes to the left and follows the ridgetop through a hardwood forest.

0.9   The trail begins a gradual descent toward Laurel Fork.

1.0   The trail forks. The sign at this location is somewhat misleading, as it mentions only the Sawmill Trailhead and the Indian Rock House. You should follow the left-hand trail. (The trail straight ahead completes the Middle Creek Loop Trail.)

1.5   The trail passes beside a rock wall with an open field above it.

1.8   The trail divides. Take the trail to the right toward Indian Rock House and Laurel Fork Creek. The trail to the left crosses Fork Ridge Road near the Sawmill Trailhead.

2.3   A spring emerges from the base of the small rockhouse. *Be careful to treat all spring water and water from streams within the park before drinking.*

2.5   Past a sign giving mileages, the trail joins an abandoned road that comes in from the left. It then passes a rock wall and a spring.

2.6   The trail forks. Straight ahead within a few yards is the Indian Rock House. This large rockhouse at the base of a high bluff is approximately 30 yards wide and 25 yards deep. This is a particularly good place to look for a variety of animal tracks.The path to the right continues the trail to Laurel Fork Creek and West Entrance Trailhead.

2.9   Trail junction. The trail to the left is a portion of the Slave Falls Loop. Continue to the right.

3.0   Steps carved out of the rock lead downhill and bring the trail under the cliffs over which the trail has just passed. *Be careful: These steps are extremely slippery when wet.*

3.2   The trail reaches Laurel Fork and the first of the eighteen fordings on this section of the trail. Although Laurel Fork Creek is at least 8 feet wide in most locations, high water in the spring makes bridges along the creek impractical. Each summer for several years the Corps of Engineers placed huge rocks to be used as stepping-stones in the stream, only to have many washed away in the spring. Note the debris high in the overhanging trees. It is easy to understand how Laurel Fork was named when you note the profusion of mountain laurel and rhododendron filling the creek valley.

3.24   Ford the creek.

3.4   Ford the creek. There is a rock wall above the creek. The trail follows the floodplain.

3.5   An old road joins the trail from the left. If you were hiking this trail in the opposite direction, this intersection could be confusing, as there is no sign.

3.6   Walk downstream in the streambed approximately 25 feet. You will see where the trail leaves the creek on the right bank.

3.65   Ford the creek.

3.8   The creek falls over a series of rock shelves. Approximately 80 yards past these shoals, the trail leaves the old roadbed and climbs left up the rock steps. Keep watch because this turn is easily missed.

3.9   Notice the rock wall rising above the small tributary creek to the left. The upper portion of this wall is sandstone, and the lower section is shale.

3.94   Ford to the right side of the creek, travel down the rocky streambed approximately 25 feet, and then cross to the left bank. The trail is not well marked. You will see the marked trail again at a stand of seven medium-sized hemlocks downstream on the east (left) bank.

4.1   Ford the creek. Travel downstream approximately 25 feet in the creekbed to join the trail on the right bank. The trail is on a floodplain. Watch closely for blazes, as the trail is hard to see.

4.25   Ford the creek.

4.28   Ignore the old roadbed that goes straight; your trail leads off to the right.

4.4   Ford the creek.

4.5   Ford the creek. When the trail forks on the far side of the creek, take the trail to the right.

4.6   Cross the small drainage. Within a few yards the trail passes a path leading up to a high bluff.

4.7   Ford the creek. To your left, up the branch that joins Laurel Fork Creek, is a wet-weather waterfall. You can see it best while fording the creek. After crossing the creek, you can get a good view of the bluff behind you. Laurel Fork Creek now flows below the rock wall on the east bank.

4.9   Ford the creek. Watch carefully for the blazes in this section since the trail joins and leaves the old roadbed many times. The trail crosses a wide floodplain with a lush undergrowth of ferns.

5.5   Ford the creek. Although the roadbed continues straight, the trail veers to the right.

5.6   Ford the creek. The trail again leaves the roadbed and goes to the right.

6.0   Ford the creek.

6.2   Ford the creek. The creek is slightly deeper here than in the previous fordings. Approximately 50 yards uphill past the creek, the trail forks. Take the right-hand trail that goes downhill.

6.5   Ford the creek. This is the last fording on this section of the trail. A short distance beyond the creek you will see a sign directing you to either West Entrance Trailhead or Station Camp Crossing. The trail straight ahead continues along Laurel Fork Creek to Station Camp Creek and is covered in two separate sections in this guide on page 54 (below Jacks Ridge Trailhead) and 46–49 (Station Camp Creek).

       Your trail to the right follows the old roadbed out of the Laurel Creek drainage and up to the ridgetop and the West Entrance Trailhead. The first portion of the trail is very steep.

6.7   Leaving the roadway to the left, the trail will rejoin it in approximately 100 yards. Several switchbacks lessen the incline.

6.9   Here you emerge onto the ridgetop. The trail continues less steeply uphill. The thin layer of soil that covers the plateau has eroded away here, exposing the bare sandstone. The trail continues to follow the old roadbed.

7.9   As the trail turns right, leaving the old roadbed, you can see TN 297.

8.2   The trail crosses the Bandy Creek Road.

8.3   West Entrance Trailhead.

5. Sawmill Trailhead

Sawmill Trailhead is named for a sawmill that stood just south of the parking area prior to the establishment of the park. The trails from this trailhead lead northeast to Slave Falls, Charit Creek Lodge, and the Twin Arches Loop; southeast to the Slave Falls Loop and the Laurel Fork Creek Trail. Sawmill Trailhead is located in the western portion of the park near Middle Creek Trailhead. To reach Sawmill Trailhead from Bandy Creek Campground, take TN 297 west to its junction with TN 154. Go right (north) on TN 154 for 1.8 miles. Turn right onto Divide Road. Following Divide Road past Middle Creek Trailhead and turn to the right onto Fork Ridge Road. You will reach Sawmill Trailhead in 2.2 miles.

Slave Falls Loop

Distance: 3.7 miles
Rating: Easy
Suggested time: 2 hours
Blaze: Red arrowhead
Special considerations: Short, steep climbs; wooden footbridges beneath
   drip line (ice)

To reach the Slave Falls Loop, begin at the Sawmill Trailhead. Follow the trail that goes left, paralleling Fork Ridge Road. Within 0.1 mile the trail intersects a trail going north and south. The trail to the right reaches Slave Falls in 1.2 miles. The trail to the left is part of the Slave Falls Loop Trail. Except for the large Indian Rock House, there are no outstanding scenic features on the trail until you reach Slave Falls in 2.5 miles.

Mileage Description

0.0   Trailhead. The trail parallels Fork Ridge Road.

0.1   To begin the loop take the trail to the left, crossing Fork Ridge Road. The trail soon forks. Follow the trail to the left toward Indian Rock House. The trail to the right is a connector trail to the Middle Creek Loop.

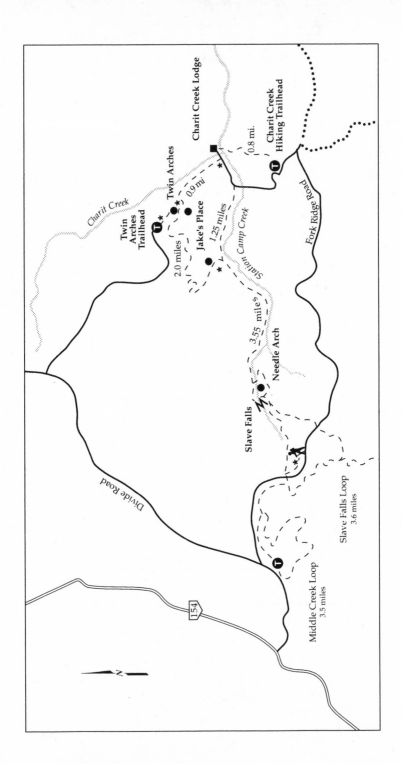

Trail Map 5. Sawmill Trailhead

0.6   Beneath an overhang the trail crosses several small footbridges. In the winter you must watch for ice on such overhangs. *Be careful: Falling ice poses a real threat when the trail passes immediately below the drip line.*

0.8   Past the directional sign the trail enters an eroded roadbed.

0.85   A spring trickles from the rock wall to the left of the trail. Within a short distance, at the base of a high bluff, you can see the impressive Indian Rock House, 30 yards wide and 25 yards deep, with a side trail leading to it. A variety of animal tracks can usually be found in the soft dirt floor. After you have explored the rockhouse, return to the loop and travel south. You'll have two short, steep climbs on this section of trail.

1.1   At a directional sign the trail forks. Take the trail to the left.

1.18   The trail briefly has been following an old roadbed. Now it abruptly leaves the roadbed. Because there is no sign, you might miss this section of the trail; look for this left turn a short distance before you reach the bottom of the hill.

1.2   Cross the footbridge.

1.4   After you cross the large footbridge, the trail follows alongside a rock wall on the left.

1.5   You won't see much of interest for the next 0.8 mile. Go left on the old roadbed. Within 20 yards the trail comes to a 4-wheel-drive road. Go left. Within 40 yards the road forks. Follow the road to the right.

1.6   The trail goes to the left, leaving the roadbed. There is a hikers-only symbol on the trail.

1.66   The trail crosses Fork Ridge Road as it begins the second part of the loop.

1.7   When the trail forks, keep to the right.

1.74   The trail forks again; go left this time.

2.2   Continue on the old roadbed. Do *not* turn left on the road marked with the no-motorcycle symbol.

2.3   Pass between the posts that block the road to traffic. You'll see a no-motorcycle symbol as you follow the trail.

2.35   You have reached the junction with the main Slave Falls–Charit Creek Trail. If you go to your right a few yards, you will intersect the 0.2-mile spur trail that leads to Slave Falls and Needle Arch is only about 0.2-mile past this intersection. (You can read more about Slave Falls and how it was named on page 67.)

After viewing the falls and arch, retrace the path to where the loop first joined the Slave Falls–Charit Creek Trail.

3.2   Cross the footbridge over the small stream. You'll find several varieties of lush fern growing along the trail.

3.6   The trail returns to Fork Ridge Road. Go left on the trail paralleling the road.

3.7   Sawmill Trailhead.

Charit Creek Lodge via Slave Falls

Distance: 4.8 miles one way (11.2 miles round trip by way of Twin Arches Loop)
Rating: Difficult
Suggested time: All-day hike or 2-day backpacking trip
Blaze: Red arrowhead
Accommodations: Charit Creek Lodge
Special considerations: Several options, steps, steep climbs, narrow trail, boulder-scrambling, footbridges (possible high water)

You have several options along this trail. To see Slave Falls, one of the larger overhanging-ledge waterfalls in the park, you may hike an easy 1.2 miles to the falls and return by the same route.

The same trail will reach Charit Creek Lodge in 4.8 miles. Charit Creek and Station Camp Creek have formed a beautiful, steep-sided valley, where a National Park Service concessionaire runs a backcountry lodge. This latter section of the trail between Slave Falls and Charit Creek Lodge is rated moderate.

To return to Sawmill Trailhead from Charit Creek, you may choose to retrace your steps or return by way of the Twin Arches Loop. The loop, although rated difficult due to the steepness of the trail leading up to the Twin Arches and the boulder-scrambling required to complete the loop past the arches, is one of the outstanding scenic trails within the Big South Fork Area.

To travel from Sawmill Trailhead to Charit Creek and return by way of the Twin Arches Loop, you will hike a total of 11.2 miles.

Mileage Description

0.0   The trail to Slave Falls and Charit Creek begins on the north side of Fork Ridge Road. For almost 200 yards it goes west, paralleling Fork Ridge Road. The sign at this junction gives directions for the Slave Falls Loop, Slave Falls, and Charit Creek Lodge. Follow the trail to the right along the ridgetop through a hardwood forest.

0.5   Cross the small footbridge.

0.9   The trail now runs along the edge of the ridge with a good view of the bluffs across the valley.

0.98   Junction with the Slave Falls Loop Trail. To the right this loop will lead in 1.5 miles to Indian Rock House. Go straight to continue to Slave Falls.

1.0   Junction with 0.2-mile spur trail to the left that leads to Slave Falls. Along the spur trail you'll find a short, steep descent by rock steps, several rockhouses, and a large bluff immediately to the left of the trail. There is a fenced overlook beneath Slave Falls.

     Over the eons, the Big South Fork River and its major tributaries cut through the sandstone rock layer, forming cliffs up to 500 feet high. Because small, intermittently flowing streams such as this one were unable to keep up with the erosive power of the river and its tributaries, they formed waterfalls along the cliffs or bluff lines. Over the years the power of the falling water has caused the sandstone to erode the base of the falls, forming hanging waterfalls like the one you see here. Numerous waterfalls of this type are found throughout the Big South Fork area. (S. Smith 1986)

     Local legend attributes the name Slave Falls to the belief that escaping slaves were hidden in this area. The independent subsistence farmers of the Big South Fork, who had little sympathy for the institution of slavery, supposedly assisted slaves in their flight north (H. Duncan 1986).

     Returning to the main trail, turn left to continue on to Charit Creek.

1.1   The trail turns downhill to the right and leads past Needle Arch. A wayside exhibit explains how the erosion of a rockshelter created this thin, delicate arch resembling the eye of a needle lying on its side. Needle Arch is approximately 10 feet high and 30 feet wide.

1.36   Stop to examine the hole in the roof of this rockshelter. Needle Arch may have looked like this in its early stages of formation.

1.44   The trail begins to descend and turns back west toward Slave Falls. Now you are traveling below the ridge. The trail will eventually make a U-turn again below the falls. The hillside slopes steeply, and in places the trail is quite narrow. The trail descends quickly at first but levels out as you near the bottom.

1.54   The small footbridge crosses the drainage.

1.89   Cross the creek below Slave Falls. The trail now returns to its eastward course.

1.91   Another 0.1-mile spur trail turns sharply to the left to give you a view of Slave Falls from the north. This trail, which is on a gently sloping hillside, doesn't pass the impressive rock formations seen on the other side. Continue straight ahead. The trail to Charit Creek now follows a course about halfway up a steep hillside.

2.14   Rock steps descend into a small drainage. In about 150 yards you'll pass above a wet-weather waterfall.

2.54   Notice the shelf waterfall above the trail.

2.84   The trail gradually descends through an area of large white pines, beech, and hemlock.

3.24   Leaving the steep-sided valley, the trail now veers closer to the creekbed.

3.44   A power-line clearing crosses the trail. Red cedars grow in the poor soil.

3.55   A footbridge crosses the north branch of Station Camp Creek. Beyond the footbridge is the junction with the Twin Arches Loop Trail. While the sign gives 1.5 miles to Charit Creek. We found it only to be 1.25 miles after a portion of the original trail was abandoned and is now blazed to follow the road.

3.85   The trail passes through an old field now covered with red cedars.

4.35   You can see to the right the gravel road used as a horse trail and a supply road for the Charit Creek Lodge. There are some good campsites beneath the hemlocks across the creek. Because there is no bridge, you must ford the creek to reach the campsites. The trail now parallels the horse trail road.

4.45   The trail joins the road.

4.65   A large, solitary boulder stands to the left of the trail.

4.8   Charit Creek Lodge. After reaching Charit Creek Lodge you may reverse your trail (9.6 miles total) or finish by way of the Twin Arches Loop (11.2 miles) If you choose to hike the loop, turn to page 77 for a more detailed description of the hike beginning at 3.9 miles.

5.71   Twin Arches. Be sure to explore the South Arch before continuing your trail underneath the North Arch. Turn to page 75 and begin at 0.7 mile for a more detailed description of the section of trail continuing to Jakes Place. In the next mile you will find massive rock walls and overhangs, some of the largest in the area.

7.60   Jakes Place.

7.65   Slave Falls Trail Junction. To return to Sawmill Trailhead where you began, take the right trail toward Slave Falls and retrace your route.

11.2   Sawmill Trailhead.

6. Twin Arches Trailhead

The new road to the Twin Arches Trailhead makes the arches, once reached only by 4-wheel-drive vehicles, more accessible. From Bandy Creek Campground, take TN 297 west to the junction with TN 154. Turn right and travel north on TN 154 for approximately 1.8 miles to a dirt road on the right, Divide Road. In 1.3 miles the road divides, with Fork Ridge Road going right and Divide Road going left. You should follow Divide Road. In 2.7 miles the road forks again. The road to the right leads to the Twin Arches Trailhead in 2.4 miles.

Twin Arches

>**Distance:** 1.4 miles round trip
>**Rating:** Moderate
>**Suggested time:** 1 hour
>**Blaze:** Red arrowhead
>**Accomodations:** Picnic tables, pit toilet
>**Special considerations:** Stairs, sheer bluffs, no camping on or under arches

Twin Arches, sometimes called Double Arches, is the largest natural bridge complex in the state of Tennessee. According to James X. Corgan and John T. Parks' *Natural Bridges of Tennessee,* very few natural bridges in the world are as large if both arches are taken as a single landscape feature (1979: 75). The Double Arches are unmistakably twins. They are located within a ridge that is a major drainage divide. Weathering and seepage of rainwater on both sides of the drainage caused the cliffs to be undercut by headward erosion where streams or rivulets eroded the base of the cliff. Further erosion created caverns, which through the centuries eventually broke through and formed the nearly perfect arches that you see today.

The larger South Arch has a clearance of 70 feet and a span of over l35 feet. (The famous Natural Bridge of Virginia is taller but not as wide.) The North Arch has a 5l-foot clearance and a 93-foot span. Downhill creep of the rock on top of the sandstone floor may have caused a joint to widen, forming the

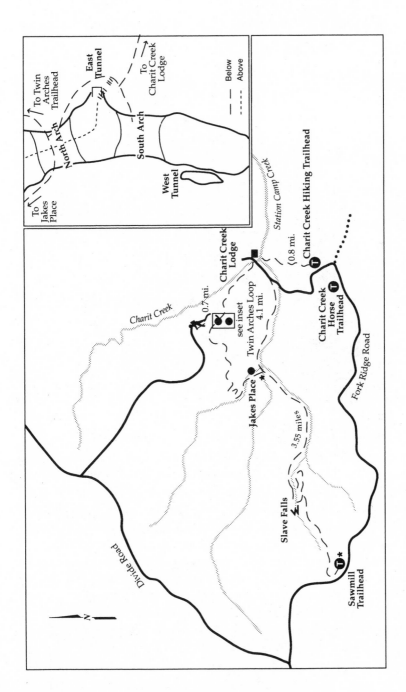

Trail Map 6. Twin Arches Trailhead

large, natural tunnel on the west side of the South Arch. Reaching a height of 6 to 8 feet, it narrows at one point to about 20 inches wide. The east tunnel in the center pillar of the Twin Arches was probably formed by groundwater flow.

Mileage Description

0.0   The trail begins at the far end of the parking area.

0.16   Warning Sign. You are entering a potentially dangerous area with high bluffs. You should remain on the trail or boardwalk, not only for your own protection, but also for the preservation of the arches.

0.23   The trail intersects an old roadbed. Follow this roadbed to the right for approximately 50 feet. A sign directs you to turn left; however, since the trail is a loop, you may also continue straight ahead.
       Our directions will take you to the left, as signed.

0.26   Two sets of long, steep stairs allow you to descend quickly to the base of the bluff.

0.3   Don't miss the switchback to the right.

0.4   Within 1000 feet the trail will cross three drainages on wooden footbridges. In mid to late May you may see Catawba Rhododendron blooming near the blufftops. You'll pass several huge stumps, all that remains of the once magnificent American Chestnut.

0.5   As the trail rounds the bend, you will have a grand view of the North Arch.

0.7   North Arch. A wayside exhibit explains the extraordinary formation of the Twin Arches. The trail going under the North Arch is part of the Twin Arches Loop Trail leading to Jakes Place and the junction with the Slave Falls Trail. To reach the South Arch, follow the trail to the left.

0.75   From near the base of the stairs you have an excellent view of both arches. Continue on and explore the South Arch. Walk through the west tunnel. By turning either left or right at the end of this fat man's squeeze, you will be walking around the end of the Twin Arches Ridge. Try your hand at catching doodlebugs living in the sand below the arch.

0.9   To finish your loop trail, ascend the stairs between the two arches.

1.0   After walking across the top of the North Arch, you will climb a second set of stairs.

1.1   A side trail offers an excellent view of Hatfield Ridge and bluffline. Return to the trail and go down a short flight of steps.

Twin Arches: North Arch (Audney Lloyd)

1.15   Walking along the narrow Twin Arches ridgetop you can see Fork Ridge to your left.

1.2   Trail junction. The trail turns left, leaving the old roadbed.

1.4   Twin Arches Trailhead.

Twin Arches Loop

Distance: 5.5 miles
Rating: Difficult
Suggested time: All-day hike
Blaze: Red arrowhead
Accommodations: Charit Creek Lodge
Special considerations: Steps, stairs, steep climbs, boulder-scrambling

Twin Arches: South Arch (Audney Lloyd)

The Twin Arches are also part of a loop trail that includes Jakes Place and Charit Creek Lodge. You may enter the loop from the Sawmill Trailhead, the Charit Creek Lodge Hiking Trailhead, or the Twin Arches Trailhead.

From Sawmill Trailhead, the hike to the intersection with the loop trail is 3.55 miles. At that point our directions take you down to Charit Creek Lodge, up to the Twin Arches, boulder-scrambling along the bluff, past Jakes Place, and back to the point where you entered the loop. Since the loop itself is approximately 4.1 miles, the hike is 11.2 miles round trip.

Entering the loop at Charit Creek is shorter but still difficult because you must hike the steep, 0.8-mile trail from the Charit Creek Lodge Hiking Trailhead (near the end of Fork Ridge Road) to the beginning of the loop.

The shortest, easiest way to enter the Twin Arches Loop is to hike the 0.7-mile trail from the Twin Arches Trailhead to the North Arch. The round trip on the Twin Arches Loop from the Twin Arches Trailhead is approximately 5.5 miles.

0.0   From the trailhead, follow the trail down the stairs and around the base of the bluff to the North Arch.

0.7   Go underneath the North Arch and continue on the trail to the right as it makes its way along the base of the bluff. The next mile includes massive rock walls and overhangs, some of the largest in the area.

0.87   The trail passes beside a sheer rock bluff.

0.98   Notice honeycombed effect on the rock surface resulting from the erosion of finer silt pockets. The trail goes downhill to the left and uses stone steps to cross a drainage.

1.12   Follow the steps leading up beside the boulder. In wet weather water may be flowing among the rocks to your right.

1.17   Larger than the previous rockshelters, this one shows clearly how the sedimentary rock was deposited in layers.

1.25   The trail follows beside a sheer bluff.

1.34   While passing this lower rock bluff, notice the small caverns and arches carved by erosion just up from its base.

1.37   Touch the lighter shades of rock and notice how the fine particles of sand just fall away. The trail passes through a gap in the bluffline. To your right you will see a long vertical fissure where the rock is separating from the main bluff.

1.44   Nearly white, beach-like sand covers the trail beneath this bluff. Turn back and take a second look at that vertical split in the rock.

1.53   A wet-weather waterfall sometimes spills over the lip of this huge semicircular bluff. The trail is more difficult to follow in this rockshelter as it winds its way among the boulders and up rock steps.

       The cobbles littering the floor are the results of niter mining. The sandstone rock of the Cumberland Plateau contains a greater concentration of nitrate than the guano-rich cave soils mined in areas like Mammoth Cave. Niter, or saltpeter, is an essential ingredient of gunpowder which is composed of 75% niter, 15% charcoal, and 10% sulfur. With fewer processing steps, the sandstone derived niter was an especially attractive source. Examples of cliff faces exhibiting niter mining can be found throughout the area. Frequently associated with such cliffs are old wagon roads, pry-bars, metal tools and wooden troughs. If you discover other sites, please inform our archaeologist. (DesJean 1992)

1.7   Look for the hole whose vertical distance extends through the rock to the top of the bluff where the sky can be seen. The metal tags on rockshelters assist archaeologists in keeping track of significant data. Most of the rockshelters in the Big South Fork area were dug without regard to proper techniques and valuable history was lost forever.

1.8   The trail has reached the end of the ridgetop and begins to descend towards Jakes Place.

2.1   The trail crosses two small drainages.

2.32   Two switchbacks with stone steps allow you to follow the drainage downhill to the valley floor.

2.5   These bottomlands were once cleared for farming. Cross the footbridge over a small tributary of Station Camp Creek.

2.6   Jakes Place. The sandstone chimney standing alone in the middle of the clearing is the lone reminder of the busy farmstead that once occupied this valley. In *Jonathan Blevins, Sr. of Virginia and His Descendants* (Blevins and Blevins 1982: 87–90), you can read how Jake Blevins brought his bride to this homestead in 1884. The house was already old when Jake and Viannah moved here.

       The Blevinses were totally self-sufficient mountain farmers who made everything from food and clothing to the guns Jake used for hunting. Jake was a skilled farmer, builder, miller, blacksmith, gunsmith, and shoemaker. Viannah gardened, canned, spun and wove for her family of five boys and four girls. The Blevinses lived on the farm and carried on this pioneer way of life until the 1930s.

       Once a popular backcountry campsite, Jakes Place became so heavily impacted that in 1991 it was posted as off limits for camping. The chimney was vandalized when campers removed stones to build a fire ring. The fate of the now unstable double chimney remains in question.

       On a nearby knoll you can find the gravesites of two of Jake and Viannah's children.

2.65   Intersection with the Slave Falls Trail. (If you entered the Twin Arches Loop here, coming in from Sawmill Trailhead, you have now hiked 7.64 miles. You have only 3.54 back to the trailhead to complete your 11.2 mile hike.) While the sign indicates that it is 1.5 miles to Charit Creek, we found it only to be 1.25 miles. (At one

time, according to faint blazes still visible on some trees, the trail
left the old roadbed and veered off to the right; however, that section
of trail was abandoned and the road was blazed as the hiking trail.)

2.7   After crossing two footbridges, the trail follows the hillside above
      Station Camp Creek.

3.0   The trail turns away from Station Camp Creek. Red cedar grow on
      what was old farmland. Cross the footbridge.

3.15 You will cross two drainages. The second one does not have a
      footbridge across it.

3.22 The trail returns to follow Station Camp Creek.

3.47 Below you can see the road that serves as administrative access and
      horse trail into Charit Creek.

3.57 After crossing a footbridge, the trail enters the gravel road leading to
      Charit Creek in 0.3 mile. Although there was no major military
      encounter in this area during the Civil War, there was a great deal of
      guerilla warfare. Scott County seceded from the state of Tennessee
      when it learned of the state's secession from the Union. Surrounded
      on all sides by Confederate sympathizers, it was easy prey for
      Confederate guerillas. (Sanderson 1974:187) The Tackett family
      lived in a cabin near the present day Charit Creek Lodge. The
      chimneyfall is located near a big rock along this road. In 1863 a
      group of rebel sympathizers suddenly came to the homestead. Joe
      Simpson relates the fate of the Tackett boys in this manner: An old
      woman was there with the two teenaged boys and she was afraid that
      they would be taken and killed. The only way that she could think to
      hide them was to put them under the feather mattress, get into bed
      on top of them, and pretend to be too sick to move. Apparently this
      ruse worked and the men eventually left. Unfortunately, when the
      covers were removed, the boys had suffocated. They were buried
      near the big, square boulder just out the cabin door. (H. Duncan.
      1992)

3.9   Charit Creek Lodge. You are at the bridge over Charit Creek. Charit
      Creek meets Station Camp Creek in this small, secluded valley
      bordered on the north by Hatfield Ridge and on the south by Fork
      Ridge.

Charit Creek was the location for one of the station camps (base camps) established by longhunters who came into the area from Virginia and North Carolina in the late 1700s.

As more permanent settlers moved into the Big South Fork area, they moved up the fertile drainage valleys. Although it is not certain who first settled Charit Creek, architectural studies suggest that the original structure within Charit Creek Lodge could have been constructed as early as 1816. The west end of the lodge, minus the back porch and the board-and-batten boxed area on the south, is the original story-and-a-half log saddlebag house. A saddlebag house is characterized by a center door that looks in upon a central chimney opening to a room on each side. The massive hewn-sandstone fireplace is still the focal point of this section of the lodge. The one-story, single-pen corn crib on the property was built during the same time period.

In the 1920s, Jack Blevins, Oscar's father, built the barn and log smithy. The large barn, a replica of the original one destroyed by fire, was a two-story, four-crib, log barn made of hand-hewn hemlock and oak logs with half-dovetail corner notching. The style of both the single-pen house and the barn are characteristic of an earlier period, as buildings here were still being constructed in the 1920s in a style that had not been used since the nineteenth century in other areas. Two characteristics of local architecture are the continual adding on to existing structures and the use of materials at hand. All of these structures have been rehabilitated or stabilized.

After World War II, many inhabitants moved away from the Big South Fork area. In the 1960s, Joe Simpson converted the farm into a hunting camp. The house was extensively modified to create a lodge, which was called Parch Corn Creek Hunting Camp, or the Hog Farm by locals, since people came from all over the country to hunt imported wild boar (U.S. Army Corps of Engineers 1986: 14–19; Blevins 1987). Today the lodge serves hikers, mountain bike and horseback riders, as well as hunters.

4.2   After crossing the clearing, you begin a steep ascent out of the Charit Creek valley. The trail goes up several sets of steps. Notice the large beech and shagbark hickory trees dotting the hillside.

4.67   After hiking uphill by way of seven switchbacks, you finally reach the end of the ridge. You probably caught glimpses of the arches through the trees on your way uphill.

4.8   You are now at the sign for Charit Creek Lodge. (A quick calculation reveals that the trail that you just climbed was not 1.1 miles but only 0.9 miles. Although signing has the loop at 4.6 miles in length, twice our measurements have arrived at the same 4.1 mile figure.) Take time to explore the South Arch. Return to the Twin Arches Trailhead by climbing the stairs between the two arches. Read the Twin Arches Trail on page 72 for details beginning at 0.9 miles.

5.5   Twin Arches Trailhead.

7. Rock Creek Loop Trailhead

To reach the Rock Creek Loop Trailhead from the Bandy Creek Campground, travel west on TN 297. At the junction with TN 154, turn to the right. In 1.8 miles turn right onto Divide Road. In 1.3 miles the road forks. Continue left on Divide Road. In another 2.7 miles the road divides again. The road to the right leads to the Twin Arches Trailhead. Remain left on Divide Road. In 0.4 mile Divide Road will again fork. Follow the gravel road to the left toward the Hattie Blevins Cemetery. If you miss this turn and reach the intersection called Three Forks, you have gone 0.1 mile too far. Rock Creek Loop Trailhead is 2.9 miles down the road to the Hattie Blevins Cemetery.

Rock Creek Loop

Distance: 7.1 miles
Rating: Difficult
Suggested time: All-day hike
Blaze: Red arrowhead/JMT/Sheltowee
Special considerations: Optional starting points, road (vehicular traffic),
    steep climbs, rocky terrain

The Rock Creek Loop begins on a ridgetop and descends to Massey Branch. It then follows Massey Branch to Rock Creek, a clear, rock-bottomed tributary of the Big South Fork River. The trail then winds up and down the bank of Rock Creek before it returns to the ridgetop by way of an extremely steep 0.3-mile trail. You will find limited parking at the trailhead near the Hattie Blevins Cemetery. Notice the wooden benches for graveside services. The sign states that Rock Creek Loop is 9 miles long, but we found it to be closer to 7.1 miles. Please note that it is a difficult trail and certainly may seem longer.

Mileage Description

0.0   Follow the dirt road leading past the cemetery.

0.2   As the trail starts downhill, the road divides. Go left. After rounding
      a curve and traveling slightly uphill, the trail then levels off for an
      easy walk along the ridgetop.

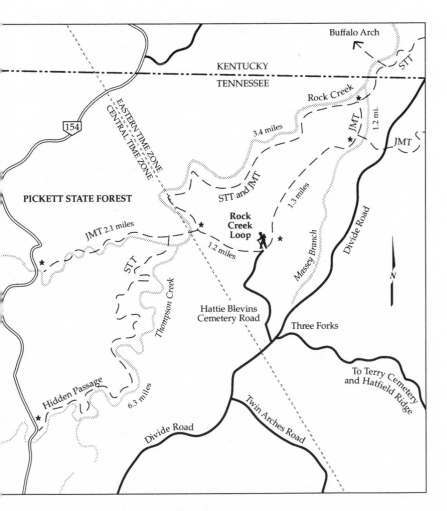

rail Map 7. Rock Creek Loop Trailhead

0.5   The road divides. Go to the right.

0. 9   Leaving the roadbed, the trail goes to the right.

1.2   The trail begins the steep descent to Massey Branch by way of several switchbacks.

1.3   A wooden bridge crosses Massey Branch to the right of the trail. The trail that crosses this bridge is a portion of the John Muir Trail. It leads within 0.5 mile to Divide Road. (The Rock Creek Loop may be started at that point; however, there is parking for only one vehicle where the JMT crosses Divide Road.)

To continue the Rock Creek Loop Trail, do *not* cross the bridge but continue straight ahead. The Rock Creek Loop and the John Muir Trail will coincide for the next 5 miles.

1.55   The trail passes through a narrow cut alongside Massey Branch. The old railroad ties are remains of the Stearns logging railroad that once traveled this route between Bell Farm, Kentucky, and the outlying timberlands of the Stearns Coal and Lumber Company in Pickett and Fentress Counties.

You can see vertical drill marks in the bluff. Rock was blasted away since only flatcars could make it through this section. The overhanging rock shelters the remaining railroad ties and as a result they are in better condition here than in other places along the line. The ties were cut from the surrounding hillsides, flattened on each side and laid in place without any type of preservation. Crumbling piles of sulfur and alum cover the trail. Crevices in the rock provide a habitat for the brown bat as you will discover if you hike here around dusk. You will see a small rock-ledge waterfall along Massey Branch. The branch soon begins to etch its way lower into the valley as the trail follows the hillside. As the trail continues northwest around the hillside, Massey Branch joins Rock Creek at the bottom of the hill.

1.9   Notice the large boulder standing alone on the left side of the trail. You have a good view of the tall bluff across the creek. Sulfur has leached from the sandstone, causing yellow stains in the bluff. See if you can spot the 1953 U.S.G.S. bench marker. According to this geological survey your current elevation is 1308 feet.

2.3   The trail has now rounded the hillside and passes below smooth, scalloped-looking bluffs.

2.4   The old railroad bed continues straight ahead. Your trail veers off to the right and begins a series of switchbacks leading downhill.

2.5   The trail forks. The John Muir Trail now joins with a section of the Sheltowee Trace, blazed with a white turtle. The trail to the right goes into Kentucky to the Great Meadow Campground. The trail to the left follows the JMT into Pickett State Park. Take the left trail.

You will follow Rock Creek, hiking up and down the hillside until you reach the Pickett State Forest boundary. Within 100 yards you'll find some good campsites on the right between the trail and the creek.

2.8   The trail rejoins the railroad cut.

2.9   The trail is very indistinct. There is a floodplain to the right, where it appears that the trail might go downhill and closer to the creek, but the trail actually goes uphill to the left, passing a large beech tree. The trail climbs steeply uphill.

3.1   The large footbridge crosses the steep drainage. The trail soon passes through a grove of large beech and hemlock trees, where the forest floor is covered in ferns.

3.3   Cross the stepping-stones in the stream.

3.6   Notice the large moss- and lichen-covered boulder between the trail and the creek. Where mosses and lichens have broken up the rock into soil, ferns have begun to grow from the cracks.

3.75   You can find some good camping spots along the creek on this section of trail.

3.8   The small footbridge crosses the drainage.

4.3   The trail makes a sharp right among some large boulders. You must watch closely for the white blaze in this area. After descending to the creek, you soon come to a small footbridge. Continue to follow the meandering path up and down the hillside.

5.5   Cross the large footbridge over the drainage, then cross another large footbridge within 100 yards.

5.6   Pickett State Forest boundary. The trail now follows the easily seen, orange-blazed boundary line.

5.9   Remnants of an old railroad track lie across the trail. In approximately 50 yards, the trail divides. The John Muir Trail goes downhill to the right and fords the creek. You will follow the Rock Creek Loop trail up the drainage to the left. This is the trail, although at first it looks more like an animal path. The next 0.3 mile of trail is extremely steep and rocky.

6.1   You will find a rockhouse in the bluff to the right of the trail.

6.2   The trail crests the ridge and levels out for the remainder of the loop. Within a short distance the trail joins an old roadbed.

6.5   The trail intersects another old roadbed. Continue to your right.

6.6   The road divides. Remain to the right.

6.7   The trail returns to the gravel road leading to the Hattie Blevins Cemetery. Go left.

7.1   Rock Creek Loop Trailhead.

8. Leatherwood Ford Trailhead

Leatherwood Ford has been a low-water crossing point on the Big South Fork River for nearly 3000 years. The combination of shallow water and gaps in the bluffs on both sides of the river made it a natural place to ford. Shell middens left from the collection of mussels remain as evidence of early Indian occupation. Longhunters and their descendants continued to use the crossing. The name Leatherwood Ford came from the abundance of Leatherwood trees found at this location. The tree derives its name from its bark, which is as strong as leather when stripped from the trees. Indians used the strips of bark from the Leatherwood tree to make bow strings, fish lines and baskets. Settlers used the bark for shoe laces.

One of the first crossing places was just upstream of the modern-day bridge. A logger, Mr. G. W. Gragg, lost a brand new team of mules and the wagon they were pulling when the mules were swept downstream into a hole and became entangled in their harnesses and drowned. Following this unfortunate incident, he and his logging crew built a log crib bridge that was used from 1929 to 1933. Remains of the log cribs can still be seen on the west side of the river. Then, in 1938 Mr. Gragg designed a concrete pier and planked bridge and was foreman of the Works Progress Administration (WPA) crew that constructed it. The bridge was built entirely by hand except for a small gasoline pump to keep water out of the pier support holes. Although flooding has washed away parts of this low-water bridge numerous times, it continues to serve the area well. In the 1980s the U. S. Army Corps of Engineers completed a steel bridge across the gorge, but the low-water bridge is still an important river access for paddlers and fishermen as well as a crossing for hikers. (H. Duncan 1986, 1992; Malanka 1992)

Leatherwood Ford is located on TN 297 between Jamestown and Oneida, Tennessee. The trailhead at Leatherwood Ford is on the east bank of the Big South Fork River and north of the highway. Many people use the river by the old bridge as a swimming area. It also serves as a canoe access.

Accommodations at the trailhead include the following: Restrooms; outdoor shower and changing stalls; large gazebo with benches, bulletin boards, and brochure racks; river boardwalks and benches; picnic tables; trash cans; recycling bins; telephones. *Be warned: During high water, the river frequently covers the low-water bridge and walkways along the riverbank.*

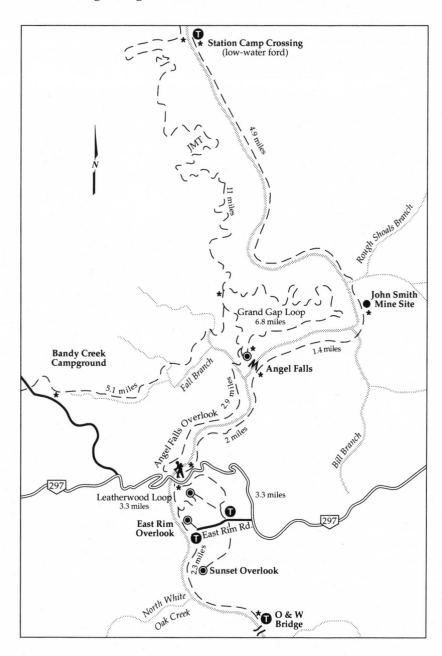

Trail Map 8. Leatherwood Ford Trailhead

O & W Bridge

Distance: 4.6 miles round trip
Rating: Easy
Blaze: JMT
Suggested time: 2 to 3 hours
Special considerations: Steps, bridge; however, first one-quarter mile is handicapped accessible

From the Leatherwood Ford Trailhead go south under the bridge spanning the gorge to the trail following the east bank of the river.

Mileage Description

0.0   A sign on the trail shows 2.3 miles to the O & W Bridge. The trail, blazed with a blue silhouette, is a portion of the John Muir Trail. The trail follows the river through a beech and maple forest interspersed with hemlock, white pine, mountain laurel, and rhododendron. You will see many large rock outcrops.

0.2   A good camping spot is located to the right of the trail.

0.25   You can see the Bandy Creek–Echo Rock Rapid, from the footpaths leading off the trail to your right. Wooden stairs lead through a jumble of huge boulders.

0.5   The trail to the left climbs uphill to the overlook on the Leatherwood Loop Trail. Continue to the right.

0.8   Sand Branch forks, and the trail crosses both streams. A sandy flood-plain stretches between the trail and the river. The branch is forested with a dense thicket of mountain laurel. A short distance past Sand Branch, an old logging road goes off to the left. Keep right.

0.9   The trail appears to end at a large rock outcrop, but it actually begins a couple of switchbacks that lead further up the hillside.

1.25   Another old logging road joins the trail from the left.

1.75   From here you can see the river and the massive boulders on its banks.

2.0   Notice the large jumble of boulders with unusual erosion patterns.
       Soon after the large, boulder-filled drainage, the trail passes through deep cuts in the bank. In *Dusty Bits of the Forgotten Past,* H. Clay Smith relates that years ago J. R. Reed, a railroad investor, attempted to build a spur railroad from the O & W Bridge to Leatherwood Ford, but the enterprise proved so costly that he went bankrupt (1985: 230–31).

The O & W Bridge (Audney Lloyd)

Ranger Howard Ray Duncan's grandfather told him that loggers later used his railroad cut, building a pole road along the route. Benita Howell explains: "Pole roads were tracks of parallel, peeled saplings, 8–10 inches in diameter, joined at the ends like sections of log pipe. Heavy flatbed wagons were pulled over these tracks by mules or horses. These cars had cast iron wheels with a concave rolling surface that fit over the poles" (1981: 118).

2.2   You'll see a huge sandstone boulder blocking the old road. The trail veers to the right around it.

2.3   You can see the O & W Bridge, which served the Oneida and Western Railroad.

The O & W Railroad was a logging and mining railroad between Jamestown, Tennessee, and Oneida, where it joined the Southern Railway. O & W shareholders owned the timber and mining rights along its route. During its heyday in the 1920s, the railroad thrived as it served the numerous mining communities along North White Oak Creek as well as the independent loggers who rolled their logs down to the railway. The train also carried passengers, mail, and goods on its three daily round trips between Jamestown and Oneida. The Depression and labor unrest at the Zenith coal mines caused the railway to decline in the 1930s. When it was finally dismantled in 1954, the mining towns along its path disappeared (U.S. Army Corps of Engineers 1982: 20–22).

Notice the huge boulder that serves as support for the west end of the bridge. The original timber supports under the east end of the bridge gave way in a flood, the Big Tide of '29. Having undergone modifications to permit various types of usage, the final disposition for the O&W Bridge will not be determined until the roads and trails management plan is complete. In any case, it will almost certainly remain open to hikers. This bridge allows access to North White Oak Creek for fishing and is an excellent vantage point for watching whitewater paddlers negotiate the Class III, O & W Rapid.

To return to Leatherwood Ford, retrace the trail along the river.

Leatherwood Loop

Distance: 3.3 miles
Rating: Moderate
Suggested time: 2 hours
Blaze: JMT/Red arrowhead

Special considerations: Alternate beginning point; highway (vehicular traffic); steps; long, steady climb; overlook/sheer bluff

The Leatherwood Loop leads you from the banks of the Big South Fork to a river overlook on top of the ridge and back again.

Mileage Description

0.0   The loop begins at the south end of the parking lot of the Leatherwood Ford Trailhead. Walk under the bridge where signs indicate the loop. Our directions will take you counterclockwise, beginning along the riverbank. The trail, marked with the blue and white blaze, joins the John Muir Trail for 0.5 mile. The construction of the modern bridge over the gorge destroyed some of the shell middens but some still remain on the left as you begin this loop.

0.2   The large, steep-sided boulders on either side of the trail were originally part of the sandstone bluffs.

0.25   You can see the Bandy Creek–Echo Rock Rapid if you follow the footpaths that lead off the trail to your right.

0.5   The trail forks. The trail straight ahead continues to the O & W Bridge. Your trail, leading uphill to the left and blazed with the red arrow, is the Leatherwood Loop. It begins a steady, 1.2-mile, uphill climb through a series of switchbacks and steps.

1.0   Notice the large, moss-covered boulder on the right with trees growing from the top of it.

1.2   Cross the small, rhododendron-filled drainage and climb the stone steps. In approximately 70 yards the trail passes beneath a rock overhang; then a switchback brings the trail back across the top of the overhang.

1.3   After a short, level walk along the drainage, you will cross the branch and start uphill again. Large hemlocks dot the hillside.

1.5   Junction with a 0.1-mile trail to the river overlook. The trail leads to a lichen- and moss-covered bluff with a beautiful view across the Big South Fork River Gorge. You can see the Leatherwood Ford Bridge to your right. Returning from the overlook, continue along the trail, which gently rises and soon joins an old roadbed.

1.7   The trail now levels out. In approximately 75 yards the old roadbed begins a slight descent and then takes a sharp right. Where the road turns, the trail leaves the roadbed on the left side. Watch carefully. This trail is easy to miss because there is no sign, but the trees are blazed. (If you reach a newly overgrown field and gate, you have missed the trail.)

1.9   Junction with the 0.2-mile spur trail leading to the East Rim Road and the Leatherwood Loop Trailhead, an alternate place to begin the Leatherwood Loop Trail. A wooden sign at the junction will direct you on around the loop trail that continues through the hardwood forest covering the ridge.

2.0   The trail passes next to a small, lily-covered pond surrounded by cattails. Cross the bridge and turn to the left. The trail will continue along the edge of an open field to your right. Open fields provide habitat for deer, rabbits, quail, and other animals.

2.1   Reenter the woods.

2.2   Go left on the old roadbed.

2.3   Begin your descent to the river. The old roadbed will soon disappear.

2.5   The trail now passes below the bluff line. Because the trail follows a drainage branch downhill, there are many switchbacks.

2.7   You can hear a small waterfall. To see it you must leave the trail to the left.

3.0   You can see TN 297 a short distance below.

3.2   The trail reaches the highway and follows the left shoulder of the road. *Be careful, especially if you have children along.*

3.3   Rock steps on the left side of the highway lead down to the Leatherwood Ford Trailhead.

Angel Falls

Distance: 2 miles one way
Rating: Easy
Suggested time: 2 hours
Blaze: Red arrowhead
Special considerations: Misleading name, *dangerous* rapid (rock-hopping not recommended)

Note before you begin that Angel Falls is not a typical waterfall, but rather a Class III-IV rapid with a bad undercut. This trail closely follows the river's edge with scenic views of the river, several rock shelters, rocky streams, and a hardwood forest interspersed with white pine and hemlock on the hillsides.

Mileage Description

0.0   The Angel Falls Trail is quite possibly the best wildflower trail and is
certainly the most accessible for all ages. From the delicate pink
Lady's Slipper in spring to the brilliant red Jack-in-the-Pulpit berries of
fall, this trail has something new to see almost every week. Numbered
posts along the trail correspond to a tree guide available at the gazebo
or Visitor Center. The trail to Angel Falls begins at the gazebo and
follows the walkway to the north end of the parking area.

0.3   Go straight past the gate, along the old roadbed. During the winter
months, the small rapids in the river as well as the rock formations
on the hillside become intriguing focal points. You will soon cross a
wooden bridge over an unnamed stream.

0.8   Coal slag darkens the sandy trail. Coal has long been an important
part of Big South Fork history. The Stearns Coal and Lumber Company and the Tennessee Stave and Lumber Company had numerous
mines throughout the Big South Fork Area. From 1880 until 1930
coal and lumber brought temporary prosperity to the area. Although
after the Depression neither company regained full strength, small
operators continued to mine along the valleys of the Big South Fork.

0.95   A wooden footbridge crosses Anderson Branch. The hillside above
is a good example of a slag deposit in the process of being reclaimed. Once considered dead from the coal mining activity that
took place at its headwaters, this branch is beginning to recover and
now supports some aquatic life.

1.45   The high sandstone bluffs you see across the river and downstream
are the bluffs overlooking Angel Falls. The trail along the opposite
side of the river is the John Muir Trail, leading to the top of the bluff
and the Angel Falls Overlook.

On the rock face on the right side of the trail you can see the major
rock types that make up the Cumberland Plateau—sandstone, shale,
coal, then more shale. The location of much of the coal in the Big
South Fork area was discovered simply because of the exposed seams.
Small operations by families to dig out coal for their own use in addition to selling what they could was quite common. (H. Duncan 1992)

2.0   The wooden platform to the left of the trail offers an excellent view
of Angel Falls. (The trail going up the hill to the right leads to the
old John Smith Mine Site in 1.4 miles. This same trail continues past
the mine site for another 4.8 miles to Station Camp. The trail that

continues straight ahead across the footbridge is for canoeists who portage Angel Falls.)

The "Falls" truly described the site at one time, for the Big South Fork River did tumble over a 6- to 8-foot rock ledge. Then, in the early 1950s, The Falls was dynamited in an effort to improve the boating along this section of river. The effort was not entirely successful, because instead of clearing the river the blasting created an extremely technical, very dangerous rapid. During the Southeastern Annual Canoe Races, it was decided that Tennessee needed some feature to counter a rapid in Kentucky known as Devils Jump, so The Falls was renamed Angel Falls (H. Duncan 1986). Rated as a Class IV rapid, Angel Falls is a long, difficult rapid whose undercut rocks create hydraulics and which may claim the lives of those unprepared for the challenge. The prominent sheer bluff of the Angel Falls Overlook serves as a silent but ominous warning to canoeists to look for the portage trail on river right. *Be warned: Wet rocks are slippery, and rock-hopping around the falls can be fatal.*

To return to Leatherwood Ford Trailhead, retrace the trail along the river.

Station Camp Crossing
via Angel Falls and the John Smith Mine Site

Distance: 8.3 miles one way
Rating: Moderate
Suggested time: Half-day hike
Blaze: Red arrowhead
Accommodations: Leatherwood Trailhead facilities, Station Camp: picnic tables, pit toilets
Special considerations: Maintenance questionable, fordings (possible high water)

The trail to Station Camp Crossing follows the Angel Falls Trail for the first two miles. Near the Angel Falls viewing platform, the trail going uphill to the right leads to the John Smith Mine Site in 1.4 miles and Station Camp Crossing in 6.3 miles. For the most part, the trail follows the floodplain near the Big South Fork River, but you won't always be able to see the river. Usually somewhat overgrown, the trail is not particularly scenic, but it does provide fishermen with a long stretch of relatively easy river access. You will need to make shuttle arrangements unless you want to retrace your route, making a 16.6-mile round trip. To drive to Station Camp Crossing, take TN 297 east through the park. At the Terry & Terry Store, 4.3 miles east of the park boundary, turn left and follow Station Camp road approximately 8 miles to the river crossing. Be sure to look for the two Chimney Rocks on your left just before you reach the river.

Mileage Description

0.0   Leatherwood Ford Trailhead

2.0   Angel Falls Rapid. Continue to the right on the old roadbed.

2.1   A gate blocks the trail to vehicular traffic. Continue to follow the red arrowhead blaze. Horses and mountain bikes are allowed north of this gate.

3.0   Within 50 yards past a spring-fed branch, you'll find a campsite near the river.

3.2   The trail comes to Bill Branch, a medium-sized branch, with some large boulders upstream. You can ford it on stepping stones. Across the stream the road forks. Either way brings you to the reclaimed mine site.

      During low water, horses sometimes ford the river near this area to access the ridgetop road leading through the Grand Gap Loop on the west side of the river. This large gap in the bluffline led to the naming of the Grand Gap Loop

3.37   At the top of the steps, the trail enters an open area just south of the John Smith Mine Site.

3.4   John Smith Mine Site. A reclaimed mine site is the only reminder of a colorful character in the history of the Big South Fork. Leaving the logging business and moving to Pine Creek, John Smith returned with his family to the area around Bill Branch and made his home there for thirty-five years. He worked at various jobs to earn a livelihood. Just upstream from his boat landing, John built a v-shaped dam out of logs and river rock with a fish trap in the center. Often filling several fifty-five gallon drums with fish, he would take them by wagon down to the O & W Railroad where they were taken to Jamestown and sold. Farming both sides of the river from Spring

Branch to Rough Shoals, John also raised sheep, cattle and hogs. He even tried his hand blacksmithing at a shop that he built in Oneida. In 1943 declining health forced John to leave his home on the river he loved so much. (*Scott County News*, December 15, 1988)

4.1   During high-water periods you must wade Rough Shoals Branch. Although the trail continues straight ahead, you may wish to take a side trip to the left and follow the creek to its confluence with the Big South Fork River. You may be lucky enough to see one of the reintroduced river otters that have accepted a new home along the Big South Fork.

4.4   You pass an overhanging rock shelter.

5.0   As you pass the pond, the trail is quite overgrown with weeds.

5.2   You can see a barbed wire fence up the hillside. Many families once lived in this area near Station Camp.

6.6   Fording a branch, you enter an area of large beech trees.

8.2   After passing through the road barrier, take the fork to the right.

8.3   Station Camp Crossing. The Station Camp Creek valley on the opposite side of the river was once a well-populated valley filled with subsistence farms. Area residents forded the Big South Fork River at this point on their way to Oneida, Tennessee. By the early 1950s no families remained in the valley. The old hunting lodge at Charit Creek opened in the early 1960s.

Hunters, horseback riders, and hikers continue to use this low-water crossing of the Big South Fork River to reach the many trails converging at Station Camp Creek. Station Camp East, a few miles east of the river, is a horse trailhead. The gravel road leading past the chimney rocks to the ridgetop is Station Camp Road.

Angel Falls Overlook via Fall Branch

Distance: 2.9 miles one way
Rating: Difficult
Suggested time: Half-day hike
Blaze: JMT
Special considerations: Steps, ladder, steep climbs, rocky terrain, narrow ledge crossing, sheer bluffs, unprotected overlook

The trail to Angel Falls Overlook begins at the Leatherwood Ford Trailhead. The trail is blazed with the blue silhouette of the John Muir Trail, which continues north along this same route. The hike to Fall Branch is 1.9 miles over a moderate trail. Continuing for approximately 1 mile from Fall Branch to the Overlook, the trail becomes more difficult as you climb to the top of the ridge by a series of switchbacks. One of the most scenic trails in the Big South Fork Area, it gives you a spectacular view of the river and gorge.

Mileage Description

0.0   Cross the old Leatherwood Ford Bridge and climb the wooden steps.

0.2   Walking beside a sheer rock face, you can see the first in a series of rapids. For the next 1.6 miles the trail will follow a relatively level course along the west bank of the river.

1.8   The trail begins to turn away from the river as it follows Fall Branch.

1.9   Fall Branch is a large stream that drains the area between the Bandy Creek Campground and the river. Its cool, clear waters tumble over and around huge rocks, creating pools and small falls. The crossing over the large footbridge gives a beautiful view of the rhododendron overhanging the stream. From 1910 to 1940 several small sawmills were located along Fall Branch and its tributaries. There was also a stave mill where slabs of white oak were cut for making barrels. (Malanka, H. Duncan 1992)

2.0   Crossing the bridge and following Fall Branch back towards the river, the trail leads to a series of stone steps. At the top, the trail turns left, where it begins its ascent to the top of the ridge. The footpath leading downhill from the bottom of the stone steps offers some excellent camping sites near the river.

  Located just downstream from the mouth of Fall Branch is the "Alf Dump," a chute used by the old time lumbermen to transfer valuable white oak and poplar from the blufflines to the banks of the Big South Fork River. From here, during one of the winter's big tides, the rafted logs would be floated down to Burnside, Kentucky, and from there on to Nashville, Tennessee. (Malanka 1992)

2.2   You will see a huge, tilting boulder indented with large potholes. Go left at the top of the steps beneath this large boulder.

2.4   Continue to the left around the base of the sheer, rock-faced cliff.

2.5   A large overhang shelters the trail. Opposite the overhang you'll see
       a footpath leading to a ledge and a beautiful view of the Fall Branch
       watershed. Often you will see turkey vultures soaring over the hill-
       sides. *Be careful: The sheer drop from this ledge is extremely dan-
       gerous, as are several points along this trail.*

2.53   The trail seems to disappear around some large boulders. However,
       by climbing up the rocks in front of you to the rocky ledge and care-
       fully making your way around to the right, you will find the trail
       leading between two rock walls.

       While this gap is not the "Grand Gap," this passage through the
       break in the bluffline is truly beautiful. The gap for which the Grand
       Gap Loop was named descends to the river from the east side of the
       loop and is used by horseback riders to access a low water ford.

2.6   A ladder makes climbing up to the next ledge easier. A series of
       quick switchbacks brings you to the Grand Gap Loop. You have
       gained approximately 450 feet in elevation since leaving Fall
       Branch. Follow the loop to the right.

2.9   Angel Falls Overlook. *Be very careful: This is an unprotected over-
       look.* Because the falls are hidden by the trees in summer, you can
       see them better from the Grand Gap Loop Trail 1 mile past the over-
       look. (To learn how Angel Falls got its name, see page 93.)

       Also, just 0.2 mile past the overlook is a small arch that was left
       standing when the backside of the rockshelter eroded. An unofficial
       trail has developed here as a result of hikers climbing the hillside
       and joining the Grand Gap Loop just west of the Angel Falls
       Overlook intersection, creating a small inner loop.

       The trail continuing past the Angel Falls Overlook is the 6.8-mile
       Grand Gap Loop Trail. (For a complete description of this loop, see
       pages 30–32.)

       Retrace your route to Leatherwood Ford.

9. East Rim Overlook and Leatherwood Loop Trailheads

The paved road leading to the East Rim Overlook is located on TN 297 just inside the eastern park boundary. Turn left and follow the East Rim Road south, remaining right at the fork, 0.7 mile to the parking area where a paved walkway leads to the overlook.

From Bandy Creek Campground, take TN 297 east through the gorge to reach the East Rim Road on the right.

The Leatherwood Loop Trailhead also lies only 0.2 mile down the East Rim Road on the right. You may begin the Leatherwood Loop at this trailhead or at the Leatherwood Ford Trailhead.

Across the road from the Leatherwood Loop trailhead, you will also find a short 1.3-mile trail leading to the Sunset Overlook, with a beautiful view of North White Oak Creek.

East Rim Overlook

Distance: 100 yards
Rating: Easy
Suggested time: 15 minutes
Blaze: Red arrowhead
Special consideration: Sheer bluff, handicapped accessible

The East Rim Overlook is the most accessible gorge overlook within the park. At the far end of the East Rim Overlook parking area a paved walkway leads into the woods and in less than 100 yards emerges onto a wooden platform with a beautiful view of the Big South Fork River Gorge. Leatherwood Ford is around the bend to the right. Upstream you can see the large drainage basin of North White Oak Creek, where the old timber and mining railroad, the O & W, once operated between Oneida and Jamestown, Tennessee. A short graveled path through the woods leads back to the parking area, creating a small loop trail.

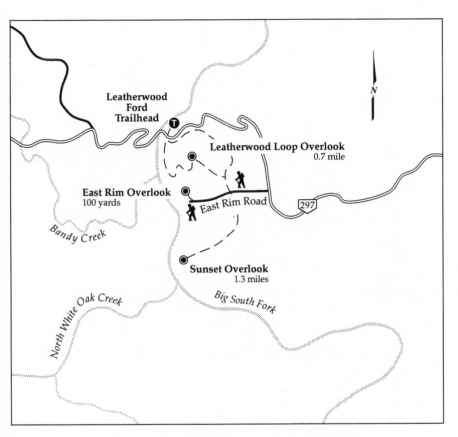

Trail Map 9. East Rim Overlook and Leatherwood Loop Trailheads

Leatherwood Loop Overlook

Distance: 1.4 miles round trip
Rating: Easy
Suggested time: 1 hour
Blaze: Red arrowhead
Special considerations: Alternate beginning point, sheer bluff

A short, level trail connects the Leatherwood Loop Trailhead on the East Rim Road with the Leatherwood Loop Trail, forming a route to a river overlook and to Leatherwood Ford or the O & W Bridge. (We describe the complete Leatherwood Loop trail on pages 89-91. Your trail enters the loop at the 1.9-mile point in that description.)

Mileage Description

0.0   From the Leatherwood Loop Trailhead parking area, follow the gravel path leading into the woods.

0.1   Enter the woods. The trail veers to the right.

0.2   Go left at the junction with the Leatherwood Loop Trail.

0.4   The trail joins an old roadbed. Go right.

0.6   To reach the overlook, leave the loop and follow the spur trail to the right.

0.7   Leatherwood Loop Overlook. Wooden guardrails protect a lichen- and moss-covered bluff with a beautiful view of the river gorge and the Leatherwood Ford Bridge.

    Return to the loop on the spur trail. The portion of the loop to your right descends by numerous switchbacks to the river valley, where you can hike upstream to the O & W Bridge or downstream to the Leatherwood Ford Bridge and Trailhead. It is 1.9 miles to the Leatherwood Ford Trailhead.

    By taking the trail to the left, you may either retrace your route to the Leatherwood Loop Trailhead on the East Rim Road or continue along the Leatherwood Loop, exiting at the Leatherwood Ford Trailhead in 1.4 miles. This part of the loop leads past a pond and open fields maintained for wildlife habitats. The trail then follows a drainage branch down to the Leatherwood Ford Trailhead.

Sunset Overlook

Distance: 1.3 miles one way
Rating: Easy
Suggested time: 1-2 hours
Blaze: Red arrowhead
Special Considerations: Unprotected overlook

This trail offers a beautiful view of the North White Oak Creek drainage basin. In the summer you won't be able to see the rapids, but the green canopy that shades most of the trail offers a cool walk on warm days.

The trail begins across road from the parking area at the Leatherwood Loop Trailhead.

0.0　Cross the footbridge and enter the woods.

0.13　The trail crosses the gravel road leading to the firing range. Used by Law Enforcement Rangers to qualify, this reconstructed range poses no danger to hikers.

0.26　Amid low thick growth, the trail passes by a small pond and then begins to follow a small creek. A large beech tree stands beside the trail.

0.29　Cross the creek on a footbridge.

0.4　The trail skirts a larger pond and crosses a footbridge.

0.57　Turn right, leaving the old roadbed.

0.7　The trail rejoins the roadbed.

1.2　As you near the end of the ridge, the sky seems to open up on three sides.

1.3　Sunset Overlook. Use extreme caution if you venture down the stone steps and out onto the bare rock bluff. It is not recommended that children be down this far without an adult firmly in tow. From the vantage point on the end of this ridge you can see the Leatherwood Ford Bridge and the railings for the East Rim Overlook to your right. You can hear the sound of rapids in the river below. Take time to enjoy the peace and beauty before returning to the trailhead.

10. Burnt Mill Bridge Trailhead

To reach the Burnt Mill Bridge Trailhead, take U. S. 27 south from Oneida, Tennessee. After crossing New River Bridge, drive 0.6 mile to the crest of the hill, where a park sign directs you to turn right. Drive 1.4 miles to the small country store and Exxon Station on the right. On the far side of the Exxon Station, turn right and go one block to the brick Mt. View Missionary Baptist Church. Turn left. Drive 2.0 miles to the 4-way intersection. A Burnt Mill Bridge sign will direct you to turn right. The road will fork in 0.5 mile. Go left at the fork. You will reach the bridge in 0.3 mile. Cross the bridge. You will find parking for the trailhead on the left.

Coming from the south on U. S. 27, turn left at Elgin onto TN 52. In 0.3 mile turn right onto a paved county road. (This road is 6.3 miles east of Rugby on TN 52.) Follow this road for 3.3 miles to the 4-way intersection mentioned above. The road straight ahead leads to Burnt Mill Bridge.

To reach Burnt Mill Bridge from the west, follow the directions on page 107 for the Honey Creek Trailhead. Continue 3.1 miles past the turn off for Honey Creek.

Burnt Mill Bridge is one of the primary locations where outfitters begin their rafting and canoeing trips. Watching their careful preparations is interesting even if you are not making the trip yourself.

Burnt Mill Bridge Loop

Distance: 4.3 miles
Rating: Moderate
Suggested time: Half-day hike
Blaze: Red arrowhead
Accommodations: Picnic tables, pit toilet, canoe access, good primitive campsites (at 3.1 miles) for larger groups
Special considerations: Steps, ladder, steep climb, rocky terrain

The Burnt Mill Bridge Loop is one of the more scenic short hikes within the

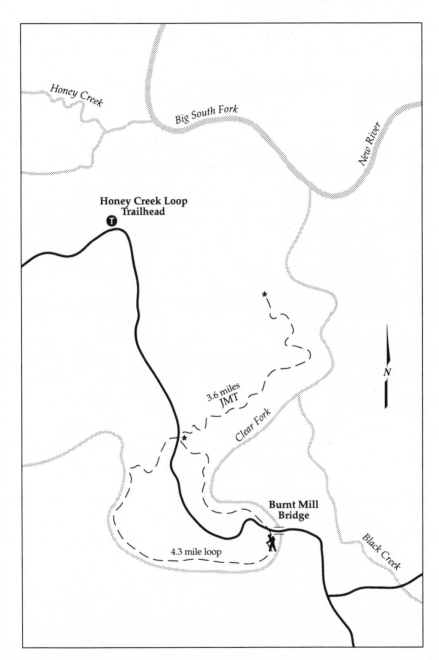

Trail Map 10. Burnt Mill Bridge Trailhead

Big South Fork Area. Most of the trail goes along the banks of the Clear Fork River and follows its boot-shaped course. The river, whose banks are lined with rock walls and overhangs, is swift-running and clear, with many rapids and large boulders. The valley is lush with rhododendron, laurel, and hemlock. Over fifty species of wildflowers have been identified on this trail.

We will begin the Burnt Mill Bridge Loop on the north side of the road, opposite the parking area.Two trails go down from the road. The one on the right simply goes down to the Clear Fork River.

Mileage Description

0.0   Take the trail to the left down the rock steps. This portion of the trail coincides with the John Muir Trail for the first 1.3 miles. Much of the first mile of trail will be rocky as it follows the hillside above the west bank of the Clear Fork River.

0.1   The trail passes beside a rock wall and beneath overhangs as you scramble among boulders.

0.4   Ladder-like steps down the bank lead to an overhanging rock ledge.

0.5   You can see small rapids in the river.

0.7   There is another series of rapids in the river.

0.9   The trail now turns away from the river as it goes under a rock ledge and then passes a large rock crevice to the left of the trail. The drainage branch on the right tumbles over a series of rock ledges.

1.0   Two small footbridges cross the branch. The trail begins a short, steep, uphill climb on an old roadbed.

1.2   Leaving the roadbed, the trail turns left. The climb is now less steep. Within 150 yards the trail rejoins the old roadbed. Go left at the junction.

1.3   The trail divides. The John Muir Trail goes to the right. This section of the JMT will eventually connect with the main portion of the JMT at the O & W Bridge crossing, but the trail is incomplete and dead-ends approximately 2 miles north of this point. To continue the Burnt Mill Bridge Loop, go left at the junction as the trail follows the ridgetop. The trail crosses Burnt Mill Bridge Road.

1.6   Cross the wooden footbridge. The trail passes through a hardwood forest on the ridgetop.

1.9   Descending toward the Clear Fork River, the trail will travel down-
      hill by way of a steep-sided drainage valley filled with laurel, rhodo-
      dendron, and hemlock. The branch flows over rock ledges, creating
      beautiful waterfalls in wet weather.

2.1   The trail returns to the north bank of the Clear Fork River.

2.5   The river, scattered with boulders above and below this point, wid-
      ens into a calm area. The trail becomes sandy. The rocks to the left
      are so flat-surfaced that they seem carved by man. In about 100
      yards a road turns steeply uphill to the left. You should remain right
      on the trail.

2.7   The trail passes close to the river, where you can see a series of
      rapids.

2.8   The large table-top rock between the trail and the river makes an
      excellent picnic site. About 75 yards past the table rock, water trickles
      over a high rock ledge and tumbles down a small drainage to the
      river. Take the steps to the left of the trail for a good view of the
      waterfall.

2.9   The trail passes by a large rock overhang.

3.0   Rock steps go along the left side of a large boulder, once part of the
      rock wall above.

3.1   A wide, sandy, open area between the river and the low rock bluff is
      an excellent camping spot. The trail now joins an old roadbed. An-
      other excellent camping site lies within 300 feet.

3.4   When the road forks, stay to your right.

3.7   The trail narrows as it passes a tall rock wall to the left and rapids in
      the river to the right. It then passes under a large rock overhang.

3.9   Turning left, the trail now leaves the roadbed for approximately 500
      feet to avoid the deep ruts in the road. If you miss the trail, you can
      follow the road.

4.0   The trail returns to the roadbed.

4.2   If you watch for ascending rocky ledges in the old roadbed, you
      won't miss the trail leading to the right.

4.3   Burnt Mill Bridge Trailhead.

John Muir Spur Trail on the Burnt Mill Bridge Loop

Distance: 3.6 miles one way
Rating: Moderate
Suggested time: Half-day hike
Blaze: Red arrowhead/JMT
Special considerations: Unfinished trail, no year-round source of water

This section of the John Muir Trail is incomplete. It follows the first 1.3 miles of the Burnt Mill Bridge Loop and then veers off for an additional 2.3 miles before it dead-ends. The Park Service hopes to eventually connect this trail with the Honey Creek Loop and then link up with the existing John Muir Trail, crossing the gorge at the O & W Bridge. As most of the trail beyond the Burnt Mill Bridge Loop simply follows the ridgetop through a hardwood forest with few glimpses of the valley below, this section of trail is less scenic than most within the park. *Note: No year-round source of water is available after you leave the Burnt Mill Bridge Loop.*

To hike this section of the John Muir Trail, follow the instructions for the first 1.3 miles of the Burnt Mill Bridge Loop.

Mileage Description

1.3   As the trail diverges, the blue-and-white blaze of the JMT leads you to the right.

1.5   The trail leaves the roadbed and goes along the ridge to the left.

1.8   The trail crosses an old roadbed.

2.7   Although the trail is no longer blazed, it's still easy to follow. Cross the footbridge over the drainage branch.

3.4   The trail crosses the large wet-weather branch.

3.6   The trail ends at a junction with three old roads. Retrace the path back to Burnt Mill Bridge.

11. Honey Creek Loop Trailhead

To reach the Honey Creek Loop Trailhead from Allardt, Tennessee, begin measuring mileage at the 4-way stop on TN 52 in Allardt. Traveling east on TN 52, turn left in 5.4 miles onto the Mt. Helen Road. Remain on the main road for 4.8 miles. Turn left on the tar-and-chip road just before the old country store located in the forks of the road of the Mt. Helen Loop. The road forks in 3.4 miles, becoming a gravel-and-dirt road. Remain left. In 0.9 mile the road forks. Remain left. The road is now a dirt road leading through a recently burned area of forest. In another 0.9 mile you will see on your left the short road leading to the Honey Creek Trailhead.

To reach Honey Creek from the east, follow the directions to the Burnt Mill Bridge on page 102. Cross the bridge and continue following the dirt road for approximately 3.1 miles until you see the sign on your right.

Honey Creek Loop

Distance: 5.63 miles round trip
Rating: Very difficult
Suggested time: All-day hike
Blazes: Red arrowhead (NPS signing may be incomplete; if so, look for various colored older blazing)
Special considerations: Registration recommended, steps, long ladders, steep climbs, narrow trail, rocky terrain, boulder-scrambling, unprotected overlooks, sheer bluffs, fordings (possible high water)

The Honey Creek Loop contains extremely rugged but amazingly beautiful terrain. Waterfalls abound. Because the trail crosses creeks and often follows the creekbed itself, it is undesirable during high-water periods. You must wear proper clothing and footwear for a safe and comfortable trip. Having to use your hands and knees to climb over and among boulders makes the trail a very difficult one. Parts of the trail are narrow, and the overlooks are unprotected. The long, steep ladders down cliffs are enclosed in wire for safety. Watch children carefully. We recommend that you don't take young children on this trail. Although the entire trail system is only 5.63 miles in length, travel time is slow.

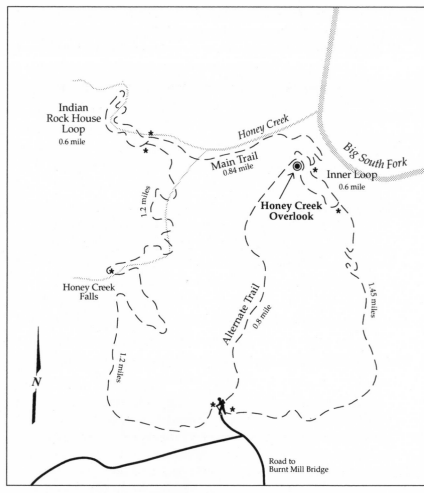

Trail Map 11. Honey Creek Loop Trailhead

Trying to find the trail after dark is nearly impossible and extremely dangerous. Allow plenty of time (1 mile per hour at a minimum) for full enjoyment and safety. Despite its difficulty, this trail offers a very rewarding experience in hiking.

Backpackers should plan to set up camp within the first mile of trail, or if reversing the trail, before reaching Honey Creek Falls. The remainder of the trail is unsuitable for backpacking because of the rugged terrain.

Honey Creek was originally a pocket wilderness set aside to be preserved in its natural state by the Bowater Company. Bowater owns and manages large tracts of land in the South to supply trees for their pulp and paper mills. They believe that an industrial forest can be managed to provide timber and used for outdoor recreation at the same time (*Bowater Trails Special Maps*). Now located within the boundaries of the Big South Fork National River and Recreation Area, the original wilderness trail will be blazed with the red arrowhead and signing improved. Trail work on the eastern section of the Honey Creek Loop Trail and the Inner Loop Trail was completed in July, 1992. When all blazing is in place, reversing this trail should no longer be a problem. (If the trail continuing up Honey Creek and the Indian Rockhouse Loop do not have the red arrowheads in place, follow the older orange blazes.) Warning signs at the bottom of the inner loop and near Honey Creek Falls will emphasize the difficult nature of this trail.

Honey Creek offers several options. The main hiking trail goes up steps to the right and through a mixed pine and hardwood forest. In approximately 1.45 miles it leads to a point where you must choose either the upper Overlook Trail or the lower trail down past Echo Rock. The two trails rejoin to form the main trail before descending closer to the Big South Fork River and then continuing up the Honey Creek drainage. *Please note: The blazed trail does not descend to the riverbanks. Several side trails have evolved through frequent use, but they are not a part of the established trail system and we don't include them in this guide. Use extreme caution if you deviate from the main trail.* An alternate trail leads from the trailhead down the gravel road to the Honey Creek Overlook Parking Area.

Mileage Description

From the Honey Creek Trailhead sign, walk down the graveled road 135 feet.

0.0   Begin the loop trail by climbing the steps to the right.

0.3   Follow the hillside through the mixed pine and hardwood forest.

0.4   A brown sign with arrow points straight ahead. The trail crosses an old roadbed and starts downhill.

0.6   The trail begins to parallel a small creek. Mountain laurel lines the banks.

0.8   Cross the small wooden footbridge. Large hemlock tower overhead and lush ferns fill the hollow.

0.9   As you ascend the wooden steps, the creek begins a sharper decline into a rhododendron-filled drainage.

0.93   The trail passes beneath a rock ledge with two small rockhouses. The sandstone has eroded away, leaving exposed ridges of iron extending from the walls.

1.0   At the end of the bluffline, the trail turns downhill.

1.01 At the bottom of the switchback, you will discover the first of many waterfalls as the creek pours over an undercut ledge. Beside the trail a huge fallen tree lies rotting, nourishing new plants as nature continues its cycle of life. The trail climbs over a step cut into this fallen giant.

1.09 The trail leaves a low bluffline to turn downhill. The creek descends ledge by ledge as water cascades over the rock shelves.

1.12 A short-cut path to the right goes down to the base of Moonshine Falls, but the main trail goes uphill to the left and past a rockshelter, then follows a switchback to the right. You may see another trail that goes down to the creek and crosses just above the drop-off at Moonshine Falls. Although some hikers have short-cut the trail in this manner, don't do it; it could be extremely dangerous in high water. Instead follow the trail continuing left and upstream.

1.16 Cross the creek. In about 300 feet you will come to an intersection. Go right and follow the trail to the base of Moonshine Falls.

1.25 As you look for the best way to cross the creek you'll discover that the crystal clear water drops over the ledge into a pool and then disappears underground briefly, creating a land bridge except in very high water.

1.27 Use caution as you recross the creek. The moss-covered rocks can be very slippery. This could be a dangerous crossing in high water as the creek begins another sharp descent, cascading over rock shelves.

1.28 Cross the narrow wooden footbridge and follow the left wall rock wall down to the creek. The water has cut deeply through the rocks and continues to fall steeply downhill.

1.32 The trail appears to fork. Take the uphill trail along a rock ledge. You'll climb over and through large boulders.

1.33 A sign on a hemlock instructs you to "Follow Bluff to Beech Tree."

1.38 You are now at the base of a 100 foot sheer bluff wall. The trail will remain close to the bluffline as you climb steeply uphill to reach the beech tree with a brown directional arrow sign.

1.45 The trail divides, making an inner loop. You may choose either (1) the Honey Creek Overlook Trail that comes in from the left or (2) the lower trail by Echo Rock. A separate description of each route follows.

Option 1: Overlook Trail - Upper Portion of Inner Loop

Use extreme caution, especially with children, along this portion of the trail. It has very steep climbs, narrow paths, and deadly drop-offs from unprotected overlooks.

1.45   Turn left and follow the steep up-hill trail to the base of the ladder encased in wire. The trail goes left at the top of the second ladder and then climbs further uphill by way of wooden steps.

1.51   At the top of the wooden steps the trail appears to come to a "T" intersection. Turn right. The trail levels out.

1.54   You can see the river through the trees to your right.

1.59   A spur trail to the right takes you out to an unprotected overlook. Downstream to your left are the Honey Creek (aka Surprise!) Rapids. Upstream, just out of view around the bend, are a close series Class III-IV (extremely dangerous) rapids. Double Drop, Washing Machine, and The Ell are known as the "Big Three." Some of the wildest and most remote whitewater rapids in the Eastern United States are found between Burnt Mill Bridge and Leatherwood Ford.

1.67   Cross the creek above the high waterfall known as Hide-Out Falls. Be extremely careful. The moss-covered rocks may be slick and the trail is very close to the lip of the falls.

1.71   The trail passes very near the edge of high bluffs.

1.72   Erosion on the top of a small rockshelter has created a low arch.

1.74   The trail forks. Within 50 feet the trail to the left leads to the Honey Creek Overlook. Continuing another 145 feet beyond the overlook brings you to the Honey Creek Overlook Parking Area, an alternate trail access. The trail straight ahead follows *dangerously* close to the edge of a sheer bluff.

1.78   A series of three ladders descend the bluff to join the lower portion of the inner loop trail

1.80   Continue to the right, close to the rock wall.

1.84   The trail forks underneath a huge rock wall. The trail to the left leads downhill toward the river and then continues as the main trail up the Honey Creek drainage. The trail straight ahead completes the inner loop, taking you back to the point where you chose Option 1, the Overlook Trail.

Option 2: Lower Portion of the Inner Loop Trail

1.45   Continue straight ahead.

1.47   The trail appears to fork. Your trail goes uphill to the left.

1.51   The trail passes close to the bluff and a large low-ceiling rock shelter before turning back downhill.

1.53   You will walk through a maze of huge boulders before turning downhill at a big beech tree.

1.54   Watch for the long vertical crack in the bluff as you near the bottom of the drainage. Just beneath this fissure is where you should listen for the roar of the rapids as the sound bounces off Echo Rock. The trail continues downhill and crosses a small drainage filled with lush ferns.

1.57   Climb over the rocks and boulders as you pass through a large rock shelter.

1.61   Water from Hide Out Falls plunges nearly 100 feet to the rocks beside the trail.

1.66   A short distance past the falls, the trail forks. The Honey Creek Overlook is 0.1 mile to the left and up the ladders to the top of the bluff. An 0.8 mile walk down the graveled road will take you back to the Honey Creek Trailhead. The main trail descends sharply downhill to the right toward the river before it turns to go up Honey Creek.

Main Trail Continuing up Honey Creek

Since the mileage on Option 1 (1.66 miles) and Option 2 (1.84) is different, we will begin a new mileage where the two rejoin to form the main trail up the Honey Creek watershed. For the purpose of giving the mileage of the entire Honey Creek Loop Trail, the 1.84 was added to the 3.79 to arrive at the total mileage of 5.63 miles.

0.0   The trail goes steeply downhill as you descend the drainage from Hide-Out Falls.

0.1   The trail levels out as you follow a low bluff for about 300 feet. You are paralleling the Big South Fork River which can be seen to your right.

0.18   Pass under the small rock overhang. The narrow trail travels along a steep hillside. While you may see several unmarked trails leading down to the river, keep in mind that these are not part of the main trail system.

0.21   The trail now begins to go up the Honey Creek watershed.

0.29   A huge red maple tree towers above the trail on your right.

0.33   Honey Creek. Follow the creekbed a short distance upstream, keeping to the left bank. Climb up and over the lower boulder. Follow the creekbed.

0.37   For the next 260 feet reassuring brown signs with an arrow direct you to stay along the creek.

0.42   At the bottom of a rock cliff, the trail goes to the right between two large boulders. Follow the arrows up a large boulder in the middle of the creekbed. A beautiful waterfall spills from the ridge.

0.46   In a fat man's squeeze, the trail passes through a tight place between two massive boulders.

0.49   Go up the short ladder and make a sharp left turn uphill between the large rock and the downed tree.

0.54   The trail returns to the creek. Water tumbling over and between large boulders creates beautiful small waterfalls in the creek.

0.64   The trail goes uphill to the right.

0.72   As you hike around a huge honeycombed boulder, to your right you can see a small waterfall below.

0.74   Large boulders create another fat man's squeeze.

0.84   You may follow the sign indicating a shortcut to the trailhead, or go right to complete the Indian Rockhouse Loop. Our directions include the loop. The Indian Rockhouse Loop becomes even more difficult.

0.87   A wooden sign directs you to "Follow Creek." Climb over the boulders and continue to walk upstream in the creekbed.

0.96   The large Indian Rockhouse is on a ledge within the bluff. You must climb up the ladder to get inside. Just after passing the rockhouse, you leave the creekbed on the right bank to bypass a narrow gorge in the creek. Return to the creekbed and follow it until you see a sign on the left. (some hikers have short-cut the trail to avoid the thick overhanging rhododendron.)

1.02   Wooden "Main Trail" sign. The trail goes uphill.

1.04   At the base of the bluff, go right past the rockhouse.

1.10   Follow the trail under a low overhang and up the drainage. Go left.

1.33   Notice the thin rock shelf forming the roof of the large rockshelter, unofficially dubbed "The Great Room." After leaving the rockhouse, follow the wall at the base of the bluff.

1.42   The trail forks. To your left the trail goes downhill 80 feet to the instersection mentioned earlier with the Indian Rockhouse Loop and Main Trail. Go straight ahead to continue the main trail to the Honey Creek Trailhead.

1.44   A wooden sign with an arrow directs you downhill.

1.49   The trail takes a big step off a rock.

1.69   Descend to the creekbed. Boulder House Falls is named for the huge boulders in the creekbed below the falls. Crossing the creek and climbing through the boulders you will come out above the top of the falls. Cross the creek and go up a steep hill. There is a rock ledge at the left. The trail goes right.

1.89   Large rock overhang.   .

1.92   Climb over the boulders. A wooden sign indicates a 100-foot trail going straight ahead to Tree Top Rock. If you take this route, after turning uphill and passing underneath thick laurel, you will come to the base of a huge exposed rock surface. However, climbing up onto the rock is very difficult and you miss Ice Castle Falls. We recommend that you follow the main trail downhill at this sign. You will eventually cross Tree Top Rock anyway.

2.0   At the bottom of a steep descent, a short side trip to your right will bring you to a wonderful secluded waterfall. The trail turns left.

2.03   Cross the creek and climb steeply uphill.

2.06   Still visible during the summer, but more easily seen during the winter months, a large boulder resembles the bow of a ship.

2.12   You have looped back, crossing the creek at the top of the waterfall. The trail continues upstream.

2.15   The trail leaves the creek and then forks. Ice Castle Falls is 100 feet to the left. Go right to continue the main trail. (The map at the Honey Creek Trailhead indicates a loop at this point. No connecting trail exists, but it is possible to cross the creek beneath Ice Castle Falls and follow the creek upstream near the left bluffline and reach Honey Creek Falls.) Again, we recommend sticking to the blazed trail.

2.25 You are now on top of Tree Top Rock. Follow the arrows across the exposed rock surface. Take care not to walk on the fragile plantlife.

2.32 The trail divides, but returns to the same point. The shorter, left fork is blazed as the main trail.

2.51 Cross the small footbridge over the creek.

2.62 A wooden sign directs you to Honey Creek Falls. The 150-foot spur trail curves around the bluffline and drops down to the pool at the base of the falls. Retrace your steps and follow the Main Trail sign.

2.72 An earthen dam has created a pool beneath a bluff. Much of the Big South Fork's earliest history was lost forever by random digging beneath rockshelters such as the two you see on your left.

2.76 Cross the small stream.

2.83 The trail comes near the top of the ridge.

2.90 Cross the old logging road. Although you are heading north, the trail will soon turn south.

3.05 Follow the trail southward along the east bank of the creek.

3.40 You begin leaving the creek.

3.43 Cross an old logging road.

3.76 Continuing an easy, uphill walk through the woods, again cross an old logging road.

3.79 The trail ends at the parking area about 65 feet from the Honey Creek Trailhead sign.

Alternate Trail: Honey Creek Overlook and Inner Loop

If time permits only a short hike, you may want to walk or drive to the Honey Creek Overlook Parking Area by way of the Alternate Trail or road. The Honey Creek Overlook offers a spectacular view of the Clear Fork River and is handicapped accessible. Attention: While the short inner loop is only 0.6 mile, don't under estimate the difficulty. (See Options 1 and 2)

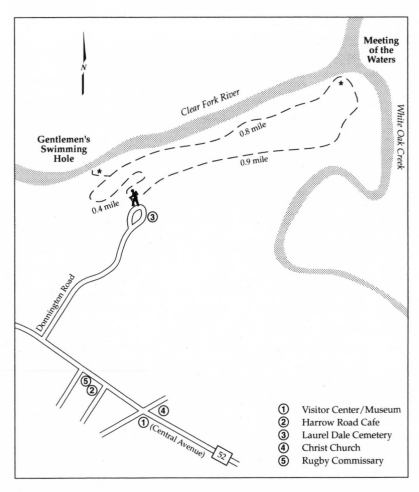

Trail Map 12. Historic Rugby

12. Historic Rugby

After traveling through the Cumberland Plateau with its small farms and depressed mining communities, you will find this Victorian village almost as surprising as Brigadoon. In 1880, Thomas Hughes, author of *Tom Brown's School Days* and a renowned social reformer, established the experimental community of Rugby in the midst of the Tennessee backwoods. His goal was to provide an alternative for younger sons of English gentry, who were deprived of inheritance by the laws of primogeniture that left all estates to first sons.

The fascinating story of Rugby is well told in the Rugby Museum and on tours operated by Historic Rugby, Inc. To reach Rugby from Jamestown, Tennessee, follow TN 52 East through Allardt. Driving from Oneida, Tennessee, follow U.S. 27 south to Elgin and turn west onto TN 52.

One demonstration of Thomas Hughes' progressive thinking was his plan to set aside parklands for the use of the residents of Rugby. Land along the Clear Fork River was preserved as park land, and several trails were constructed leading to the area. One of the most popular trails led to the Gentlemens Swimming Hole on the Clear Fork River (*Historic Rugby*).

Gentlemens Swimming Hole

Distance: 0.4 mile one way

and the Meeting of the Waters

Distance: About 0.8-mile beyond the Gentlemens Swimming Hole

Total distance: About 2.4 miles round trip
Rating: Difficult
Suggested times: 1 hour - 2 hrs.
Blaze: Red arrowhead
Accomodations: Picnic tables, nearby Harrow Road Cafe and Rugby
   Commissary
Special considerations: Steps, steep climb, rocky terrain, possible high
   water (option to the Meeting of the Waters)

In July 1988, the National Park Service relocated a portion of this trail, formerly on private property, across land owned by Historic Rugby, Inc. to give park visitors access to the Gentlemens Swimming Hole and the Meeting of the Waters. From the Schoolhouse Visitor Center and Museum on TN 52, drive west approximately 0.2-mile. Turn right onto the road leading to the Laurel Dale Cemetery. Upon reaching the circular drive at the cemetery you will see the trailhead to your left.

0.0   Trailhead. A self-guided brochure featuring flora and historical information is available at the Bandy Creek Visitor Center as well as the Schoolhouse Visitor Center in Historic Rugby. (S. Duncan 1991) The trail leads downhill through a mixed hardwood forest.

0.1   Continuing downhill past an old fence line, the trail enters a wooded area that was once grazed by livestock. Large hemlock trees can be found along the trail.

0.2   Cross the small drainage branch on stepping stones. The trail goes down a flight of stone steps as it merges with the historic trail to the river.

0.3   Water cascades over rock shelves in the branch beside you as you follow the steep, rocky trail downhill. Rockshelters and overhangs, including the Witch's Cave on your left, have weathered from the ancient bluffs.

0.35   Turn left at the trail intersection. The trail straight ahead continues to the Meeting of the Waters.

0.4   The Gentlemens Swimming Hole features a beautiful, rock-strewn sandy beach and a deep pool in the Clear Fork River.
        The Gentlemens Swimming Hole was frequented by the English gentlemen of the Rugby community. The Ladies Swimming Hole was upstream, and a separate trail was built to this pool because, as the local paper noted at the time, certain of the gentlemen refused to

bathe in the British fashion, preferring to bathe "à la Francais" (*The Rugbeian,* July 16, 1881).

Today the Gentlemens Swimming Hole remains popular with area residents. Clear Fork's cold water, pebbly bottom, and deep pools provide excellent swimming. We don't recommend diving into the river, but if you do, *always check the depth of the water first,* because water levels vary greatly. It's fun to float through the small rapids on tubes (remember: feet up!) and sunbathers will find the large boulders in the river ideal for tanning. The only disadvantage to the Gentlemens Swimming Hole is the steep, uphill climb back to the trailhead, especially if you are carrying coolers, picnic baskets, towels, rafts, and tubes.

Meeting of the Waters

The trail to the Meeting of the Waters continues straight past the turnoff for the Gentlemens Swimming Hole. Hiking around the end of the bluff, you will weave your way up and down the narrow strip of land between the bluff line and the Clear Fork River. Sections of this trail may be flooded during high-water periods. The 0.8-mile trail passes through rhododendron thickets and beneath several rock overhangs. You will see massive boulders in the river-bed. Although the trail appears to dead-end at a rock wall, it actually veers sharply downhill for a short, hold-on-to-the-trees descent. Standing on the rock ledge after you descend, you can see where White Oak Creek joins the Clear Fork River at the Meeting of the Waters. The rock walls across White Oak Creek rise steeply to the ridgetop. Retrace your steps to return to the trailhead.

At lower water levels it is possible to cross the rock shelf and climb a steep 0.1-mile trail to an old roadbed. By remaining to your right at each road junction, you can follow dirt roads back to the trailhead for a total loop trail of 2.1 miles. While not scenic, the roads offer a shorter, more level route.

Bluff view of the Big South Fork gorge, with the O & W Bridge (Audney Lloyd)

13. The John Muir Trail

The John Muir Trail, blazed with a blue silhouette of a man's head on a white background, covers nearly 50 miles within the Big South Fork Area. Beginning at the O & W Bridge, the trail follows the Big South Fork River as it flows northward. After leaving the riverbank near Angel Falls Overlook, it follows the ridgetop, offering beautiful views of the gorge and the plateau beyond. It then descends the ridge and travels through the valleys created by Station Camp and No Business creeks. From No Business Creek, the trail leads up to the top of the ridge and the John Muir Overlook.

Continuing across the plateau and descending to Massey Branch, it then winds its way up Rock Creek. Skirting the old railroad tunnel, the John Muir Trail crosses TN Hwy. 154 and continues upstream to the headwaters of Rock Creek on the western boundary of Pickett State Park.

The John Muir Trail was conceived in 1971 as one of the seven scenic trails selected by the State Legislature for incorporation in the Tennessee Trails System Act. This trail was named in honor of John Muir, noted wanderer and naturalist, who is considered the father of our National Park system. In *John Muir's America*, DeWitt Jones and T. H. Watkins tell of John Muir's crossing the Cumberland Plateau on his thousand-mile, cross-country hike in 1867 (1976: 39–40). He was traveling from Indiana to the Gulf of Mexico, where he hoped to continue on to South America. In Florida a severe bout with malaria abruptly ended his adventure. Muir mentions that while hiking to the Gulf, he spent the night near Jamestown, Tennessee,   before continuing on to the Obed–Emory River near Kingston (Muir [1916] 1981: 20). He probably never saw the Big South Fork River, however, as he came from Kentucky through the Wolf River Valley.

Until the southwestern portion of the John Muir Trail is completed, the trail begins at the O & W Railroad Bridge on the Big South Fork River. To drive to the O & W Bridge, travel east on TN 297 for 4.2 miles past the eastern park boundary to the Terry & Terry Store. Turn right at the junction and go 3.3 miles. Turn right at the small subdivision. The street sign reads Verdun. If you come to an elementary school, you have passed the turnoff. Follow this road 1 mile to Verdun, where the road forks. The road to the right will follow the old O & W Railroad route across several high, narrow, wooden trestles for 8.1 miles to the parking area at

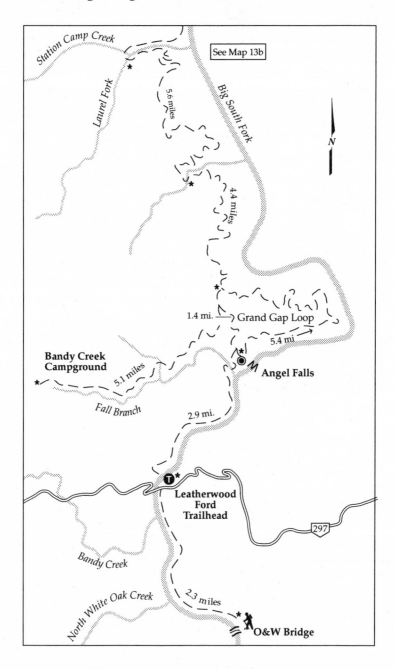

Trail Map 13a. The John Muir Trail:
O & W Bridge to Station Camp Creek

the O & W Bridge. (An improved parking area and hiking trail down to the river are planned for 1993.)

The John Muir Trail is a long-distance trail that requires careful planning. Throughout the guide we mention possible camp sites along the trail. You'll find resupply or access points at Station Camp Crossing and Divide Road.

To drive to Station Camp Crossing, follow the directions above to the Terry & Terry Store. Turn left at the junction onto Station Camp Road. This graveled road passes the Chimney Rocks and leads down to the river crossing in 7.9 miles. You must ford the river to reach the trail from Station Camp Crossing. Because the river can rise rapidly, this fording is not always possible. *Never try to ford the river if the depth or current looks at all questionable.*

To drive to Divide Road, take TN 297 west through the park to the intersection with TN 154. Turn right onto TN 154 and go 1.8 miles to Divide Road. Turn right and remain on Divide Road until it forks. Remain left on Divide Road for 5.4 miles. Watch carefully: Signs mark the trail crossing, but there is no parking area.

Except for the telephones at Leatherwood Ford Trailhead, there are no telephones or stores nearby or along the route. Although there is a large campground at Pickett State Park, there are no supplies available at the park.

Before beginning the John Muir Trail, you should register with the National Park Service at the Visitor Center in the Bandy Creek Campground.

John Muir Trail

Distance: Approximately 50 miles
Rating: Moderate to Difficult
Suggested time: 5-day backpacking trip
Blaze: JMT
Begins: O & W Bridge
Ends: Pickett State Park Forest's western boundary
Alternate ending: Pickett State Park Office, TN Hwy 154
Access/resupply points: Leatherwood Ford, Station Camp Crossing (low-water fording only), Divide Road
Accommodations: Leatherwood Ford Trailhead (telephones), Pickett State Park

Special considerations: Backcountry permit suggested, isolated trailhead/
alternate, conjunction with horse trail, steps, stairs, ladders, steep climbs,
narrow ledge, unprotected overlooks, sheer bluffs, fordings (possible high
water), limited sources of water (from mile 4.2 to mile 20.4)

The O & W Railroad was a logging and mining, shortline railroad between
the Southern Railway at Oneida to the east and Jamestown, 38 miles to the
west. The O & W's officers and shareholders owned the timber and mining
rights along its route and in the 1920s profited from the industrial development and prosperity of the area. Unfortunately, the area declined as quickly as
it developed. The great Depression and labor unrest that brought the mining
town of Zenith to national attention caused the O & W Railroad to become
unprofitable. It was dismantled in 1953 (Howell 1981: 39, 134–35).

Mileage Description

0.0   The trail goes to the left, away from the roadbed around a huge
      boulder that fell from the cliffs and now blocks the old road.

0.1   The trail follows the road originally cut in an attempt to build a
      railroad spur from the O & W to Leatherwood Ford. For approxi-
      mately 0.2 mile the railroad cut is evident, but it then leaves the trail
      and is so overgrown that you must watch carefully to see where it
      bears to the left and dead-ends at the river bank. (You can read more
      about this railroad venture on page 87.)

0.2   A stream tumbles among large boulders. For the next 1.2 miles the
      trail follows the beech- and maple-covered hillside, permitting only
      glimpses of the river.

1.0   The trail forks. Stay to the left.

1.4   Two sharp switchbacks lead you closer to the river where the trail
      passes through numerous rock outcrops. The hardwood forest is
      interspersed with white pine, hemlock, and rhododendron.

1.5   The trail crosses the two small forks of Sand Branch. The drainage
      basin is filled with rhododendron. Sand Branch forms a sandy flood-
      plain below.

1.8   The trail leading uphill to the right is the Leatherwood Loop Trail.
      The John Muir Trail continues straight ahead.

2.0   The trails to the left lead closer to the river, where you can see the
      Bandy Creek–Echo Rock rapid.

2.3   Leatherwood Ford is one of the major trailheads in the Big South
        Fork Area. (For more information about it, read page 85.)

        Continuing the John Muir Trail from the Leatherwood Ford Trail-
        head, cross the river on the old bridge, climb the short series of
        wooden steps, and hike north along the west bank of the river. Since
        you will be following the Angel Falls Overlook trail described on
        pages 95–97, our description here will be brief.

4.2   Cross the large wooden bridge over Fall Branch.

4.3   The trail climbs a series of stone steps, turns left, and begins its
        steep ascent to the ridgetop. You can find some good campsites near
        the river if you follow the footpath leading downhill from the base
        of the steps toward the river.

4.5   Go left at the top of the steps beneath the huge, tilting boulder.

4.7   Continue to the left around the base of the sheer, rock-faced cliff.

4.8   A large overhang shelters the trail. Opposite the overhang the footpath
        leads to a ledge with a beautiful view of the Fall Branch watershed.

4.83   When the trail seems to disappear, climb to the rocky ledge and
        carefully make your way around to the right. You will see the trail
        leading between two rock walls.

4.9   Climb the short ladder to the next ledge. A series of quick switch-
        backs brings you through a gap to the ridgetop.

5.0   You are entering the Grand Gap Loop.

        The Grand Gap Loop Trail follows the bluff line above the Big
        South Fork River with excellent views up- and downriver for approxi-
        mately one-third of its distance. *Be careful: The trail sometimes passes
        within a few feet of sheer cliffs.* The remainder of the trail continues
        through the hardwood forest on top of the plateau. (You may enjoy
        reading a more detailed description of the loop on pages 30–32. You
        are entering the loop at 1.3-miles.) You may travel either direction at
        this intersection, as the entire loop is part of the John Muir Trail.

Loop Option: Counterclockwise (5.4 miles)

Mileage Description

5.2   Angel Falls Overlook.

5.4   Notice that a natural arch is being formed at the back of the small
        rock shelter.

6.25   Just beyond the sharp switchback, the trail returns to the bluff line. Looking back upriver, you have a good view of Angel Falls. *Be extremely careful if you approach the edge of the bluff.*

6.4   The trail passes a rockhouse.

7.0   An old road crosses the trail past the drainage branch.

8.2   The trail very briefly travels along the roadbed and then turns to the left.

8.7   The trail emerges onto an overlook. You can see where Rough Shoals Branch enters the Big South Fork.

9.1   Cross the old logging road.

10.4   Intersection with northbound John Muir Trail.

Loop Option: Clockwise (1.4 miles)

Please note that the mileage on the clockwise shortcut will not be cumulative. Hiking to the left on the Grand Gap Loop will bring you to the same intersection with the northbound John Muir Trail in 1.4 miles.

Mileage Description

0.2   A large sandstone ledge offers a view of both the Fall Branch drainage and the Big South Fork River.

0.6   The small gravestone of Archie Smith stands to the right of the trail. (You can read about the Smith family on page 31.)

1.3   The trail going downhill to the left leads to Bandy Creek Campground. Cross the old road.

1.4   Intersection with northbound John Muir Trail.

JMT continued

The John Muir Trail to Station Camp continues from the northwestern corner of the Grand Gap Loop. Although the signs at the junction read 10.4 miles to Station Camp, it is actually 11 miles to the river crossing.

10.9   *A river overlook is atop a dangerous overhang: Be careful.* The trail will follow the cliff for a short distance.

11.4   You can see a rockhouse approximately 50 yards to the left of the trail.

11.8   The soil has almost completely eroded from the sandstone cap in this area. Lichens, mosses, and small pines cover this soil-poor area.

12.3   Pass beneath the rockhouse. You can see another rockhouse higher up the cliff. The trail then goes along a drainage lined with hemlock.

12.4   Cross the large, wet-weather drainage branch on stepping stones.

12.5   Pass the old road and continue straight ahead.

12.7   Cross the small footbridge, then continue through the laurel-filled drainage and over another footbridge.

12.9   There is a short series of wooden steps.

13.3   The trail divides. Go straight to the river overlook. From the overlook you have a good view of the Cumberland Plateau and the sandstone cliffs rimming the edge of the gorge. Make a U-turn to the left to continue the trail to Station Camp.

13.4   You will pass under two consecutive rock ledges.

13.7   The trail divides. Go straight to the river overlook. Although unnamed on the latest topographic maps of the area, the drainage branch to your left is the largest one on this section of the trail. You will be hiking around it for the next 3.3 miles. You can also see the Big South Fork River to the north.

14.0   *Be careful: You are hiking close to the edge of high cliffs.*

14.6   Cross the footbridge over the small branch.

14.8   A large wooden footbridge spans the branch. Although the sign shows 4.3 miles to Station Camp Creek, the mileage is incorrect. It is 5.6 miles from this point to Station Camp Creek. This branch through Duncan Hollow is the only year-round source of water on this section of the trail. Approximately 50 feet up the branch you will find several good campsites where the forest floor is open and covered with pine straw. Cross the bridge and continue to follow the trail around the large drainage branch. You will hike for nearly 2 miles before returning to the bluff line.

15.4   Hike past the large rock wall.

15.9   The stacks of rocks that you see may have been used as building foundations for a cabin.

16.7   The trail leaves the branch and leads north along the cliffs above the Big South Fork River. This is the last time that you will see the river until the trail reaches Station Camp Crossing. For the next 2 miles the trail will follow the ridgetop through an oak forest.

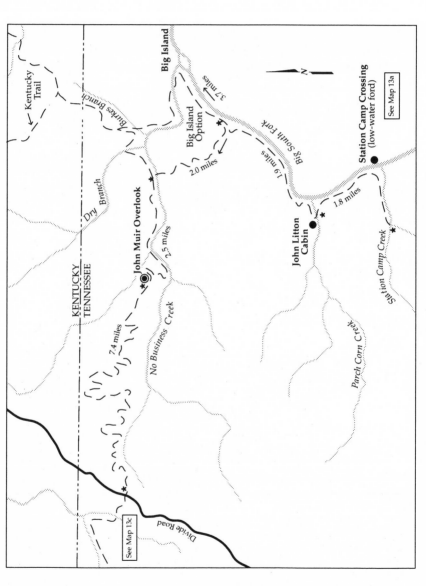

Trail Map 13b. The John Muir Trail: Station Camp Creek to Divide Road

18.2 The trail passes beneath the rock overhang.

18.3 Cross the old road.

18.7 An old road joins the trail from the left. The trail follows the roadbed for about 0.3 mile. Leaving the roadbed, the trail turns left and begins the long descent from the ridgetop.

19.15 Cross the footbridge and descend the steps cut in the trail. You will begin to see large beech trees.

19.4 After crossing another footbridge and going through an area of large boulders, the trail begins a series of switchbacks. The trail descends the ridge so gradually that many switchbacks are required. Watch carefully to avoid missing them. The trail goes down some rock steps, skirts a large boulder, and continues the switchbacks.

20.4 The trail reaches the bridge over Laurel Fork. The Laurel Fork of Station Camp Creek, one of the major streams within the Big South Fork area, originates near the Middle Creek Trailhead.

From the bridge you can see Fork Ridge rising to the west. On the far side of Fork Ridge is Station Camp Creek valley, bounded on the north by the steep-sided Hatfield Ridge. A short distance downstream, Laurel Fork enters Station Camp Creek. It is about 1 mile to the Big South Fork River.

Although this valley is now covered by overgrown fields, in the early decades of this century it was a well-populated area of subsistence farmers with a school, church, and post office.

After crossing the Laurel Fork bridge, the trail turns right in conjunction with a horse trail. Although the land here is level, it is overgrown with tall weeds and grasses, making it very buggy for camping in the summer.

20.44 The trail forks. The trail to the left leads to Charit Creek Lodge, 3.4 miles west. The John Muir Trail continues to the right. In approximately 50 yards the trail goes left through tall grass, leaving the horse trail. It crosses the footbridge over Station Camp Creek and then rejoins the horse trail. The trail parallels the creek.

21.0 The old road you have been following forks. Stay right. In approximately 50 feet the trail leaves the roadbed on your left. The somewhat overgrown trail passes among the remnants of several old buildings.

21.11 Trail junction. The trail leading west goes to Charit Creek Lodge. The trail going downhill and to the east leads in 0.2 mile to Station

Camp Crossing, the low-water ford of the Big South Fork River. You may use this route to enter or exit the John Muir Trail. If you hike down to the riverbank, you can see where the old Station Camp Road entered the river from the east side.

The trail following an uphill course to the east (to the left of the trail to the river crossing) is the continuation of the John Muir Trail. The trail joins the horse trail. Ignore the Station Camp East and Peters Mountain Trailhead signs for horse trails.

Within 200 yards a spring emerges from a limestone outcrop to the left of the trail. You can locate it by the drainage ditch crossing the trail. One of the old schools at Station Camp was located on the hillside above the spring, and schoolchildren used this spring for drinking water. (H. Duncan, 1986) Remember to *treat any water in the park before drinking it.*

21.2   The trail veers to the left, leaving the horse trail, to follow the hillside toward Parch Corn Creek. You can see the river during the winter months.

21.7   The trail crosses the wooden footbridge over the rocky drainage and then rejoins the horse trail.

22.04   Leaving the river, the trail passes through the overgrown fields at the mouth of Parch Corn Creek.

22.11   The trail once again leaves the horse trail to cross the footbridge over Parch Corn Creek. Although the trail passes through tall weeds, it is well signed.

22.15   Cross the wooden footbridge over a side branch.

22.2   Another wooden footbridge spans Parch Corn Creek. After crossing the bridge, go to the right. In about 40 yards the trail meets an old roadbed. The John Muir Trail continues to the right. You may wish to go left a few hundred yards in order to see a log house representative of the houses built by settlers throughout the Big South Fork area. Built in 1881 by John Litton, the house is a story-and-a-half, single-pen (one-room) log house of hewn hemlock and poplar. Its loft was used as sleeping quarters (U.S. Army Corps of Engineers 1986: 10). Characteristically, Litton later added a shed on the back for cooking and dining, and a porch on the front and side. John Litton may have lived in this house before moving to a farm on North Fall Branch around 1900. That farm can be visited by hiking the

ıe John Litton Cabin (Audney Lloyd)

John Litton/General Slaven Farm Loop. More information about the Litton family is found on page 36.

Although you cannot camp within the house or on its immediate grounds, you will find some suitable camping spots upstream along Parch Corn Creek. There is a spring approximately 200 feet west of the front door of the log house, just past the road that goes up hill. *Again, be sure to treat the water before you drink it.*

22.23 Return to the John Muir Trail. It veers to the left, leaving an old roadbed.

22.5 The wooden footbridge crosses Harvey Branch. For the next 1.4 miles, the trail will leave and then rejoin the horse trail numerous times. The horse trail is actually the old wagon road that led from the community at No Business Creek to the Station Camp Creek community. The trails are generally in sight of one another. The hiking trail diverges to avoid deep ruts in the old road and to use the bridges across two small branches. If you should miss some sections of the hiking trail, you can follow the old road, since both trails lead to No Business Creek.

23.9　Cross the bridge over Big Branch. A Civil War incident occurred in this vicinity. Some say it happened at the mouth of Parch Corn Creek, while others say it occurred near Big Branch. A mass grave of Confederate guerrillas with a rock wall surrounding it is located in this area west of the Big South Fork River. Although Tennessee seceded, Scott County voted to remain with the Union. Surrounded by Confederate sympathizers and living in isolated river valleys, many Scott County residents were natural prey for Confederate guerrillas.

During the war a group of about thirty men came from Rock Creek (in present day Pickett County, Tennessee, and McCreary County, Kentucky) into the No Business Creek settlement and then down the river toward Station Camp with the intention of terrorizing Union sympathizers. Along this section of trail between No Business and Station Camp was the home of Jonathan Burkes. The Confederates took possession of the house, set out pickets, and prepared to spend the night.

During the night, the pro-Union Home Guard surprised the Confederates and killed seven of them in the house. One Confederate fled to the river, jumped in, and drowned. The next day his body was found on Big Island and was buried there. The remainder of the band fled to Fentress County, a Confederate stronghold.

The seven men killed in the house were buried in a shallow mass grave. Later, when they found dogs disturbing it, neighbor women built a rock wall around the grave (Sanderson 1974: 61–69). The wall was reported to be still standing a generation ago, but its exact location is not known. (H. Duncan 1986)

This incident was just one of many which took place in the Big South Fork area, where the Civil War was a war of neighbor against neighbor.

24.1　The trail forks. The John Muir Trail goes left up the hill and over the ridge. It passes beneath huge sandstone bluffs, where you have a good view up the No Business Creek drainage. Our mileage for this book will continue with "JMT continued" on page 134.

The trail to the right follows along the river to the mouth of No Business Creek across from Big Island and then continues up No Business Creek to a junction with the John Muir Trail. This trail is easier to hike because it is more level, but you must ford No Business Creek. We will call this section of trail the "Big Island Option."

Big Island Option (3.7 miles)

Mileage Description

0.0   Junction with the John Muir Trail. Take the trail to the right that parallels the Big South Fork River. The trail is often contiguous with the horse trail. On the hillside above the trail you notice a number of sandstone foundations and one old chimney. Approximately sixty years ago over 125 people lived in the No Business area. Today only one house, a few run-down barns, and numerous stone foundations remain.

0.3   The large wooden footbridge crosses the wet-weather drainage.

0.5   To the left of the trail, notice the large boulder with a stairstep crack.

1.0   You can see Big Island in the middle of the river. This is a low-water crossing of the Big South Fork River. An old Indian trail from Huntsville, Tennessee, crossed at this location and traveled along No Business Creek before climbing the ridge and heading for Monticello, Kentucky. This trail was also used as a wagon road by early settlers. The stores in No Business brought their supplies over this road. During high water, they would dismantle their wagons and ferry the wagon beds, front and back wheels, and supplies across the river in a dugout. (H. Duncan 1986)

      Hudson Burke, who lived in the No Business area, helped cut the road to Monticello. He made his living by selling niter to the powder mills. Leached from the sandstone and dried on the roof of his cabin, the niter was taken to Monticello where it was then sent by train to Lexington. Niter, or saltpeter, is an essential ingredient of gunpowder and was needed by everyone on the frontier from the early longhunter to the pioneer farmers. The military, in two different conflicts, the War of 1812 and the Civil War, used large quantities of the locally derived niter. The hidden nature of the coves and valleys in this remote area provided an ideal setting for the production of niter for the Confederate Army during the 1860s. (DesJean 1992)

      Where No Business Creek enters the Big South Fork, turn left on the old road and go west.

1.3   Ford No Business Creek. You can easily see where the road enters and then exits the creek about 50 yards upstream. You will find a fair amount of water in this creek all year.

1.4   Continue west after exiting the creek. A sign gives directions to Divide Road. Continue in the same direction. The other trail behind you is a horse trail. On the hillside above this junction stood the one-room schoolhouse that served the No Business Community. The schoolhouse also doubled as a church for two Baptist congregations, each using it one Sunday per month (U.S. Dept. of Interior 1981: 86).

1.5   There is a fence along the left side of the road. The trail parallels No Business Creek.

2.0   You can see the remains of an old barn to the left of the trail. The barn was built level with the road for ease in filling the loft. Many of the abandoned, decaying buildings along No Business Creek were destroyed by a series of tornadoes that hit the area in 1974. Within 100 yards the trail leaves the road. Go right and cross Burkes Branch.

2.1   The trail forks. The short, 1.4-mile trail to the right makes it possible to hike nearly the total length of the Big South Fork area by joining the John Muir Trail to the Kentucky Trail. (We describe the Kentucky–John Muir Connector on page 184.) You should simply reverse the directions to hike north to join the Kentucky Trail. Your trail to the left continues the Big Island Option.

2.4   The large footbridge crosses Dry Creek.

3.3   After crossing two more footbridges, the trail joins an old road and goes to the right.

3.7   The Big Island Option trail rejoins the John Muir Trail.

JMT (continued from page 132)

Mileage Description

24.1   If you decide not to take the Big Island Option, follow the trail uphill to the left. A rock overhang to the right displays layers of shale and sandstone. The trail offers a view of the Big Branch drainage. At first the incline is gentle, but then the trail begins to steepen as it travels uphill and crosses a wet-weather drainage. Although we did not see any wild hogs, we did notice, especially in the No Business area, where they had been rooting for acorns.

24.7   Two switchbacks take the trail further uphill. In the winter you can see two huge, vertical chimney rocks to the right above the trail.

24.8   After another switchback you'll see a large, sandstone bluff to the left of the trail.

24.9 As the trail crests the ridge, you can still see the large chimney rocks. Laurel and holly grow in profusion around the base of the bluff known as Burkes Knob.

25.0 The trail rounds the end of the bluff. Large boulders separated from the bluff litter the hillside on the northeast. Notice the large numbers of hemlocks on the north side of Burkes Knob.

25.1 The trail begins to descend from the ridge.

25.3 You can see the large bluffs on the ridge across from No Business Creek.

25.5 Watch carefully: You could easily miss several switchbacks that lead downhill.

26.0 The trail first crosses Betty Branch on the small footbridge before crossing the large wooden footbridge over No Business Creek.

There are some good camping spots to your right after you cross the bridge to the north side of No Business Creek.

The large, two-story, tin-roofed house called "the boarding house" by locals, was destroyed by the park service in 1992 since it was not considered to be an historical structure. Constructed about 1930, the board-and-batten house was the only two-story house within the Big South Fork Area (U.S. Army Corps of Engineers 1986: 10).

When you look around this deserted valley, it is hard to imagine the vigorous community existing here sixty years ago. As at Station Camp, the Scotch-Irish and German longhunters were the first Europeans to enter this valley. Some eventually settled here, and their children and grandchildren cleared and farmed the land.

At the beginning of the century there were two general stores, a gristmill, a blacksmith shop, a school, two churches, a post office, and numerous farms along No Business Creek.

The people who settled here had large families. Marriage was generally between families within No Business or Station Camp, their nearest neighbor. Fewer than ten family names dominated the history of the area from the 1790s until the 1950s, and these same names still predominate in surrounding counties.

Most people along No Business Creek were subsistence farmers. For cash income the earliest settlers hunted and trapped. Their descendants logged and gathered wild plants to sell to the local general stores, which in turn shipped them to pharmaceutical manufacturers.

When the Stearns Coal and Lumber Company operated in the first decades of this century, some of the No Business residents sold moonshine to the company miners and loggers.

After World War II the community began to decline. The Stearns Company, after depleting the timber and coal resources, began to pull out. Electricity, city water, and automobiles were a big attraction in the world outside the secluded valleys of No Business and Station Camp. Manufacturing jobs in the North offering eight-hour work days attracted the hardworking subsistence farmers. Dewey Slaven, the last resident of No Business Creek, left in 1960 (U.S. Dept. of Interior 1981: 91).

26.1   On the hillside above No Business Creek, the Big Island Option rejoins the John Muir Trail. Go left on the road. The trail now parallels No Business Creek. Split-rail fences, picket fences, sandstone foundations, and log barns are reminders of the once-thriving community of No Business.

27.0   Large slabs of sandstone bridge the small drainage. Several log barns stand in the field to the left of the trail.

27.08   A spur road goes uphill to the right. Stay on the road along the creekbank.

27.13   You must ford Tackett Creek. A dry fording across stepping stones is usually possible.

The earliest known settler on Tackett Creek was Elisha Slaven. When the area surrounding his farm in Kentucky became too settled, he sold the farm for a hog rifle (Kentucky long rifle) and a pair of horseshoes and moved into the Tackett Creek valley. He was still primarily a hunter, but his family raised a garden and grew some crops.

Later generations of Slavens made their own bullets out of lead found near Tackett Creek. Since silver and lead are often found together, this practice gave rise to the local belief that there was a lost silver mine somewhere on Tackett Creek (Howell 1981: 57).

You'll find a good camping spot about 20 yards west of Tackett Creek. The trail continues to parallel No Business Creek.

27.3   The trail takes a sharp turn to the right, leaving the old roadbed. It passes between wooden posts and begins to climb to the ridge. This will be a steady, often steep climb. You have an excellent view of the bluffs overlooking No Business Creek.

27.4   The trail intersects an old road. Go right on the road.

27.7   The trail leaves the roadbed and goes uphill to the left. Because the blaze is not easy to see, begin looking for it when you notice the road ahead becoming overgrown.

28.0   You can see beautiful bluffs directly above the trail when the trees are bare.

28.2   A ladder ascends the small bluff.

28.3   The trail follows the base of the large bluff.

28.4   You must scramble up a portion of the bluff. The trail is not clear at this point. When it looks like the trail has ended, simply climb straight up the sloping shelves of rock in front of you, and you will rejoin the trail. Now the trail is no longer steep but gently inclined.

28.5   At the top of the ridge you once again have an excellent view of the bluffs above Tackett Creek.

28.6   The John Muir Overlook is an eroded-rock outcrop on top of a steep bluff overlooking No Business Creek. *Be very careful because it may be slick when wet.*

    After leaving the John Muir Overlook, you descend a short ladder and cross a narrow, eroded ridgetop. The next section of trail is relatively level with few outstanding scenic features, but it is quickly traveled and has several good camping spots. Although there are numerous streams, not all of them are year-round ones.

28.8   The trail joins an old road. Go left.

29.2   The road is barricaded. The trail goes to the left of the barricade.

29.5   Within the next 0.5 mile you will cross an old roadbed three times. The many roads crisscrossing the area are reminders of the logging boom from the 1880s until the 1920s when most of the accessible timber had been cut. The reforesting of the area was begun in the late 1950s.

30.2   You now begin to hike through a large area of downed trees. On April 3, 1974, several tornadoes touched down in this area, leveling large sections of forest in Pickett State Park and the No Business section of the Big South Fork.

30.5   Cross the small wooden footbridge beside the overhang with a flowing spring.

30.7   Enter the grove of hemlocks and cross the small wooden footbridge.

31.3   Cross another small wooden footbridge next to a large hemlock.

32.0   The trail passes through another area of storm-damaged trees.

33.3   The thin soil has totally eroded away in places, exposing the bare sandstone. Only mosses, lichens, and pines grow here.

33.4   Two footbridges cross the stream. The trail passes through another area of exposed sandstone.

33.6   Cross the footbridge and follow the rock wall along the creek.

33.7   The trail passes a small overhang and then follows the switchback to the top of a small bluff and another bare hillside.

34.6   Descend the long, slanted ladder used as steps into a small drainage where a stream has cut its way through the sandstone, leaving a steep wall on one side. There is a long series of footbridges at the base of the rock wall.

34.7   You will see a wet-weather waterfall just before the trail crosses a footbridge.

35.0   The trail passes between the small rock wall to the right and the branch to the left.

36.0   Leaving the branch, the trail reaches Divide Road, a possible exit or resupply point along the trail. Cross Divide Road and follow the trail through the hardwood forest on the ridgetop.

36.2   Begin to descend the switchbacks into the drainage carved by Massey Branch.

36.5   A large wooden bridge crosses Massey Branch. The trail divides, creating the Rock Creek Loop trail. The John Muir Trail turns to the right and for the next 5 miles will follow a portion of that loop.

36.75   The trail passes through a narrow cut alongside Massey Branch. Old railroad ties still lie across the trail. As the trail goes northwest around the hillside, Massey Branch joins Rock Creek at the bottom of the hill.

37.5   Within 500 feet after passing below some smooth, scalloped-looking bluffs, the old railroad bed continues straight ahead. The trail, which veers off to the right, begins a series of switchbacks that lead downhill.

37.7   The trail forks. The trail to the right goes past the Great Meadow Campground. The John Muir Trail goes left, following a portion of the Sheltowee Trace (blazed with a white turtle). Traveling up-

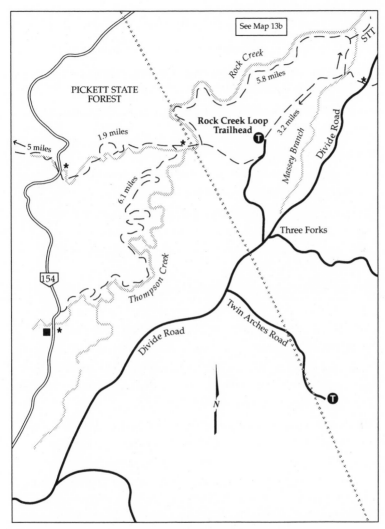

Trail Map 13c. The John Muir Trail: Divide Road to Pickett State Park

stream, you now follow Rock Creek over the trail that goes up and down the hillside until it reaches the Pickett State Forest boundary. Within 100 yards you'll find some good campsites on the right between the trail and the creek.

38.0   The trail rejoins the railroad cut.

38.1   The trail is very indistinct. Disregard the floodplain to the right where the trail seems to go downhill; your trail actually goes uphill to the left. There is a large beech tree about 25 feet up and to the left of the trail. The trail now goes steeply uphill.

38.3   The large footbridge crosses the steep drainage. The trail soon passes large beech and hemlock trees.

38.5   Cross the stepping stones over the stream.

38.8   A large moss- and lichen-covered boulder lies between the trail and the creek. Ferns have begun to grow where mosses and lichens have broken up the sandstone into soil.

39.0   You can find some good camping spots along the creek. Cross the small footbridge over the drainage branch.

39.5   The trail takes a sharp right among some large boulders. You must watch closely for the blaze in this area. The trail descends closer to the creek, crosses the small footbridge, and continues its meandering path up and down the hillside.

40.7   The large footbridge across the drainage will be followed by another large footbridge within 100 yards.

40.8   Pickett State Forest boundary. The trail now follows the easily-seen, orange-blazed boundary line.

41.1   Old rails from the Stearns railroad lie across the trail. In approximately 50 yards the John Muir Trail leaves the Rock Creek Loop Trail, goes down the creek bank, and fords Rock Creek. Cross the small, rocky floodplain in the bend of the creek and continue west (left) along the north bank of the creek. Beside Rock Creek you will see the remains of a railroad bridge.

41.3   The John Muir Trail joins Pickett State Park's brown-blazed Rock Creek Trail. The signpost marks the point at which the John Muir Trail and the Sheltowee Trace separate. You may choose either option. (1) The trail straight ahead, the John Muir Trail, leads to a point on TN 154, 3 miles north of the park office, where it then crosses the highway and ends at the Pickett State Forest boundary 5 miles west along Rock Creek. (2) The trail to the left going immediately down to the creek is a continuation of the Sheltowee Trace that merges with Pickett State Park's Hidden Passage Trail and ends near the park office and campground.

Option 1

Mileage Description

41.3   Trail junction. To finish the John Muir Trail, continue straight ahead.

41.4   The trail appears to dead-end, but follow the narrow, rocky, north bank of the creek, and you'll see the trail again. Following the old railroad bed, the trail passes through the steep-sided valley carved by Rock Creek.

41.9   The trail passes a high rock wall on the right with a larger bluff higher up the hillside. The wall, which includes an overhang, continues to line the trail.

42.1   The old trail descended to Rock Creek and led through the abandoned railroad tunnel. Because of the extreme hazards of this tunnel, the trail has been rerouted to the right. *Don't enter the tunnel:* Even now, large boulders and timbers still fall inside it. You will be able to see inside the tunnel from the other end when you follow the trail to the right. If you look carefully, just before the steep descent to the creek, you'll see an arrow on a small rock to the right of the trail. The arrow points uphill to the narrow trail leading over rocks and beneath an overhang. You should follow this trail.

42.2   The trail drops steeply to a small branch with a overhanging-ledge waterfall to the right. Most of this trail will be narrow and difficult until you join the old trail on the other side of the tunnel.

42.3   There is another short, but steep, climb into and out of the small drainage.

42.4   The trail enters an area of thin soil where the ground is covered with lichens and mosses. Eastern red cedars, which grow in poor soil, and hemlocks forest this area.

42.5   The trail rejoins the old trail route just past the bridge leading into the tunnel at your left. Continue to the right.

42.6   Ford Rock Creek. In approximately 200 yards a small footpath leaves the trail to the right. This path goes to an impressive waterfall that tumbles over a thick, rock ledge. There is also a good camping spot nearby.

42.9   Ford the creek. You can find another good camping spot to the right of the trail. The trail veers to the left and soon passes a large area of pines with a clear forest understory.

43.1   Ford Rock Creek. There are picnic tables and campsites to the left of the trail. The trail joins a road and travels north (right) along the creek. The several parking and primitive camping spots in this section are close to the highway.

43.2   The trail reaches TN 154. To continue the John Muir Trail, cross the bridge and look for the sign on the left side of the road a short distance beyond the bridge. The trail is marked with the blue-and-white blaze. This unfinished section of the John Muir Trail goes 5 miles further along Rock Creek, continuing to follow the old Stearns Logging Railroad. It crosses the creek twenty-seven times in 5 miles. There are stepping stones in most crossings.

48.2   The trail dead-ends on the Rock Creek Road (also called Boundary Road) on Pickett State Forest's western boundary. When completed as planned, the JMT will extend to the Alvin C. York Grist Mill Park on Wolf River at Pall Mall, Tennessee, on U. S. 127. For now, unless you have arranged for a shuttle, retrace your route to TN 154 and follow it south to the Pickett State Park office. (Use extreme caution when hiking along highways!)

Option 2

Mileage Description

41.3   Trail Junction. Leaving the John Muir Trail, go downhill to your left to the creek. Ford Rock Creek. Since the creek is approximately 20 feet wide and can be fairly deep, use caution in fording. The small floodplain at the junction of Rock Creek and Thompson Creek makes an excellent camping spot in dry weather. The trail follows the brown Rock Creek blaze up Thompson Creek. The M. I. Thompson Lumber Company operated a narrow-gauge railway on Thompson Creek in the late 1920s. It joined the Stearns Logging Railroad at Rock Creek. This narrow-gauge railroad passed under the natural bridge near what is now the swimming area at Pickett Lake in Pickett State Park. (H. Duncan 1986)

41.4   The trail leaves the creek and heads steeply uphill.

41.5   Continuing steeply uphill, the trail requires some hands-and-knees climbing.

41.7   The trail reaches the ridgetop above Thompson Creek. It is narrow and close to the bluff line.

41.8   Across the valley you can see Thompson Overlook.

42.0   You can hear a waterfall from the trail.

42.1   Junction with Hidden Passage Trail. Go left for approximately 50 feet and cross the creek on the small wooden bridge. You will now see the green Hidden Passage blaze as well as the white Sheltowee turtle. To the left of the trail you can see the falls that you previously heard.

42.3   You are now hiking out toward the end of Thompson Ridge. *Be careful: This is an area where the trail passes above steep cliffs.*

42.55   The trail reaches the end of Thompson Ridge. The large bluffs across the gorge are streaked yellow by the sulfur that has leached from the sandstone. At the end of the ridge, the trail takes a sharp right turn uphill to the Thompson Overlook. At the top of the overlook, the road to the right leads to the Group Campground in Pickett State Park. Go left, along the south rim of Thompson Ridge.

42.9   Below the bluff you reach the junction with the 1-mile spur trail to Double Falls. This beautiful spot is well worth the extra mileage. The trail passes beneath a rock bluff that rims the valley. Continue straight along the bluff.

43.06   Pass under the boulder-filled rock shelter. Sand eroded from the overhang covers the ground.

43.14   The trail now goes by a larger rock shelter.

43.24   Follow the streambed beneath the rock shelter. You can rest on a wooden bench behind the wet-weather waterfall. In the late 1930s the Civilian Conservation Corps (CCC) constructed all the wooden benches along the Hidden Passage Trail out of American chestnut, now virtually extinct. (H. Duncan 1986)

43.4   The side trail to the left offers another view of the rock shelter through which you have just passed.

43.7   The trail crosses the end of the ridge.

44.0   Cross the small stream that tumbles over an 8-foot waterfall.

44.1   The steep switchback brings the trail back under the large bluff.

44.2   A steep climb brings you to the base of the large bluff. As you travel beneath the bluff you will see several sandstone boulders that have eroded to unusual mushroom shapes.

44.4   The trail now goes around the end of a ridge and to another bluff passing along a steep cliff.

44.7   A small overhang shelters the trail.

45.0   The rock shelter that becomes a waterfall in wet weather has a bench beneath it.

45.2   You pass another medium-sized rock shelter.

45.6   The trail passes an old road that joins the trail on the right.

46.1   You are back on a steep cliff.

46.2   Only lichens and mosses adorn the bare sandstone hillside. The trail now travels along the rim of the bluff.

46.4   *Be careful: The trail crosses the lip of the narrow waterfall.* The series of tall ledges is Crystal Falls.

46.42   A short spur trail leads down to the bottom of Crystal Falls. The small stream tumbles over tall ledges into a crystal-clear pool at the base.

46.46   The trail reaches Hidden Passage. The passage winds through a low-ceiling rock shelter littered with boulders. Beyond the overhang you will hike the switchback to the right. You'll see a stone pillar to the left of the trail.

46.6   When the trail reaches the Hidden Passage Loop junction, go to the left.

46.8   Rock steps lead up to the right.

46.9   Cross the small stream with the waterfall below.

47.0   You can see another small waterfall below the trail.

47.1   The trail reaches TN 154. The Pickett State Park Office and campground are 0.3 mile to the left along the highway.

Kentucky Trails

The Kentucky portion of the Big South Fork Area features numerous overlooks, several loop trails, two long-distance trails, and a connector trail.

The Blue Heron Loop and Catawba Overlook offer insights into the era of coal mining along the Big South Fork. While traveling to or from Blue Heron, be sure to see Stearns, Kentucky. Stearns was the headquarters for the Stearns Coal and Lumber Company, begun by Justus Stearns in 1901. The company, which once owned over 200,000 acres of land and employed 2,000 people, dominated the economic and social life of the area for the first half of the century. The Stearns Coal and Lumber Company built the Kentucky and Tennessee Railroad to service its mines and timberlands. The main office is still the most prominent structure in the town, and many of the houses in Stearns were once company houses (U.S. Dept. of Interior 1986: panels v-13, v-15). The Big South Fork Scenic Railway offers those unable to hike the trails a view of the Big South Fork wilderness. Colorful autumn leaves make the Fall excursions very popular. The railroad operates from mid April until the end of October.

The Bear Creek Scenic Area features a river overlook and an unusual natural arch.

The Yahoo Falls Scenic Area covers several short, concentric loop trails with a combined length of less than 4 miles. Although they can be hiked separately, they connect with the Sheltowee Trace and the Yamacraw–Yahoo Loop.

The Yamacraw–Yahoo Loop trail begins at the Yamacraw Bridge and stretches north to Yahoo Falls and Arch, offering a challenging, 15.4-mile hike through some of the most beautiful scenery in the Big South Fork Area.

The Kentucky Trail is entirely within the park boundary. It begins at Peters Mountain Trailhead on the western boundary of the Big South Fork National River and Recreation Area near the Kentucky-Tennessee border and ends at the Yamacraw Bridge on KY 92. By using the Kentucky–John Muir Connector trail, you can hike almost the entire length of the park.

The Sheltowee Trace is a trail developed by the Daniel Boone National Forest. Because much of the land within the Kentucky portion of the Big South Fork National River and Recreation Area was transferred from the Daniel Boone National Forest, sections of the Sheltowee Trace are now within the park boundary. We will describe the trail from its origin in Pickett State Park in Tennessee to Cumberland Falls State Park in Kentucky. Information regarding the remainder of the Sheltowee Trace may be obtained from the U.S. Forest Service, Stearns Ranger District. (See Appendix 3)

14. Bear Creek Scenic Area

Bear Creek Scenic Area is the site of the proposed Bear Creek Lodge. Future development of the Big South Fork area may one day realize its construction.

To reach the Bear Creek Scenic Area, take Hwy 1651 south from Stearns or north from Pine Knot to Revelo, Kentucky. Across from the Post Office in Revelo take KY Hwy 742 west for approximately 3.1 miles to the junction for Bear Creek. A sign notes the intersection where you should turn left. It will be 3.7 miles to the trailhead. (Signs at 2 miles and 2.4 miles direct you to turn right and then left, respectively.) Before reaching the trailhead you will pass a small parking area across from the Split Bow Arch Overlook. Please note that the Split Bow Arch Loop Trail is not accessible from the overlook. We recommend that you hike the loop first and then stop at the overlook.

Bear Creek Overlook

Distance: 0.5 round trip
Rating: Easy
Suggested time: 20 minutes
Blaze: Red arrowhead
Special considerations: Sheer bluff

0.0   Trailhead.

0.15   Having followed an old roadbed through open fields, the trail enters the woods

0.25   The Bear Creek Overlook, positioned high above a large bend in the river, offers a panoramic view of the Big South Fork. Retrace your route back to the trailhead.

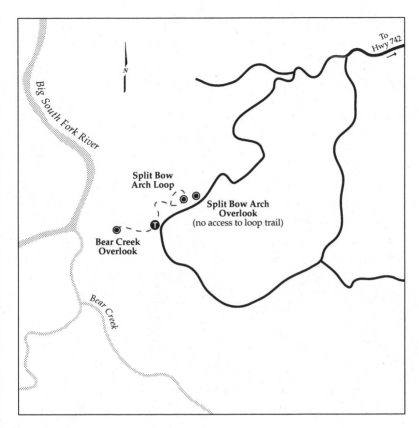

Trail Map 14. Bear Creek Scenic Area

Split Bow Arch Loop

Distance: 0.64 mile round trip
Rating: Moderate
Suggested time: 45 minutes
Blaze: Red arrowhead
Special considerations: Stairs, steps

0.0   The trail begins at the sign to the right of the Bear Creek Scenic
      Area bulletin board and proceeds down steps carved from the rock.

The sides of the trail are carpeted with Partridge Berry, an evergreen herb. In late summer the twin white flowers produce a single red berry-like fruit.

0.13   A switchback brings you below the bluffline.

0.18   The trail divides, creating a loop. Turn left and follow the steps downhill.

0.26   The trail crosses a footbridge over a small rhododendron-filled drainage and then climbs uphill by way of steps.

0.32   A rockshelter is tucked away in the bluff ahead of you. To your right, Split Bow Arch spans the wooden staircase that takes the trail through its large opening.

0.36   As you ascend the stairs, notice the large blocks of fallen rock and the narrowness of the arch above you.

0.39   While headward erosion created the Twin Arches and the erosion of a rockshelter formed Needle Arch, Split Bow Arch had a different beginning. Here, the ridgeline developed a deep fissure that eventually widened, completely separating a narrow finger of rock from the bluff. Continued weathering caused large blocks of stone to fall from the narrow, isolated ridge and Split Bow Arch was formed.

0.42   Having passed through a narrow corridor, the trail reaches the end of Split Bow Arch ridge. To your left you can see a rockshelter within the main bluff.

0.47   The trail returns to the beginning of the loop. Continue straight ahead and back up the stone steps to the trailhead.

0.64   Trailhead.

15. Blue Heron

Blue Heron is one of the two areas within the Big South Fork National River and Recreation Area selected for major development. Opened in the spring of 1989, the Visitor Center complex houses exhibits, a snack bar, and a terminus for the Big South Fork Scenic Railway. You can see ghost structures representing the superintendent's residence, a company store, a school, a church, and a typical company house with accompanying interpretive displays. Listen to the voices of Blue Heron as former residents tell the stories of their lives in this mining community. The restored coal tipple and trestle provide access to trails on the west side of the river.

To reach Blue Heron, take KY 1651 south from Stearns or north from Pine Knot, Kentucky, to Revelo. Directly across from the Revelo Post Office, take KY 742 west. After you pass the entrance to the Blue Heron Campground, the road turns to the right and goes down to the Visitor Center complex. The road to the left leads to the river overlooks.

We will begin the Blue Heron Loop at the first parking area on the road leading to the overlooks. If you do not wish to hike the entire loop, you may drive out to the second and third parking areas for short walks to scenic vistas of Devils Jump and the Blue Heron Tipple.

Although the story of mining along the Big South Fork is the main feature of the Blue Heron Loop, the trail offers outstanding scenic views of the gorge and Devils Jump as well as a climb through Cracks-in-the-Rock.

Blue Heron Loop

Distance: 6.4 miles
Rating: Moderate
Blaze: Red arrowhead
Suggested time: All-day hike and visit
Accommodations: Blue Heron Campground, Big South Fork Scenic Railroad, Blue Heron Visitor Complex
Special considerations: Protected overlooks (Devils Jump Overlook is handicapped accessible), steps, stairs, ladders, abandoned mine sites, rock-hopping discouraged (*dangerous* rapid), access to the Kentucky Trail and Catawba Overlook.

Devils Jump (Nicho Young)

Mileage Description

0.0   South from the paved parking area a path descends a few yards to meet the loop trail. The first section of the trail, which parallels the road, is level as it follows the ridgetop.

0.4   You hike past another parking lot to the right of the trail. Within 150 yards the trail will follow the bluff line.

0.7   The paved trail to the left leads to a river overlook with an excellent view of Devils Jump.

Devils Jump is a Class IV whitewater rapid. There are two theories as to the origin of the name Devils Jump. The first story involves the first commercial oil well (1819) in the United States, which was drilled 7 miles south of this point along the Big South

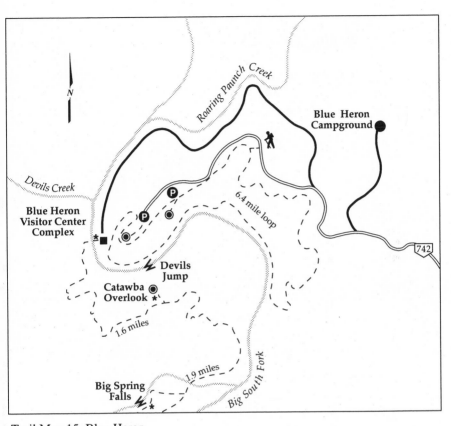

Trail Map 15. Blue Heron

Fork River. The owner, Martin Beaty, hired a man to raft the oil
downstream. He hoped to sell the oil to pharmaceutical companies,
as current uses of oil were unknown at that time. The raftsman was
extremely apprehensive because local people thought Beaty had
drilled into hell. This idea was further substantiated by the fact that
the substance spewing from the well burned so readily. While navi-
gating the rapids, the raft turned over. Upon returning to Beaty, the
raftsman reported that all was well until the Devil jumped from
behind some large boulders in the river, sank the raft, took the oil,
and disappeared up the creek. Thus the names Devils Jump and
Devils Creek (Blevins and Blevins 1982: 5).

The second theory seems more likely. This theory associates the name with the early logging days along the river. Before 1900, logs, made into huge rafts, were floated down the river during high water. The men who rode these rafts downstream were called raft devils. The boulder-filled narrows above Blue Heron had long been famous along the Big South Fork as a dangerous passage. As the massive log rafts neared these narrows, the raft devils often had to jump if it looked as if the water was too dangerous to navigate. "The devils had better jump" became a well-known saying. (H. Duncan, 1986)

Return up the paved trail. Keep left at the fork. Just below the parking area the loop trail leaves to the left of the paved trail. The trail continues west.

0.9   Pass the small rock shelter to the right of the trail.

1.0   The trail is now on the end of the ridge above Devils Jump. Located at the base of a bluff, the trail is narrow.

1.2   The tipple overlook above the trail to your right can be reached by following the blue arrowheads for approximately 775 feet.

1.25   The highly-eroded sandstone bluff has formed columns. Past the columns, the trail leaves the river and then begins to descend.

1.35   The trail descends steep steps through a gap in the bluff, then follows the base of the bluff.

1.4   Cracks-in-the-Rock. Massive cracks in the bluff wall have created tunnels through the rock. Children will especially enjoy climbing the stairs and crossing the boardwalk through the huge boulders.

1.7   Cross the small wooden footbridge.

1.8   The trail now passes the ruins of a coal mining camp. Mining camps lasted until the coal seams were depleted; then they were moved elsewhere or abandoned. Mine 18, the Blue Heron Mine, began operation in 1938. Most of the miners came from other mine sites, such as Fidelity or Co-operative. This area bustled with activity as long as the coal held out. Two hundred workers were employed at Blue Heron, and 22 company houses, an elementary school, a Baptist church, and a company store dotted the hillside.

Although they had the luxury of electricity and some had indoor plumbing, life at Blue Heron was difficult for most mining families.

Operating from 7:00 a.m. until 3:00 p.m., the noise and ever-pervading dust from the coal tipple was a day-in, day-out, nerve-grating fact of life for the families at Blue Heron. The only access to town was the K & T Railroad until the road into Blue Heron was built in 1947. Students attended high school in Whitley City, leaving at 5 a.m. and returning at 5 p.m. The camp was the social world of the miner and his family.

When Mine 18 was closed in 1962, some of the houses and other buildings at Blue Heron were salvaged, but most were left to decay.

1.9 The trail enters the Blue Heron Visitor Center area. You will want to visit all of the ghost structures and listen to the voices of former residents as they tell the story of Blue Heron. After enjoying the interpretive exhibits, return to this point and continue your hike.

2.0 Built in 1937, the Blue Heron Tipple below to the right of the trail was an engineering marvel in its day. Electric tram cars brought coal from mines on both sides of the river to the tipple. Doors in the bottom of the tram cars opened to drop the loads of coal at the top of the tipple. The coal was passed through a graduated series of grates, separating the various grades of coal. Conveyors carried the different grades of coal to chutes that dropped them into freight cars. Coal too large to fall through the grates was crushed and then loaded. The tipple could grade over fifty-five carloads of coal per day.

The train trestle crossing the river was also built in 1937. Electric trolley motors pulled as many as 30-45 coal cars at a time from the mines across the Big South Fork River to the Blue Heron Tipple. The old trestle, converted to a pedestrian bridge, connects the Blue Heron Tipple to the Kentucky Trail and to the Catawba Overlook trail on the west side of the river.

The company store stood near the foot of the tipple steps. The store, which also housed the timekeeper's office and the post office, served families on the surrounding ridges as well. Here the miners could purchase not only their clothes and boots, but also their own picks and shovels. If a miner was short of cash, he could be issued scrip to be spent at the company store and work off his debt during the next pay period. Past the sand house the trail forks. Go to the right.

2.2 A sign reads 0.4 mile to Devils Jump. To your right is the low-water ford and canoe access.

2.5   The trail forks. The trail to the right leads to the river. Continue left. Within 100 yards the trail passes a huge boulder to the left of the trail.

From 1941 to the 1950s, this area below "the Jumps" with its sandy beach was the home of a Boy Scout camp. A spring originating from underneath the high cliffs on the west side of the river provided the camp, as well as some of the Blue Heron community with water. Conley Blevins, a camper here in 1945, recalls the day his father Maynard Blevins, a member of the Kentucky and Tennessee Section Crew, helped lay the pipeline across the river just above the Jumps. Accustomed to the drenched appearance of Mr. Blevins caused by the heat and humidity of the area, his wife commented that he looked like he'd been in the river and, as a matter of fact, at least that day, he had. The pipeline is still visible to canoeists when the water is clear. (C. Blevins 1992)

2.6   The trail forks. The left-hand trail continues the loop. The trail to the right leads out onto the boulders surrounding Devils Jump. *Be careful: Climbing on the rocks can be fatal.*

2.8   The trail crosses a small earthen dam and enters a reclaimed mine site. If you look uphill just before crossing the dam, you will see wooden stairs above the reclamation site. Follow the trail up the steep hillside.

2.9   Climb the stairs. At the top of the stairs, the hiking trail joins the horse trail. Turn right. In a short distance you will see where the trails divide. The lower hiking trail affords views of the river for most of its distance.

The upper horse trail follows the old tram track that served the mines on this side of the river. There are several closed mine entrances to the left of the trail.

The mines along the Big South Fork were unusual in that stream downcutting left seams of coal exposed on the steep hillsides. Instead of entering from the surface and going downward, mines along the Big South Fork entered the horizontal seams at their sides and went straight back into the seams. As "rooms" of coal were blasted and hauled out of the mine in electric shuttle cars, pillars of coal were left to support the ceiling. Each man would be assigned a room by the mine supervisor. If assigned a good room of coal, he could

Blue Heron Coal Tipple (National Park Service)

make money because the miners were paid by the ton. Some men could load as much as fifteen tons a day with a good room of coal.

The mines at Blue Heron never became fully mechanized because the original mine openings were too small. The mines themselves were a disappointment; neither the quantity nor the quality of coal at Blue Heron met expectations. By 1962, diesel engines and increased environmental and safety regulations ended the mining at Blue Heron (U.S. Dept. of Interior 1986: panel v-17).

4.0 Trail junction. The hiking trail rejoins the horse trail. A sign states that it is 350 feet straight ahead to Laurel Branch, but you should follow the steps uphill to the left. The trail begins to ascend to the ridgetop. There are several switchbacks beyond the steps.

4.1 Climb the long series of steps.

4.3 The trail passes beneath the large overhang. It then leads upward through the gap and turns back over the top of the bluff.

4.6   The trail appears to reach the ridgetop, but it will climb gently uphill for the next 0.5 mile. This is a good section of trail for wildflowers.

4.8   The trail forks. Hikers accessing the trail from the campground will enter and exit here. Go right. In 100 yards the trail goes up steps carved in the rock. A sign directs you to either Blue Heron or the Mine 18 Road in 600 feet. This is the road on which you entered the area. Continue left toward Blue Heron to follow the loop.

5.0   Cross the small footbridges.

5.4   The trail is next to the Mine 18 Road.

5.5   The trail again nears the road but then descends the long series of steps and winds through the woods along the top of the ridge until it reaches the beginning of the loop.

6.4   Blue Heron Loop Trailhead.

Catawba Overlook and Big Spring Falls

Distance: Overlook: 3.2 miles round trip
Rating: Moderate
Blaze: Red arrowhead
Suggested time: Overlook: 2 hours
Accommodations: Blue Heron complex facilities
Special considerations: Stairs, steps, sheer bluff

The trail to the Catawba Overlook and Dick Gap Falls was created to eliminate a very unstable, slag-covered portion of the Kentucky Trail. The overlook was named for the abundance of Catawba Rhododendron found there.

0.0   From the west end of the tipple bridge, the trail to the Catawba Overlook begins to your left. Within 300 feet you will see the remains of one old steel railroad car. Three wooden ones, badly decayed, rest nearby.

0.25   The trail forks. Follow the trail to the right.

0.34   A footbridge crosses a drainage. The water in the creek drops in cascading falls.

0.44   The trail forks. Go left down the stone steps and cross the creek. This area is known as Three West Hollow.

0.55 The trail climbs steeply uphill, crossing two drainages.

0.94 Pass through boulders along the trail, cross a footbridge, and then continue uphill by way of a switchback.

1.03 Wooden stairs followed by log steps ascend to the top of the bluff.

1.13 At the base of the bluff the hiking trail intersects the horse trail. The two trails coincide for 167 feet before the hiking trail turns left and leaves the horse trail.

1.6 Catawba Overlook. Beginning on your far left, notice the yellow stains on the opposite bluff. They are caused by sulfur leaching from the sandstone. Sulfur is one of the elements—including carbon, hydrogen, nitrogen, and oxygen—that form coal. High sulfur content lessens coal's value as fuel because the sulfur and oxygen form the poisonous gas sulfur dioxide as the coal burns. (Collier 1986) Across the river you can see the Blue Heron Tipple Overlook. Upstream, to your right is Devils Jump Rapid. You may return to Blue Heron by retracing your route for a 3.2 mile round trip.

This trail continues beyond the overlook to Dick Gap Falls (2.2 miles) and Big Spring Falls (approximately 3.74 miles).

1.67 Footbridge

1.8 You will see a field to your left and an old roadbed to your right. Your trail continues straight ahead.

1.9 Descending, the trail crosses a long wooden footbridge past a low rockshelter before it climbs uphill again.

2.1 Cross over a downed tree by way of wooden steps. With tree roots still in tact, the branches have grown up as tall as trees themselves. A short flight of wooden steps descend the bluff.

2.2 Dick Gap Falls is a small wet weather waterfall in a creek. The trail continues downhill to the right.

2.4 Following a switchback, the trail begins to descend the drainage along an old roadbed.

2.5 The closed trail to the left was part of the original Kentucky trail. Do not attempt to hike it. The unstable coal slag is *extremely* dangerous. The trail to Big Spring Falls continues straight ahead for nearly one mile.

3.1   Notice the coal slag to the left of the trail. This portion of the trail is along the old railroad bed that serviced the mines in this area.

3.2   A trail goes to the right, but you should stay left.

3.34   Cross the wooden bridge over the creek. Watch closely for switchbacks. From the Kentucky Trail, a spur trail to the right will lead to the falls.

3.74   Big Springs Falls. This beautiful wet weather waterfall is approximately 100 feet high. Since the trail is located underneath the drip line, use caution, especially on the wooden footbridges. Return to Blue Heron for a round trip of 7.48 miles.

16. Yahoo Falls Scenic Area

Distance: 3.5 miles
Rating: Moderate
Suggested time: 2 hours
Blaze: Green, yellow and blue arrowheads
Accommodations: Picnic area (no running water, no camping)
Special considerations: Steps, stairs, steep climbs, high bluffs, fordings

To reach the Yahoo Falls Scenic Area follow U. S. 27 north of Whitley City, Kentucky; then turn west onto KY 700. Follow KY 700 for 4.7 miles; then turn right onto a 1.3-mile spur road that leads to the picnic area. On the right at this last intersection is the grave site of Big Jake Troxell, Princess Cornblossom's husband.

Yahoo Falls is closely associated with the legends surrounding Princess Cornblossom and the Cherokees, as told by Robert F. Collins in *A History of the Daniel Boone National Forest*. Since stories about Princess Cornblossom and Jake Troxell have been passed down orally through many generations, fact and legend are intertwined. Big Jake, so called because of his height, came to the Big South Fork during the Revolutionary War in the guise of a trader. His mission was to win the friendship of the Cherokees, who were being courted by the British. Chief Doublehead, the last great Cherokee chief of the plateau tribes, became friends with Big Jake and pledged loyalty to the American cause. In fact, some of Doublehead's tribe fought with the Revolutionaries at Kings Mountain.

Chief Doublehead's daughter, Cornblossom, was a renowned beauty of her day. She and Big Jake fell in love and were married. After Doublehead's death she became the leader of her tribe.

In 1810, Princess Cornblossom decided to lead her people to the Sequatchie Valley near Chattanooga, Tennessee, where a Presbyterian missionary ran a school for Indians. She believed that the future of her people lay in education and assimilation with the white settlers. Her tribe met at the rockhouse beneath Yahoo Falls to begin their migration south.

A small group of settlers led by Hiram Gregory heard of the trip and planned an ambush. They lined the rim of the bluff and fired into the

159

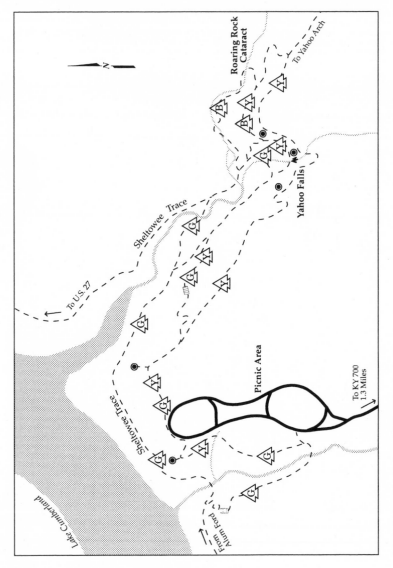

Trail Map 16. Yahoo Falls Scenic Area

Cherokees assembled below. Trapped in the rockhouse, the Indians were massacred. Princess Cornblossom and her son, Little Jake, reached the scene shortly after the massacre and killed some of the ambushers. Broken by the tragedy of her people, Princess Cornblossom died within a few days and was buried in what is now Stearns, Kentucky. Her grave site is recognized with an historical marker. Big Jake, who lacked the will to go on without his wife, died the same year. Their son, Little Jake, became an infamous renegade who terrorized settlers in the Big South Fork area for many years (Collins 1975: 136–42).

Located atop the bluff, the Yahoo Falls Picnic Area has tables and primitive restrooms. No water is available, and camping is not allowed.The trails around the Yahoo Falls Scenic Area terrace the hillside. The trails along the top of the bluff (yellow arrowhead) include five overlooks with views of Lake Cumberland (the Big South Fork River), Yahoo Creek, and Yahoo Falls. The middle trail below the bluff line (green arrowhead) follows Yahoo Creek to the base of the falls. You can see the falls from the bridge over the creek or else circle behind the falls underneath the rock shelter. The lower trail (blue arrowhead) follows a portion of the Sheltowee Trace. Briefly leaving the lower trail, a short trail to Roaring Rock Cataract squeezes between large boulders, rambles up the branch, and joins the mid-level trail shortly before it climbs the hillside to the upper trail. A sign at the upper trail junction gives the distance to Yahoo Arch as 0.8 mile to the left. You can return to the picnic area by going to the right. The short, steep, connector trails climb metal stairs, rock steps and switchbacks.The Yahoo Falls Scenic Area map on page 148 shows the connection between trails. The chart below gives blazes and individual trail lengths.

Trail Name	Legend	Roundtrip distance from parking lot
Topside	◬Y◬Y	1.2 miles
Cliffside	◬G◬G	1.2 miles
Cascade	◬B◬B	1.1 miles

Yahoo Falls with rock shelter (National Park Service)

17. Yamacraw–Yahoo Loop

Distance: 15.4 miles
Rating: Difficult
Suggested time: 2-day backpacking trip
Blaze: Sheltowee white turtle or diamond
Accommodations: Alum Ford Campground, Yahoo Falls Scenic Area (picnic)
Special considerations: Trailhead security, highways (vehicular traffic), steps, steep climbs, boulder-scrambling, narrow trail. Attention: The U.S. Forest Service logged the area south of KY 700. Contact the Stearns Ranger District for the current status of this loop.

The Yamacraw-Yahoo Loop Trail is a very long, difficult day hike. We recommend that you make it a two-day backpacking trip. The trail follows the Big South Fork River downstream, detouring occasionally to go up steep, rock-filled branches. You must boulder-scramble across some of the branches. There are several small waterfalls along the trail as well as two nearby larger ones—Princess Falls and Yahoo Falls. You will also see spectacular bluffs and a large natural arch.

To begin the loop, take KY 92 from Stearns, Kentucky, west to the Yamacraw Bridge. Parking is available on the northeast end of the bridge, but security at this trailhead has been a problem.

Mileage Description

0.0 The trail, blazed with the white turtle or diamond of the Sheltowee Trace, begins at the north end of the parking area. Ignore the short loop trail that goes down to the river and under the bridge; it is not a part of the Sheltowee.

Yamacraw was named for a small tribe of Indians originally from South Carolina who settled in this area in the latter quarter of the eighteenth century. They brought their skill in agriculture, particularly in growing corn, to the tribes of the Cumberland Plateau. They left the plateau as more white settlers moved into the area (Collins 1975: 145).

0.3 An old road joins the trail from the left. The trail follows the roadbed.

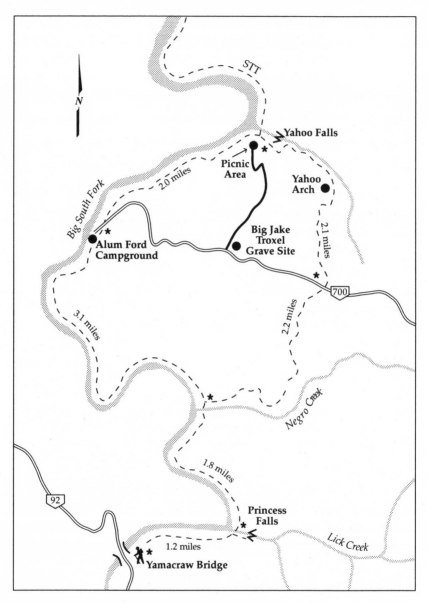

Trail Map 17. Yamacraw-Yahoo Loop

0.5 The trail forks briefly and rejoins.

0.7 The small footpaths to the left of the trail lead to camping sites along the river. Large boulders litter the banks. Within 60 yards there is a small drainage branch. A footpath beyond the large boulder overlooking the branch leads up to a 20-foot ledge waterfall. It is approximately 50 yards off the main trail.

0.9 The trail passes through a jumble of boulders.

1.0 To the right of the trail you pass a small rock shelter and then a stream flowing between large boulders. About 80 yards beyond the stream, the trail turns steeply uphill. You'll find a possible campsite to the right of the trail. The trail leaves the river to go up Lick Creek.

1.1 The trail forks. Stay right. The road to the left is where vehicles ford the creek.

1.2 Trail junction. The trail downhill to the left goes to the bridge over Lick Creek. The center trail is the Lick Creek Trail, leading to Princess Falls and Lick Creek Falls. Named for Princess Cornblossom, Princess Falls, 45 feet wide and 17 feet high, is only 0.2 mile off the loop trail and well worth the detour. An old road goes uphill to the right. Remain left and in 60 yards cross the wooden bridge over Lick Creek, a large stream with a mass of boulders filling the streambed. After crossing Lick Creek, turn left and head back toward the river. At the road junction continue straight. The lower road is the vehicle ford of Lick Creek.

1.4 Passing through an area of oak and poplar, the trail returns to the Big South Fork River.

1.6 A sandy floodplain stretches between the trail and the river. The roadbed and the trail diverge, with the road going downhill and the trail continuing straight ahead.

1.7 The trail goes up the drainage branch. As you cross the branch on the rock path, notice the series of small waterfalls above the path.

1.8 Return to the river along the floodplain.

2.5 The trail emerges onto the very edge of the riverbank and then turns back to the hillside.

2.6 Beech and hemlock indicate a small drainage branch.

2.7   Continue downstream along the bank of the river.

2.8   The trail leaves the river to go up Negro Creek. The origin of this name is uncertain; however, John Mason, a local historian, believes that a black family lived at the mouth of this creek in the 1800s. A black family was quite a rarity in the Big South Fork area because the Scotch-Irish, German, and Welsh subsistence farmers who inhabited the valleys and ridges of the area were not slaveowners.

2.9   Across from some massive boulders supporting a stand of trees, the trail makes a sharp switchback. Somewhat obscure, the trail goes down the bank and heads downstream. The trail appears to dead-end at the boulder-filled creek. Climb down the bank where it appears to dead-end, cross the small funnel made by a portion of Negro Creek, and then climb up the opposite boulder. On the other side of the boulder you'll find a split-log bridge across the remainder of Negro Creek. After crossing the log, hike the several switchbacks going up the hillside and then follow the trail back toward the river. You'll find some good camping spots near the confluence of Negro Creek and the Big South Fork.

3.0   The trail passes beneath a large, tilted boulder to which you will return later on the loop. We will follow the loop clockwise, so you should continue downriver.

3.1   The trail climbs further up the hillside and passes through an area of boulders.

3.2   Cross the small drainage branch with a series of ledge waterfalls. The trail is not far below the base of the bluff.

3.3   The trail leaves the river, turning to go up a drainage branch.

3.4   The trail passes down through boulders to the stream. To the left the stream rushes through a picturesque tunnel of boulders. Ford the creek. If the creek is high, you can climb across the top of the tunnel. *Be careful: It's a long drop to the creek.*

3.6   The trail returns to the river.

3.8   Cross the small, wet-weather drainage. Within 20 yards rock steps lead down to another small drainage branch.

4.3   The Cotton Patch Shelter, an elevated pavilion, stands to the left of the trail overlooking the river. We found no nearby source of water for camping. On the trail just past the shelter, a double-fireplace chimney marks an old home site.

4.5   You can see the river again.

4.8   Cross the small, wet-weather drainage.

5.0   Cross another small, wet-weather drainage.

5.3   Pass the small overhang to the left of the trail.

5.9   Cross the rocky branch.

6.1   Alum Ford, a boat launch area, has camping sites with tables, grills, and primitive restrooms.

6.3   The trail crosses KY 700 from Whitley City. You can see the boat launch below to your left. This portion of the Big South Fork River north of the Yamacraw Bridge is part of Lake Cumberland. Go up the left side of the highway about 75 yards, and you will find the trail.

6.5   The trail crosses an old, eroded roadbed.

6.6   The trail forks. Remain right.

6.9   Cross the rocky stream. Upstream you can see a 10-foot ledge waterfall. There is an old mine on the hillside next to the stream. The trail passes large hemlocks.

7.0   A 15-foot ledge waterfall highlights the steep drainage. You can see large sandstone bluffs across the river.

7.5   Pass another steep drainage with an impressive series of shelf waterfalls.

7.6   The trail passes below the base of a tall bluff. This is part of the bluff that Yahoo Creek has eroded upstream, creating the large rock shelter and falls at Yahoo Falls.

7.7   Trail junction. The cliffside trail to the right (green arrowhead) using a metal stairway at the bluff, leads to the Yahoo Falls Scenic Area in 0.3 mile. The picnic area has tables and primitive restrooms but no water. Overnight camping is not allowed in the picnic area. Continue straight ahead.

7.8   Cross the bridge over the drainage. Enclosed by massive bluffs and the river, this site offers a cool, secluded haven along the trail. Rhododendron fills the semicircular valley capped by a wet-weather waterfall.

8.0 The trail begins to follow the south bank of Yahoo Creek. Within 100 yards the trail forks. The trail to the right remains on the south bank of Yahoo Creek up to Yahoo Falls. It also connects with trails leading to the picnic area and the Topside trail (yellow arrowhead) that follows the bluff above Yahoo Falls.

In addition there are numerous short trails within the Yahoo Falls Scenic Area. The section entitled "Yahoo Falls Scenic Area" on page 159 will help you explore them. It is a beautiful area, and we recommend that you take time to see all of it. To continue the Yamacraw–Yahoo Loop, we will direct you on the shortest, most level route through the area.

The Yamacraw–Yahoo Loop Trail continues straight ahead.

8.1 Cross the bridge over Yahoo Creek. Within 20 yards the Sheltowee Trace makes a sharp turn to the left around a large boulder. There is no sign at this junction. You should follow the green blazed trail to the right toward Yahoo Falls. In 80 yards you will have to ford the creek. Less than 20 yards past the creek the trail forks.

The Cascade trail to the left (blue arrowhead), which seems to disappear between large boulders, involves rock-hopping, wading, and squeezing between boulders as it leads to the small waterfall called Roaring Rock Cataract. This trail will eventually rejoin the Yamacraw–Yahoo Loop, but it is a more difficult and less direct route. Our directions continue with the trail to the right, also blazed with blue.

The trail forks again in 20 yards. The Yamacraw–Yahoo Loop travels left, going uphill via several switchbacks. (A short side trip to the right will bring you to the base of Yahoo Falls.)

8.3 View of Yahoo Falls. Yahoo Falls is a 113-foot, overhanging-cliff waterfall. Take the trail to the left beneath the rock overhang. In 100 yards the trail forks. The trail to the left downhill leads to Roaring Rocks Cataract. This is where the Roaring Rock Cataract Trail rejoins the Yamacraw–Yahoo Loop Trail (if you chose that option).

The trail uphill to the right continues your trail. It bears the Topside Trail's yellow blaze.

8.4 Trail junction. The trail to the right leads to the bluff above Yahoo Falls, several scenic overlooks, and the picnic area. The trail to the left continues the loop. Follow the sign toward Yahoo Arch.

8.6 Cross the small rock bridge across a drainage. The hillsides are covered with hemlock, beech, and rhododendron. The trail leads steeply uphill in a series of switchbacks.

9.1 The trail passes the base of a large bluff. Within 100 yards the steep rock face gives way to a large rock shelter. At the far end of the shelter is Yahoo Arch.

Yahoo Arch was formed when weatherization caused cracks to form at the back of an overhang. As these cracks eroded, the front of the overhang separated from the cliff. Yahoo Arch is 17 feet high and 51 feet wide, with a 70-foot base. The trail goes beneath the arch, veers left around its outer edge, and climbs to the hillside.

9.3 The trail passes a small bluff and climbs the stone steps uphill.

9.4 You are back on top of the ridge.

9.5 The trail joins an old road and begins a steep uphill climb.

9.7 The trail levels out. You have a good view across the top of the plateau.

10.2 The trail intersects KY 700 that runs between Whitley City and Alum Ford. Go right on the road approximately 30 yards, and you will see the trail to the left of the highway. Attention: The next two miles of trail are in an area that was recently logged by the U. S. Forest Service and may not be usable at this time. You may have to reverse your trail, making the total distance 20.4 miles. Another option is to hike down the road to Alum Ford and then backtrack from that point. Use caution hiking along highways.

10.4 The power-line cut passes an eroded bluff. To descend the bluff, follow the arrows to the right to the steps cut in the rock. There are white blazes on the rock.

10.6 Cross the small branch and follow it downstream.

11.2 The trail leaves the drainage branch it has been following and heads down Negro Creek, becoming rocky, narrow, and sloped sideways.

11.3 Steps are cut in the large dead tree.

11.8 After 50 yards of steep, downhill hiking, watch carefully for the white diamond blaze, indicating a right turn.

12.1 Cross the old road.

12.2   You have a large boulder to the left of the trail and a bluff to the right.

12.3   A larger boulder sits left of the trail.

12.4   Junction with Loop Trail. From this point you will be retracing the same route by which you entered the loop. The return trail cuts back downhill to the left just before reaching a large, tilted boulder. The trail follows the river briefly and then travels up Negro Creek.

12.5   Cross the split-log bridge over Negro Creek. Cross the boulder at the end of the bridge and ease down its far side until you can jump to the opposite bank. Climb the bank to find the trail that heads downstream toward the river.

12.6   You are back at the river.

12.8   The trail continues straight ahead past numerous fallen trees. Cross the small drainage.

12.9   The trail is on the edge of the riverbank.

13.6   The trail crosses the floodplain.

13.7   After crossing the small, rocky drainage branch, you will come to another floodplain.

14.0   Leave the river and follow Lick Creek upstream.

14.1   Old road junction. Leave the old roadbed that the trail has been following and take the middle trail to the right .

14.2   Cross the large bridge over Lick Creek. The trail goes downstream to the right.

14.3   Junction with Lick Creek vehicle ford road. Remain left on the trail.

14.5   You will pass a small rock shelter to the left and then a large jumble of boulders.

14.7   Cross the drainage branch.

14.9   The trail forks briefly and rejoins.

15.1   The trail leaves the old roadbed and goes uphill to the left.

15.3   Cross the small, rocky branch.

15.4   Trailhead at the Yamacraw Bridge.

18. The Kentucky Trail

Distance: 27.2 miles
Rating: Moderate to difficult
Suggested time: 3- to 4-day backpacking trip
Blaze: Red arrowhead
Begins: Peters Mountain Trailhead
Access/resupply points: Ledbetter Trailhead, Blue Heron Visitor Complex, Wilson Ridge
Ends: Yamacraw Bridge
Accommodations: Blue Heron Visitor Center Complex
Special considerations: Connector trail to JMT, alternate trail (avoids dangerous fording of Rock Creek in high water), road (vehicular traffic), steps, ladder, abandoned mine sites, steep climbs, fordings (possible high water), trail below drip line (ice)

The Kentucky Trail travels past the first commercial oil well drilled in the United States, numerous coal mines, and the Blue Heron Tipple. It begins at Peters Mountain Trailhead and ends at the Yamacraw Bridge.

To reach Peters Mountain Trailhead, take TN 297 through the park west to TN 154. Go north on TN 154 for 1.8 miles to Divide Road, a dirt road on the right. Follow Divide Road. Remain left at the fork. You will pass the Twin Arches Road and the Hattie Blevins Cemetery Road. When you reach the Three Forks junction, go left. From this junction it will be 5.8 miles to Peters Mountain Trailhead, an equestrian trailhead.

The Kentucky Trail, blazed with the red arrowhead, is a long-distance trail that requires careful planning to hike. Once you leave Peters Mountain Trailhead, there is no vehicle access to the trail until the Ledbetter Trailhead at 12.4 miles and Wilson Ridge at 24.0 miles.

The Ledbetter Trailhead can be reached by taking KY 92 from Stearns, Kentucky, to the Yamacraw Bridge over the Big South Fork River. Turn left immediately after crossing the bridge. The road briefly parallels the river and then turns west and follows the railroad. When the road forks, remain left and cross the railroad tracks. In a short distance you will turn left onto the gravel

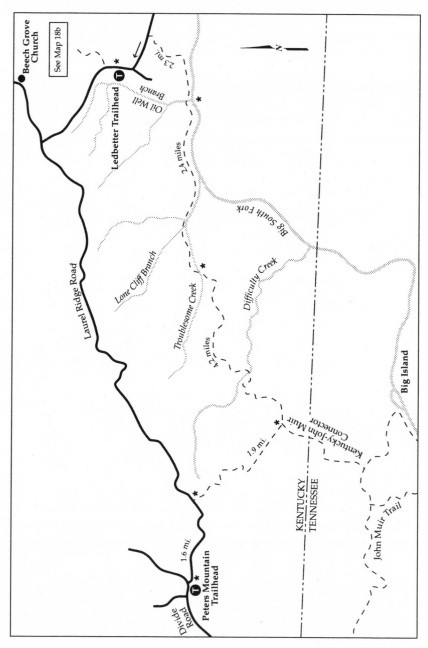

Beech Grove Church

See Map 18b

N

Ledbetter Trailhead

Oil Well Branch

2.3 mi.

2.4 miles

Big South Fork

Laurel Ridge Road

Lone Cliff Branch

Troublesome Creek

Difficulty Creek

4.2 miles

Big Island

Kentucky-John Muir Connector

1.9 mi.

KENTUCKY
TENNESSEE

John Muir Trail

1.6 mi.

Peters Mountain Trailhead

Divide Road

road crossing Rock Creek on the low concrete bridge. After crossing Rock Creek, the gravel road forks in 1.5 miles. At the fork the gravel road to the left goes out on Wilson Ridge, where the Kentucky Trail crosses it in 2.1 miles. A brown trail sign marks the trail crossing and access point on Wilson Ridge. The road to the right goes on to the Ledbetter Trailhead. In 2.5 miles it passes the Beech Grove Baptist Church. Although several roads lead off to the left in this area, you should continue straight. One mile past the church, take the road to the left. (If you should pass an old, burned-out schoolhouse, you have missed the road.) From this junction it is only about 1.5 miles to the Ledbetter Trailhead.

You can reach the Blue Heron complex on the east side of the river now that the old trestle to the coal tipple has been converted into a pedestrian walkway. Directions are given in the Blue Heron Loop section of the guide on page 149.

Mileage Description

0.0   You will begin hiking the Kentucky Trail by following the road paralleling Peters Mountain Trailhead. The Kentucky Trail joins the Sheltowee Trace for the first 1.6 miles.

0.2   The trail turns right onto a dirt road. A sign at the junction gives the distance of 6.1 miles along an equestrian trail to Big Island near No Business Creek. Although the hiking trail is inadequately blazed, you can follow it easily since it remains on the road. Disregard old park maps indicating that it leaves the road. While a trail was cut paralleling the road, it was never blazed or maintained. A future relocation of the Sheltowee Trace off of Laurel Ridge Road will probably also see a relocation of this portion of the Kentucky Trail.

1.3   The road divides, rejoins, and then forks again. Go left at the fork.

1.4   The road descends in a series of rocky ledges.

1.6   The road forks. At this intersection, the Kentucky trail goes to the right. (Although blazes indicate that the Sheltowee Trace also goes right, this is not correct. Due to a land dispute, the trail that was to have brought the Sheltowee Trace back to Laurel Ridge Road dead-ends at private property. Therefore, the Sheltowee remains left along the road at this junction.)

     This portion of the Kentucky Trail, a dirt road, varies little in elevation for the next 2.4 miles until it begins to descend from the ridge.

2.2   The trail crosses the small stream with a ledge waterfall.

2.4   The road to the left leads past an old farm site. You should remain to the right.

3.5   Trail junction. The trail downhill to the right leads into Tennessee, where it joins the John Muir Scenic Trail. (See page 184 for a description of the Kentucky–John Muir Connector.) The trail straight ahead continues the Kentucky Trail.

3.6   The trail begins to slowly leave the ridgetop. You now see hemlocks, which are not found on the drier ridgetop.

3.8   A well-marked junction shows where the trail leaves the old roadbed and travels north.

4.0   The trail descends steeply.

4.3   After going down the short ladder, the trail levels out briefly and then again becomes steep.

4.4   The trail descends steps to the base of the bluff.

4.5   The trail turns to the left, away from the bluff. You'll find a side trail that leads to a ledge waterfall.

4.53   Cross the small wooden footbridge. Notice the rhododendron surrounding the small branch and the large boulders scattered along its bank.

4.7   Cross the large wooden footbridge. This branch flows into Difficulty Creek. The trail is now level and follows Difficulty Creek. You'll find many good campsites to the left of the trail near the creek.

4.8   Cross the small footbridge.

5.0   Cross the large footbridge over Difficulty Creek. Within 200 yards you'll cross another large footbridge over a drainage branch, then yet another in 130 yards.

5.2   The trail begins a steep, uphill climb out of the Difficulty Creek drainage.

5.5   The trail reaches a narrow ridge and bears left and uphill on an old roadbed. The trail will leave the old roadbed and go right in about 150 yards.

5.7   The trail joins a 4-wheel-drive road on top of the ridge. Go right.

6.3   The trail leaves the road and begins to descend the north side of the ridge.

6.5   The trail passes below a medium-sized boulder.

6.8   The trail is below the large bluff filled with potholes. It passes below the rock overhang. There is another overhang in 125 yards. The trail is on the hillside above Troublesome Creek.

7.1   Watch closely: You will see a large boulder that appears to lean against another just beyond an easily missed switchback on the trail.

7.3   Begin to descend toward the creek.

7.4   There is a switchback to the west. The trail briefly follows an old road before switching back to the east.

7.5   Cross the footbridge.

7.7   The large footbridge spans Troublesome Creek. The trail follows the gently rolling path on the bank above Troublesome Creek.

8.1   The trail crosses Lone Cliff Branch a few feet above its junction with Troublesome Creek. Although there are stepping stones, you will have to ford in high water. After crossing the branch, go left upstream along Lone Cliff Branch. Beyond the branch the trail becomes overgrown on the small floodplain. After you leave the floodplain, the trail is obvious.

8.2   Trail junction. The sign at the junction indicates that the Sheltowee Trace goes uphill to Laurel Ridge Road. This is the trail that dead-ends at private property and should not be used. Within a few yards the old roadbed to your left will also lead to the Laurel Ridge Road, but it is not part of the trail system. (You will come out on Laurel Ridge Road east of the point where the Sheltowee leaves the road to head northward.) The Kentucky Trail continues straight ahead, downstream toward the Big South Fork River. It will follow first Troublesome Creek and then the Big South Fork River with little change in elevation. In approximately 3 miles the trail will ascend to the ridgetop.

8.3   After crossing Watson Branch on stepping stones, the trail begins a short, uphill climb and then levels off.

8.5   Hike steeply downhill for a short distance. You can hear but not see a waterfall along Troublesome Creek.

8.6   Cross the rocky branch. Hemlocks grow in abundance along the creek.

8.9   The trail joins an old roadbed.

9.0   The trail leaves Troublesome Creek and begins to follow the Big South Fork River.

9.1   Notice the large boulders resting along the banks and riverbed.

9.2   The small footpath to the right offers an excellent view of a massive boulder midstream.

9.4   Cross the large footbridge over the rocky drainage. Within a short distance is a good camping spot to the right of the trail. The stream, however, does not flow year-round.

9.7   Pass between large boulders as you go downhill.

10.1   There is a large footbridge over Oil Well Branch.

Near this bridge is the site of the first commercial oil well drilled in the United States. In 1819, Martin Beaty was drilling for brine to evaporate into salt. Instead of brine, he struck oil. It poured from his well into the Big South Fork River only a few yards away. At that time oil was mainly used in patent medicines. Beaty tried shipping it downstream and selling it for that purpose, but the neighbors downstream complained so heatedly about the oil fouling the river that he capped his well (U.S. Army Corps of Engineers 1982: 11).

You can find the well by backtracking about 500 feet along the trail. At the south end of the bridge, follow the trail as it heads toward the river. The trail curves to the right, paralleling the river, and goes up a slight rise. The trail next curves to the left. As soon as it curves to the right again, leave the trail and cut through the grass approximately 25 paces toward the river. (Improved signing and a wayside exhibit is proposed for this area.) All you can see of the well is a black pipe sticking out of the ground.

10.3   A road goes uphill to the left. This road leads to the Ledbetter Trailhead, but the trail continues to the right.

10.5   Cross the rocky drainage.

10.7   After passing by a canebrake between the trail and the river, you cross another rocky drainage.

10.9   Cross two small footbridges.

11.0   The trail leaves the river and begins climbing to the ridgetop at Ledbetter Trailhead, gaining 350 feet in elevation.

11.3   The trail is now less steep.

11.8   The trail reaches the ridgetop and joins a road. The road soon passes an abandoned house and overgrown fields on the right.

12.1   Road junction. The road on the left is the same one you passed earlier near Oil Well Branch. Continue straight.

12.4   Ledbetter Trailhead. From the abandoned fields on the ridgetop where you now are, you can see the Cumberland Mountains to the east.

   From Ledbetter Trailhead follow the road 150 yards until the trail veers off to the right. The trail is signed.

12.5   The King Cemetery is to the right of the trail. Several names common in the Big South Fork area are represented in the cemetery: King, Boyatt, and Ledbetter.

12.6   Roads diverge in many directions. The trail follows the center road, which will be blazed in a short distance.

12.8   The road forks. Stay left. The road soon becomes a trail as it leaves the ridgetop and passes through a hemlock forest.

13.0   Pass below small bluffs.

13.1   The trail intersects an old road. Go left. You can't see a blaze at this point.

13.3   Cross the footbridge over Laurel Crossing Branch. Rhododendron, holly, and hemlock surround the branch. Approximately 100 feet past the bridge the trail turns sharply to the right away from a wider path. Watch carefully: You could easily miss this right turn.

13.4   The small bridge crosses the north fork of Laurel Crossing Branch. The trail follows the narrow path between the steep hillside and Laurel Crossing Branch.

13.45 The trail moves away from Laurel Crossing Branch and passes through a hardwood and pine forest with an understory of laurel.

13.8   Two switchbacks take the trail higher up the hillside.

14.1   Cross the small footbridge. The trail is soon back on the ridgetop.

14.3   Trail sign for the Waters Cemetery and Blue Heron Tipple. The

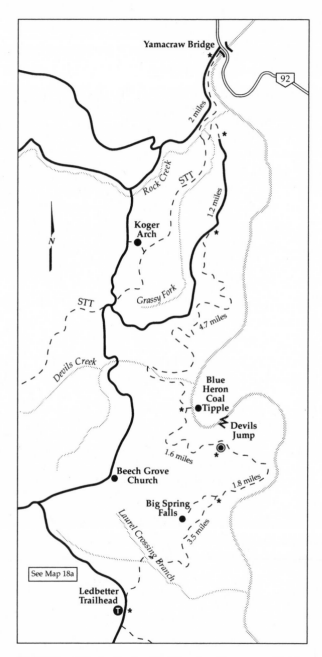

Trail Map 18b. Ledbetter Trailhead to Yamacraw Bridge

Waters Cemetery is a few yards through the woods to the left. This is still an active cemetery, and a road leads from the west end of the cemetery to the Beech Grove Baptist Church.

14.4   The trail leaves the old road it has been following and goes to the right.

14.6   The trail passes an old home site and crosses the road leading through the home site. The trail reenters the woods to the west.

14.9   To your left you can see the Waters Cemetery road paralleling your trail. The trail turns right, leaving the old roadbed it has been following.

14.95 The trail enters a large, abandoned field where grasses, weeds, and pines are invading this once-cultivated ridgetop. You have an excellent view of the Cumberland Mountains.

15.0   Ruins of a sandstone chimney remind you of the hardworking families who cleared and farmed these isolated ridgetops.

15.4   The trail leaves the ridgetop and descends below the bluff line on steps carved out of the stone.

15.6   Across the drainage branch, large sandstone bluffs cap the valley. The trail continues its descent to the valley by way of numerous switchbacks.

15.9   A short spur trail to the left leads to Big Spring Falls, a 100-foot, wet-weather waterfall in 0.3 mile. Although easy, *the trail can be extremely dangerous in the winter.* It passes directly under the drip line of the bluff, where huge icicles form; moreover, part of the trail crosses wooden footbridges that become icy sheets when the water on them freezes.

The trail to the right continues the Kentucky Trail. There is a switchback immediately past the junction with the spur trail. Watch closely for switchbacks in this area.

16.0   The footbridge crosses the creek below the falls. There are no good camping sites here because the hillsides are steep.

The trail begins following the bed of the railroad that serviced the mines along this ridge, so it is generally level.

16.84 Extremely dangerous, unstable coal slag now covers large sections of the original Kentucky trail. Do not attempt to hike past the trail closure. The trail now turns left and follows a drainage branch upstream.

17.1   At Dick Gap Falls the trail turns left and continues uphill.

17.2   Climb to the top of the bluff by way of the wooden staircase. Wooden steps assist you over a fallen tree whose branches now resemble trees themselves.

17.4   The trail crosses a long wooden footbridge past a rockshelter.

17.5   Passing a field to your right and an old roadbed to your left, your trail continues straight ahead.

17.6   Footbridge

17.7   Catawba Overlook. Take time to sit on the benches and read about the Blue Heron community beginning on page 152.

18.2   The hiking trail joins the horse trail for approximately 170 feet before leaving it on the left.

18.3   The trail descends log steps and then wooden stairs to the base of the bluff.

18.9   The trail descends Three West Hollow. The trail goes to the right.

19.3   Four abandoned coal cars (three decayed wooden ones and one of steel) sit as mute reminders of the bustle of activity that once characterized this track. The Blue Heron railroad trestle connected the mines on this side of the river with the Blue Heron Tipple. The tipple separated and graded various sizes of coal and loaded it in coal cars for shipment. The trestle now serves as a pedestrian access to Blue Herm.

19.5   Cross the stream. The concrete slab to the right of the trail was the foundation for a sub-station. It was used to boost power to operate the mining equipment. (C. Blevins 1992). An old vent fan lies alongside the trail. The wooden posts lining the old track once carried the electrical lines that ran the coal cars on the Blue Heron mining tram.

19.7   The trail starts uphill, leaving the railroad cut. Within 50 yards the trail begins a series of four uphill switchbacks. The last switchback leads onto an old roadbed. Go right on the road.

20.4   Road junction. Go right downhill toward the creek. You will find some good campsites to the left of the trail near the creek.

20.5   Ford Devils Creek. You can use stepping stones except in high water. Follow the roadbed uphill. The trail now follows the north bank of Devils Creek downstream.

20.7   Through the trees you can see large boulders in the creek. The trail levels out.

20.8   The road forks. Remain right.

20.9   Again, notice the wooden poles that once carried the railroad tram's electrical lines.

21.1   The trail rounds the end of the bluff and leaves Devils Creek drainage.

21.2   From the scenic overlook you have an outstanding view of the bluff between the Big South Fork River and Roaring Paunch Creek.

21.3   From this point the trail goes uphill. The concrete piers at the right are part of a trestle that once spanned this drainage valley. The trail now becomes occasionally steep. The drainage valley is filled with beech, hemlock, and poplar trees.

21.6   The trail levels out. Within 75 yards it will cross a small drainage.

21.63 Cross the footbridge. The roadbed continues uphill, while your trail veers to the left.

21.7   Pass next to the small rock shelter and through the boulders.

21.8   After walking beside the large bluff at the head of a drainage valley, cross the footbridge and continue straight on the trail. A road to the left has been barricaded.

22.0   The level trail passes through a hardwood and pine forest on the ridgetop.

22.1   The trail leaves the old roadbed and goes right.

22.3   The trail now parallels a county road. The orange blazes are the Big South Fork National River and Recreation Area boundary blazes.

22.5   Cross the old roadbed.

22.7   You begin descending below the bluff line. The bluff, with a small rock shelter, is to the immediate left of the trail. Notice the rhododendron, hemlock, and hardwood trees growing from the cracks in the bluff.

22.9   You are back on top of the bluff and can see the river below through
        the trees. Within 100 yards the trail returns below the bluff through a
        gap in the sandstone wall.

23.1   Small rock shelter.

23.3   Footbridge.

23.4   The trail passes beneath a large, solitary boulder.

23.5   Cross the small drainage. A large beech tree has fallen across the
        trail. The trail returns to the ridge. After passing two large boulders
        that have separated from the bluff, go left.

24.0   At the top of Wilson Ridge, the trail joins a gravel county road.
        Continue north on the gravel road. Do *not* take the dirt road to the
        right. (To reach the end of the Kentucky Trail at Yamacraw Bridge,
        you must ford Rock Creek. During high-water periods you may exit
        the Kentucky Trail at Wilson Ridge.)

24.3   As you continue on the Kentucky Trail, the gravel road passes a
        hillside scarred by a recent fire. The road and trail are along the park
        boundary.

24.5   Short, steep descent.

24.8   There is a farmhouse on the left side of the road. The gravel road
        ends past the farmhouse, and the trail continues on the dirt road.

25.2   The trail begins to descend from the ridge. Watch carefully: After a
        sharp switchback the trail turns left, leaving the old roadbed. The
        trail gradually descends as it rounds the end of Wilson Ridge. You
        can see Rock Creek and the Big South Fork River.

25.6   The trail becomes steeper, with numerous switchbacks, as it de-
        scends the west slope of Wilson Ridge to Grassy Fork Creek.

25.8   Stone steps lead down to Grassy Fork Creek. Cross the creek on the
        logs and go up the hillside a short distance to the junction with the
        Sheltowee Trace. Follow the Sheltowee Trace to the right toward
        Rock Creek.

26.0   You will come out on a small floodplain adjacent to Rock Creek.
        Walk straight across the floodplain to the series of rock steps leading
        down to Rock Creek. Large rocks have been placed straight across

the creek slightly left of the bottom step. In the spring or after a heavy rain, they are often under water and are too dangerous to cross. *Please be careful:* The creek is approximately 20 feet wide; if the depth and current look at all questionable, do not try to ford Rock Creek.

(To detour around Rock Creek, follow Grassy Fork Creek upstream via the Sheltowee Trace for 2 miles. A sign will direct you to Koger Arch. Go under the arch and follow the trail downhill to Devils Creek Road. Go to the right on the road and follow it until it crosses Rock Creek. Turn right onto the paved road leading to the Yamacraw Bridge and KY 92.)

After fording Rock Creek, walk straight uphill until you intersect a dirt road covered with coal debris. Go right. Notice the decaying trestle on the hillside, a remnant of the mining railroad that went up Grassy Fork Creek.

26.4 Rock Creek enters the Big South Fork River. The ballast-filled, concrete-arch railroad bridge spanning the river was built in 1907. At that time it was the largest of its type in the South. The Kentucky and Tennessee railroad that crossed the bridge was the main link between the far-flung timber and mining communities such as Co-operative and Bell Farm, and the main office of the Stearns Coal and Lumber Company in Stearns, Kentucky (U.S. Army Corps of Engineers 1982: 19).

(Suggestions have been made to incorporate this bridge into the trail system, crossing the river here instead of on the narrow KY92 bridge. *Do not* attempt to cross unless it is quite evident that the idea was adopted and implemented.)

26.7 Follow the trail along the river northward to the Yamacraw Bridge.

27.2 Yamacraw Bridge. You have completed the Kentucky Trail. There is a convenience store located to the west of the bridge.

19. Kentucky–John Muir Connector

Distance: 1.4 miles
Rating: Difficult
Suggested time: 45 minutes
Blaze: Red arrowhead
Special consideration: Steep, rocky terrain

The Kentucky Trail and the John Muir Trail are two long-distance trails within the park. A short, steep 1.4-mile trail connects them.

Mileage Description

0.0   In Kentucky, the connector leaves the Kentucky Trail at mile 3.5. A sign at the junction gives mileage to Difficulty Creek and Troublesome Creek.

0.5   The trail veers to the right. It has followed the ridgetop up to this point but now begins a long descent. Within 50 yards the road is barred at the state line.

0.6   There is a high rock wall to the right of the trail.

0.7   The trail forks. Go right. The trail becomes steep.

0.9   The trail briefly levels out as it follows the drainage downstream. The trail now travels along a large rock wall to the left. As you round the end of the wall, you can see that it is part of a massive bluff overlooking No Business Creek.

1.0   The trail continues to follow the branch downhill, but it now becomes very steep and rocky.

1.4   The trail levels off and crosses a branch right above its junction with another stream. In 100 yards the trail joins the Big Island Option of the John Muir Trail at mile 2.1. Travel to your right along the Big Island Option 1.6 miles to join the John Muir Trail going west. If you go to the left on the Big Island Option for 2.1 miles, you will join the John Muir Trail along the Big South Fork River above Big Island.

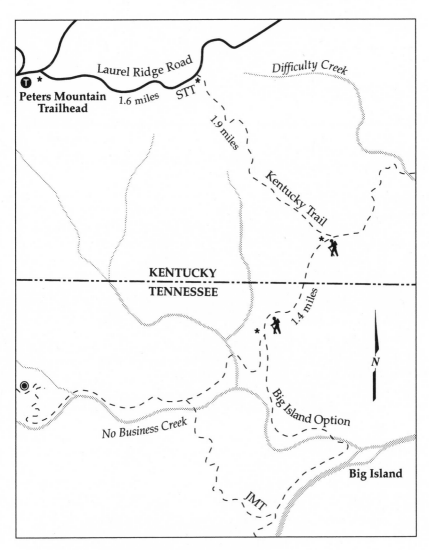

Trail Map 19. Kentucky–John Muir Connector

20.   The Sheltowee Trace

Distance: 66.4 miles
Rating: Moderate to difficult
Suggested time: 7-day backpacking trip
Blaze: White turtle or diamond
Begins: Pickett State Park, Tennessee
Access/resupply points: Great Meadow Campground, Hemlock Grove
Picnic Area, Peters Mountain Trailhead, Yamacraw Bridge on KY 92,
Flat Rock, Ky., on U.S. 27, KY 700
Ends: Cumberland Falls State Park, Kentucky
Accommodations: Pickett State Park, Great Meadow Campground,
Hemlock Grove Picnic Area, Cumberland Falls State Park
Special considerations: Incorrectly signed trail, connector to Kentucky
Trail, alternate trail (avoids dangerous fording of Rock Creek in high
water), alternate access (JMT, 1.5 miles off Divide Road), roads and
highways (vehicular traffic), steps, ladders, abandoned mine sites, steep
climbs, narrow trail, rocky terrain, fordings (possible high water), trail
below drip line (ice)

The Sheltowee Trace is named in honor of Daniel Boone, who was captured
by the Shawnee Indians in 1778 and spent the winter with them. Boone
gained such respect from Blackfish, their war chief, that he was adopted by
the tribe and given the name Sheltowee, or Big Turtle. He escaped after
learning of plans to attack Fort Boonesborough and traveled over 160 miles
in four days to warn the settlers (Collins 1975: 100-2).

Daniel Boone explored much of the land through which the trail passes. The
Sheltowee Trace, blazed with either a white turtle or white diamond, is 254
miles long. At most road intersections, you will find National Recreation Trail
symbols. Our directions begin the trail at Pickett State Park in Tennessee and
end at Cumberland Falls State Park in Kentucky. If you are interested in the
entire trail, contact the U.S. Forest Service, Stearns Ranger District. (See
Appendix 3) They can also provide you with sectional maps based on USGS
quads that cover the portion of the Sheltowee Trace described in this guide.

Long-distance trails require careful planning. There are four good resupply or access points along the Sheltowee Trace. The first is a Great Meadow Campground, 13.0 miles along the trail. (See page 13 for driving directions to Great Meadow Campground.) The next good access is Peters Mountain Trailhead, located at 17.2 miles along the trail. (Driving directions to the trailhead are found on page 171.) The Sheltowee Trace crosses the Yamacraw Bridge on KY 92 at mile 32.6, providing an easy access along a major highway with a nearby convenience store. The trailhead at Flat Rock, Kentucky (mile 47.8), 1 mile north of the Stearns Ranger District Office on U.S. 27 (just north of Whitley City), is the last good access point.

To begin the Sheltowee Trace, take TN 154 into Pickett State Park. You should check with a ranger about parking your vehicle for extended periods.

The Sheltowee Trace follows for the first 6.3 miles the Pickett State Park's green-blazed Hidden Passage Trail, the brown-blazed Rock Creek Trail, and the orange-blazed Coffee Trail.

Mileage Description

0.0   The trail begins on TN 154 just 0.3 miles north of the Pickett State Park office.

0.25   The trail crosses the small stream with a waterfall below.

0.3   Rock steps lead up to the right.

0.5   The trail divides at the Hidden Passage Loop. Go right on the loop.

0.6   After passing a stone pillar on the right, you will hike a narrow, hidden passage through a low-ceilinged rock shelter littered with boulders.

0.7   A short spur trail to the right leads to the base of Crystal Falls. We recommend that you detour to see this beautiful stream tumbling over tall ledges into a crystal clear pool at the base.

0.73   The trail crosses the lip of Crystal Falls above a series of tall ledges. *Be careful, especially in high water.*

0.9   The trail crosses an eroded sandstone hillside adorned only by lichens and mosses. Narrowing, the trail begins to follow the rim of the bluff.

1.5   An old road leaves the trail to the left. Keep right.

2.0   You will pass a rock shelter.

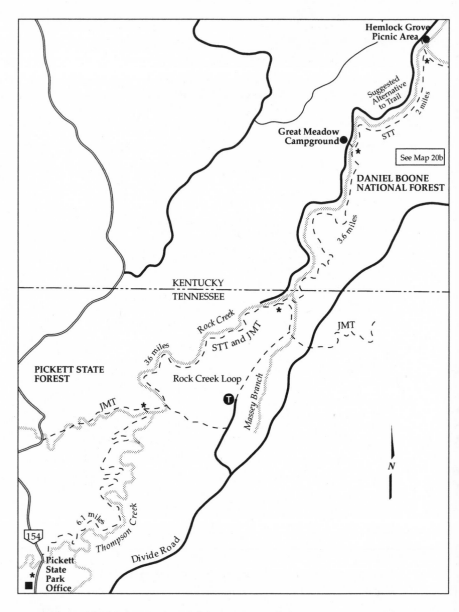

Trail Map 20a. The Sheltowee Trace:
Pickett State Park to Hemlock Grove Picnic Area

2.1   You'll see another rock shelter with a wooden bench. The benches you see along the Hidden Passage Trail were built by the Civilian Conservation Corps (CCC) out of American chestnut.

2.3   The trail passes a small overhang before continuing along the steep cliff and rounding at the end of the ridge.

2.7   Begin following the base of another bluff. Notice the sandstone boulders eroded to unusual mushroom shapes.

2.8   A steep descent leads away from the bluff.

2.9   The trail follows the base of another bluff. There is a steep, downhill switchback at the end of the bluff.

3.1   Cross the stream on the undercut ledge. The small stream tumbles over an 8-foot waterfall below. The trail then crosses the end of the ridge.

3.75   A side trail to the right offers a view of the rock shelter and wet-weather waterfall ahead on the trail.

3.9   The trail follows the streambed beneath the rock shelter. You may rest on the wooden bench behind the wet-weather waterfall.

4.1   After passing boulder-filled rock shelters, the trail goes beneath the high rock bluff rimming the valley.

4.2   Junction with the trail to double falls. Double Falls is 1 mile down the trail to the right. The Sheltowee continues to the left. After a short climb the trail levels off along the south rim of Thompson Ridge.

4.5   At the end of the ridge on Thompson Overlook, wind and water have eroded the hillside to the bare sandstone. The road traveling west from the overlook leads to the Group Campground in Pickett State Park. Your trail continues off the end of the ridge with a short, steep, downhill section before leveling off to travel the north rim of Thompson Ridge.

4.8   *Be careful: the trail passes above steep cliffs.*

4.9   You can see a tall, overhanging-ledge waterfall to the right of the trail.

5.0   Cross the creek above the waterfall on the small wooden bridge. Within a few yards the Sheltowee leaves the Hidden Passage Loop Trail, turning to the right to follow the brown-blazed Rock Creek Trail.

5.4   The trail reaches the ridgetop above Thompson Creek. After following a narrow passage close to the bluff line, the trail descends the ridge so steeply that you'll need to hold onto the rocks as you climb down.

5.6   At the bottom of the steep descent, the trail goes left, paralleling Thompson Creek as it rushes to meet Rock Creek. You must make one more steep descent before reaching the confluence of the creeks.

5.7   Thompson Creek flows into Rock Creek. The small floodplain at this junction makes an excellent camping spot in dry weather. You'll find additional campsites after fording Rock Creek. Both creeks are rocky and crystal-clear, with occasional large boulders lining their banks. A few yards upstream from the junction, ford Rock Creek to continue the trail.

5.8   A short distance uphill from the fording, a signpost marks the junction of the Rock Creek, Sheltowee Trace, and John Muir trails. To the left, the Rock Creek Trail and the John Muir Trail follow Rock Creek for 2 miles to TN 154, another possible access to the Sheltowee Trace.

The Sheltowee Trace turns right at this junction and joins the John Muir Trail for the next 3.6 miles. A short distance past the signpost, you can see the remains of the railroad bridge that once spanned the creek. (Railroading along Rock Creek and Thompson Creek is described on page 142.)

5.9   The trail emerges onto a small, rocky floodplain, where the creek makes a sharp turn to the left. After you ford the creek near the tip of the floodplain, you will find the trail a short distance up the far bank. Go left on this trail.

6.0   Old rails from the Stearns Logging Railroad lie across the trail. The Coffee Trail, the John Muir Trail, and the Rock Creek Loop all share this section of trail.

6.3   The trail now enters the Big South Fork National River and Recreation Area.

6.4   Cross the large footbridge over the drainage; then cross another large footbridge within 100 yards. The trail begins a meandering, often rocky, path up and down the hillside along the south side of Rock Creek.

7.6   After passing close to the creek and crossing the small footbridge, the trail climbs to an area of large boulders. Watch closely for the blaze.

8.1   Cross the small footbridge over the drainage. You'll find some good camping spots along the upcoming section of trail.

8.6   Cross the branch on stepping stones.

8.8   After passing through a stand of large beech and hemlock trees where the forest floor is covered in ferns, you'll cross a steep drainage on the large footbridge.

9.0   The trail descends from the hillside onto a floodplain. Go right along the creek. The trail soon joins the railroad cut.

9.4   The trail forks. The trail uphill to the right is the John Muir Trail, which crosses Divide Road in 1.5 miles. This is another possible access to the Sheltowee Trace. The trail straight ahead continues the Sheltowee Trace. Although the sign at the junction gives the distance to Great Meadow as 3.0 miles, we found it to be 3.6 miles. Continue straight ahead along the hillside above the south bank of Rock Creek.

9.6   Cross the small footbridge. The trail follows the creek.

9.75 Cross the large footbridge, over Massey Branch.

9.85 Just 100 feet beyond the Big South Fork boundary, a short access leads down to Rock Creek and the Buffalo Arch Trail. Located in the Daniel Boone National Forest, Buffalo Arch is an unusual sandstone arch that can also be reached by hiking a spur road off Hwy 1363 about 1 mile north of the Tennessee state line.

10.0 The trail overlooks a deep blue pool in Rock Creek.

10.5 After crossing two small drainages, the trail reaches a rock bluff.

10.6 Large rocks head up a small drainage crossing before you reach another view of Rock Creek with its huge boulder and rapids.

10.9 U.S. Forest Service activity changed the old road intersection previously encountered here; however, the trail is well-marked and easy to follow. The hillside across the creek has been harvested for timber. From just past the John Muir Trail junction near Massey Branch to Peters Mountain Trailhead, the Sheltowee Trace is within the Daniel Boone National Forest.

The National Forests and National Parks are two different agencies in two different branches of government. The Forest Service is administered under the Department of Agriculture, and the Park

Service is administered under the Department of Interior. Although the agencies work closely together, their policies and regulations differ. The National Parks are managed under the philosophy of preservation, which means simply preserving the land as it is. National Forests, on the other hand, are managed under the philosophy of conservation, which means using resources by careful husbandry and improvement. The agencies cooperate for the best land management. (Thorsen 1986)

11.46   The trail crosses a steep drainage. A short distance down the trail, two piles of stones lead you to speculate about what might have been here in earlier times.

11.6   The trail crosses a small branch.

12.26   The trail leaves the creek and follows a rocky path before it returns to the bank above Rock Creek.

12.33   Cross the branch. You can see a small bluff above to the right of the trail. The trail begins to diverge from Rock Creek. The Sheltowee Trace is now well marked.

13.0   Great Meadow Campground. You will have to ford Rock Creek if you want to go to the campground. At this bend in the creek, the water is fairly deep just below the rapids. Upstream you can see where additional rocks, other than those provided by nature, have been added to the streambed to help create a nice swimming hole.
    From this point it is 2 miles to the Hemlock Grove Picnic Area. In 1.3 miles, the Sheltowee will enter a 0.3-mile narrow, tunnel-like section of trail formed by the dense regrowth from the clearcut that was done along Rock Creek several years ago. With regular maintenance the trail should continue to be passable. Old signs indicated that the mileage between Great Meadows and Hemlock Grove to be 3 miles. Unable to confirm this because of the clearcut, we later (apparently along with the Forest Service) found it to be only 2 miles. Their newer signs reflect the change. If you have already crossed over to the campground, you may want to simply walk up the gravel road and rejoin the Sheltowee from the Hemlock Grove Picnic Area. At the southern end of the picnic area, you can see where Mark Branch enters Rock Creek. Ford Rock Creek and continue upstream on the south side of Mark Branch through a grassy field where a stone pillar and signs mark the trail. Two new U. S. Forest Service trails, Gobblers Arch and Mark Branch Loop, offer nice day hikes as well as dryer alternatives to

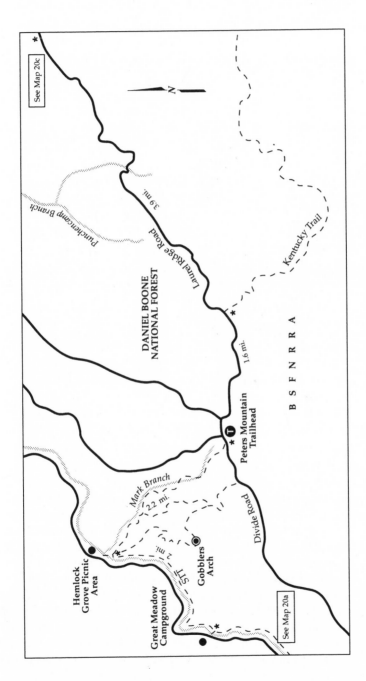

Trail Map 20b. The SheltoweeTrace: Hemlock Grove Picnic Area along Laurel Ridge Road

the trail up Mark Branch. As we come to the junctions, we will describe the alternate trails, both of which are blazed with the white diamond of the Sheltowee Trace.

14.1   The trail crosses a branch.

14.3   Thick regrowth from a recent clearcut lines the trail.

14.6   The forest opens back up again.

14.94   The trail going uphill to your right is the Gobblers Arch Trail. By following this trail you can reach Peters Mountain Trailhead in a little less than 4 miles. It is the driest, but most difficult alternative to the trail up Mark Branch. A short description of this trail will briefly interrupt the Sheltowee Trace.

Gobblers Arch Trail (Alternate Route to Peters Mountain Trailhead)

0.0   For almost 0.5-mile the trail ignores contour lines and simply climbs straight uphill. It is at times to be following an old skidder path used by loggers. It seems questionable as to whether or not this lower section of trail will hold.

0.6   A huge semi-circular gap breaks the bluffline that you have been following. Wild turkey tracks gave us a clue as to how this trail may have gotten its name. (Tracks also revealed that this particular turkey was being closely followed by a bobcat!)

0.8   Past a waterfall in the branch, the trail goes through a gap in the bluff.

0.9   Switchback to the right.

1.1   The trail rounds the end of the ridge.

1.46   Vista. A sign marks a side trail that leads to an overlook of Rock Creek drainage basin. Notice the different heights of trees that define the clearcut areas. While a carefully controlled and documented clearcut done in Pickett State Forest along Rock Creek revealed no damage to water quality, the controversial issue of clearcutting is far from being settled.

1.7   A rockshelter heads up a drainage crossed by the trail.

2.0   Gobblers Arch. The trail enters the opening to the arch and exits through a wider expanse on the far side. The lower ceiling of this arch makes its depth seem greater. A switchback brings you near the top of the arch. A sign indicates that you will reach a road, FDR 1605, in 0.2 mile.

2.25   Enter the roadbed and continue following the road.

2.86   The southwestern portion of the Mark Branch Loop trail enters the road on your left.

3.36   You have reached Divide Road (aka FDR 569). Turn left and follow Divide Road.

3.86   The Sheltowee Trace from Mark Branch enters Divide Road from your left. If you hiked the Gobblers Arch, continue the trail beginning with mileage 17.2 on page196 .

Sheltowee Trace continued.

15.00   A stone pillar, constructed by a hiker who once missed the turn up Mark Branch, marks the trail. About 300 to your left you can reach the Hemlock Grove Picnic Area on Rock Creek. To your right, the Sheltowee Trace continues up Mark Branch to Mark Branch Falls.

15.6   The trail crosses the creek and reaches the junction with the Mark Branch Loop Trail.

Mark Branch Loop (Alternate Route to Peters Mountain Trailhead)

0.0   Avoiding all but one of the creek crossings, the portion of the loop leading uphill to the right is a drier, 2.3-mile route to Peters Mountain Trailhead. While somewhat steep, it is much easier than the Gobblers Arch option, but not as scenic as the main trail up Mark Branch. It is also blazed with the white diamond of the Sheltowee Trace.

0.2   Following a switchback, the trail crosses a drainage and continues steeply uphill.

0.5   Near a rock overhang, a log bridge crosses a cascading stream.

0.6   The trail enters an old roadbed.

0.66   A sign in the roadbed marks the trail.

1.1   Following a switchback, the trail continues uphill.

1.3   The trail enters a forest service road. Turn left and go 0.5 mile to Divide Road.

1.8   At Divide Road go left for another 0.5 mile to the junction with the Sheltowee Trace.

2.3   Sheltowee Trace on Divide Road across from Peters Mountain Trailhead. Having followed this option, resume the main trail at mileage 17.2 below.

Sheltowee Trace continued.

15.7   The trail enters an area of large beech and hemlock. Cross the creek. The Sheltowee continues to wind its way up Mark Branch, crossing back and forth numerous times. Most of the crossings can be made on stepping stones, but a few places are soft and mushy. (If you are coming from Hemlock Grove just for a short hike to the falls, this is one trail that you certainly won't mind backtracking. You'll enjoy a new and different perspective of the rock formations on your return trip.)

16.1   A deep, hollow gurgling sound arises as the water disappears below a huge jumble of boulders.

16.4   Mark Branch Falls is a high, overhanging ledge waterfall formed as the branch carved the valley below. Water seeping from the bluff runs red with iron ore. The soft soil beneath the falls is also stained a deep orange-red. If you touch some of it and then try to wash your hands in the creek, you'll soon discover why it made a good dye. Switchbacks lead uphill beyond the falls.

16.6   A ship-like boulder sits beside the trail. The trail descends some rock steps. Notice the seemingly precarious position of the large hemlock as it clings to the rock ledge.

17.2   The trail follows along Mark Branch before ascending to the ridgetop and emerging onto Divide Road across from Peters Mountain Trailhead.

To the right Divide Road leads to Fork Ridge Road and TN 154. The road to the far left leads to Bell Farm, Kentucky. You can see Peters Mountain Trailhead, an equestrian trailhead, on the hillside in front of you. The Sheltowee Trace will follow the road beside the trailhead. The Kentucky Trail, originating at Peters Mountain Trailhead, will join the Sheltowee Trace for a short distance.

17.4   Road junction. Take the road to the right. The trail follows the dirt road along the ridgetop.

18.5   The road separates, rejoins in a short distance, and then forks. Go left at the fork.

18.6   Rocky ledges form steps in the roadbed.

18.8   The road forks. Take notice and please read our directions carefully: At this junction the Kentucky Trail turns to the right, while the Sheltowee Trace continues straight. This is a confusing junction because the trail to the right is clearly blazed with the Sheltowee turtle. Originally the Sheltowee was to go right at this point and return to Laurel Ridge Road near Lone Cliff Branch. However, a property dispute has halted indefinitely the construction of the trail, and at this time the trail dead-ends at private property before reaching Laurel Ridge Road. Therefore, to remain on the Sheltowee, you must continue hiking the Laurel Ridge Road. The next 4 miles of trail follow the ridgetop, with only one steep section at the Punchencamp Branch drainage. (With the proposed up-grade of Laurel Ridge Road to 2-wheel drive access, the U.S. Forest Service and National Park Service will most likely work toward relocating the Sheltowee Trace off of the road.)

19.0   The road forks but rejoins within 150 yards.

19.4   Road junction. Remain left. Within 150 yards the road will divide for a short distance.

20.0   Road junction. Remain left. The road to the right leads down to Troublesome Creek.

20.06 The road divides briefly (you can go either way); the left-hand section of the road passes a cemetery. As soon as the roads rejoin, the road forks again. Go right.

20.9   The trail begins to descend from the ridge, often steeply. You will pass two side roads.

21.3   Punchencamp Branch. Following the branch, the trail goes uphill for the next 400 yards. Ignore the road to the left and continue on the main road.

21.8   The road comes to the base of a large, highly eroded bluff. The side road to the right leads to a large rock shelter with a pool beneath it. Most of the rock shelters in the Big South fork Area are dry. Heavily used as a back-country campsite, this area would make a good place to camp if it were cleaned up.
The road now passes along the base of the bluff.

21.9   Look for the narrow arch formed when cracks caused by weatherization further eroded. The trail passes around the end of the bluff. At the far side of the bluff are several rock shelters. Stay on the main road for 0.8 mile past the rock shelters. Several smaller roads will diverge, but the main road is always obvious.

22.7   Watch carefully: The Sheltowee Trace now turns left, leaving the Laurel Ridge Road. Note that after passing the arch and rock shelters, you have less than 1 mile to this junction. The trail, lightly blazed with an occasional diamond or turtle, is an overgrown road. If you should hike on the Laurel Ridge Road until you see a large cemetery to your right, you have missed the turn. Within 70 yards after leaving Laurel Ridge Road, another road joins the trail from your right. Continue straight.

22.8   The road forks. Go right.

23.2   The trail veers off to the right, leaving the old roadbed, and follows the narrow ridgetop.

23.3   The trail down the end of the ridge is composed of eroding sandstone. *Be careful: You might slip.*

23.4   Junction with an old road. Go left. The trail is again level.

23.5   The trail enters a logged area. Shrubs, blackberries, and small pines have begun the process of reforesting. This open area offers some good views of the plateau.

23.8   The road forks. Go right.

24.0   The trail leaves the open area.

24.1   The trail passes below a bluff and around the end of the bluff. Within 200 yards the trail will make a sharp left turn. Watch carefully for the diamond blaze. This turn is very easy to miss, as the trail first appears to continue straight. The trail begins a gradual descent. Notice the highly eroded bluff with its many small rock shelters.

24.6   The trail becomes very steep as it descends into the drainage, but several rock stairs ease the descent. You can see a small wet-weather waterfall to the right of the trail. Rhododendron and hemlock line the hillsides.

24.8   After crossing the small drainage branch, turn left to ford Spring Branch on the stepping stones. The trail continues along the hillside above the branch.

25.1   The trail again fords Spring Branch and immediately crosses back to the east side. You'll find a possible campsite on the west side. If the water is high, you can stay on the east side of the branch and work your way downstream above the steep bank. Your trail is approximately 60 yards downstream along the east bank. Where the trail leaves Spring Branch, if coincides with an old roadbed.

25.3   Cross the rocky drainage branch.

25.4   Cross another small drainage.

25.5   Leave Spring Branch and start uphill.

25.6   Junction with a dirt road. Go right on the road.

25.7   Watch carefully: The trail leaves the road and follows the stone steps uphill to the left. You will have a steep, uphill climb.

25.8   After passing between two large boulders, the trail veers to the left. Ignore the animal trail to the right. The trail still climbs uphill, but not as steeply.

25.9   The trail goes along the base of the bluff. A narrow passageway to the left of the trail leads around a boulder. The trail then passes an overhang and begins to lead away from the bluff.

26.1   The trail intersects an old road. Go left on the old road. The trail levels out along a ridgetop.

26.6   The trail veers to the left, leaving the roadbed and heading downhill.

26.7   Watch carefully: The trail makes a sharp right turn that is hard to see. Rock steps aid your steep descent. Within 300 yards the trail is again below the sandstone bluff.

27.0   The trail passes between the bluff and a large boulder.

27.2   Stone steps lead up through the gap in the bluff.

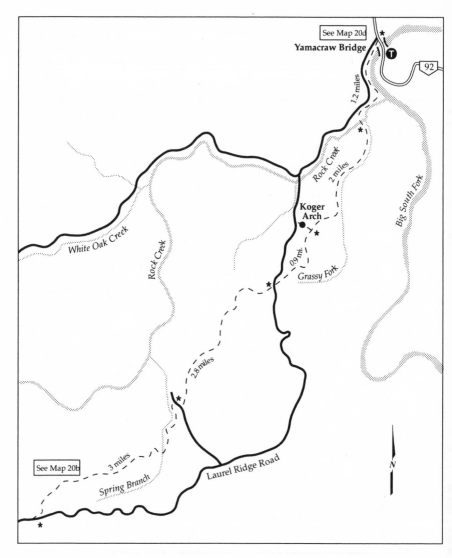

Trail Map 20c. The Sheltowee Trace: Laurel Ridge Road to Yamacraw Bridge

27.3   On the ridge the trail continues uphill, reaching a rocky knob. The trail climbs the knob and offers a spectacular view of the Cumberland Mountains and the deeply segmented Cumberland Plateau. The area to the east of this ridge is drained by the Big South

Fork River. To the west it is drained by Rock Creek, a large tributary of the Big South Fork. The trail continues along the narrow ridge. Pines grow on the thin, acidic soil of this eroded sandstone ridgetop. You will find many scenic overlooks along the ridgetop.

28.2   The trail makes a steep descent from the ridge.

28.3   Junction with a dirt road. Go left on the road. The trail is now level.

28.4   Junction with Laurel Ridge Road (Devils Creek Road). Go left.

28.5   Road junction. The road to the right leads out onto Wilson Ridge and connects with the Kentucky Trail. The road to the left is the continuation of Laurel Ridge Road (Devils Creek Road) that leads north to Yamacraw Bridge. To continue the Sheltowee Trace, go straight across the gravel road to the sandy dirt road. The road is not blazed. Although gateposts stand on either side of the road, it is not gated. This level, sandy road makes a semicircle around a logged area before leading north into the woods.

29.4   A sign to the left of the trail marks the trail junction with the Koger Arch Trail. On your left, the 0.25-mile trail to Koger Arch leaves the roadway approximately 12 paces past the sign. Koger Arch is 54 feet wide, 18 feet high, and 91 feet across at the base (Thorsen 1987). It was formed when cracks at the back of an overhang eroded until the overhang separated from the hillside. Passing under Koger Arch, a trail continues downhill to Devils Creek Road. Because the Sheltowee Trace fords Rock Creek on its way to the Yamacraw Bridge, this trail past Koger Arch provides an alternative route in case of high water.

To continue the Sheltowee Trace, take a sharp right off the road directly across from the sign to Koger Arch. Your trail is blazed and goes gently downhill.

29.5   The trail meets an old roadbed. Go left on the roadbed and continue gently downhill.

29.8   The drainage branch to the left of the trail falls sharply away.

29.9   The trail passes beneath a power line, and within 100 yards it crosses a small stream.

30.0   The road forks. Remain left and recross the stream. The trail soon crosses the larger Grassy Creek. The trail follows the creek downhill. You will find possible campsites along the floodplain and across the creek at the base of the bluff.

30.25   Ford Grassy Creek. The trail is now on the west side of the creek. Within 150 yards you can see an old coal mine to the left of the trail. You will pass numerous mine entrances and slag piles before reaching Rock Creek.

30.3   Ford Grassy Creek. Follow the stepping stones through the boggy area. Notice the large boulders lining the banks of the creek. The trail soon joins the old mining railroad cut.

30.6   Ford the branch to the west bank. Continue to follow the old railroad spur. Within 100 yards the trail begins a lengthy passage through large boulders. You'll have fun climbing and squeezing through the cracks. Massive boulders line the creek.

30.8   *Be careful:* A narrow, half-log bridge with no handrail crosses the creek above a small waterfall.

30.9   Cross another half-log bridge.

31.1   The concrete structure to the left of the trail is an old mine entrance.

31.2   Junction with the Kentucky Trail. Blazed with a red arrow, the Kentucky Trail crosses Grassy Creek and climbs to the top of Wilson Ridge before heading south for 26 miles to Peters Mountain Trailhead. The Sheltowee Trace continues straight ahead.

31.4   The trail emerges onto a small floodplain. Walk straight across the floodplain to a series of rock steps leading down to Rock Creek. Large rocks have been placed in the creek slightly left of the bottom step. *Caution: The Sheltowee ford of Rock Creek can be dangerous.* If water covers the stepping stones or the current seems swift, use the detour described on page 201. It's better to be extra careful.

   After fording Rock Creek, walk straight up the bank until you come to a dirt road covered with coal debris. Go right on this road. The decaying trestle on the hillside is a remnant of the mining railroad that went up Grassy Creek.

31.8   Rock Creek flows into the Big South Fork River. The railroad bridge spanning the river linked the timber and mining communities along Rock Creek and the main offices of the Stearns Coal and Lumber Company in Stearns, Kentucky.

32.1   Follow the trail along the river northward to the Yamacraw Bridge.

32.6   Yamacraw Bridge. *Be careful crossing the bridge:* There is no pedestrian walkway.

Turn left into the parking area at the northeast end of the bridge. The Yamacraw–Yahoo Loop Trail follows the Sheltowee Trace for the next 8 miles into the Yahoo Falls Scenic Area. We will describe this portion of the trail briefly, while continuing the mileage for the Sheltowee Trace. (For a more complete description, read pages 163-168.)

34.0   We recommend that you hike the 0.2-mile side trail to Princess Falls. Upon returning, cross the large wooden bridge over Lick Creek. The trail will cross the vehicle ford of the creek and then turn left toward the river.

34.4   A sandy floodplain stretches between the trail and the river. The roadbed and the trail now diverge, with the road going downhill and the trail continuing straight.

35.5   Having crossed two small drainage valleys, the trail now leaves the river to go up Negro Creek. You will have to look carefully to find where the trail goes down the creek bank, crosses part of the creek, climbs up the opposite boulder, and crosses the remainder of Negro Creek on a split-log bridge.

36.2   The trail descends between boulders to a stream that rushes through picturesque tunnel of boulders. If the creek is too high to ford, you can climb across the top of the tunnel.

37.0   The trail passes the Cotton Patch Shelter, an elevated pavilion.

39.0   Alum Ford Campground. Cross KY 700 and follow the left shoulder of the road for about 75 yards to find the trail.

40.5   Trail junction: The trail to the right (green arrowhead) climbs the metal stairs to the Yahoo Falls Picnic Area. The Sheltowee Trace continues straight ahead below the bluff and crosses the bridge over the drainage.

40.8   After following the south bank of Yahoo Creek, the trail forks. The trail to the right leads to Yahoo Falls and also connects with trails leading to the picnic area. The Sheltowee Trace continues straight.

40.9   Cross the bridge over Yahoo Creek. Within 20 yards the Sheltowee makes a sharp left turn around a large boulder and heads down Yahoo Falls. (You can read about the beautiful Yahoo Falls Scenic Area on pages 159-162.)
        The Sheltowee Trace, traveling along the north bank of Yahoo Creek, crosses an old wooden bridge.

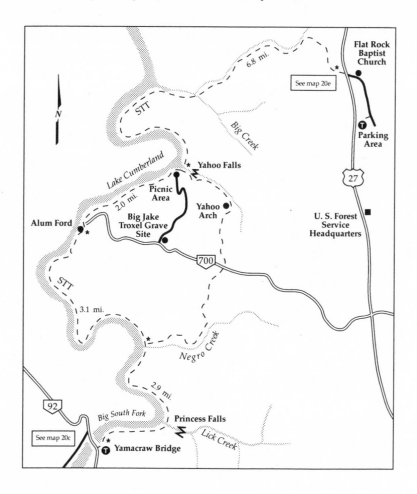

Trail Map 20d. The Sheltowee Trace:
Yamacraw Bridge to Flat Rock, Kentucky

41.4   The trail goes to the right around a boulder and heads up a small, drainage valley before crossing the stream.

41.8   The trail is near the base of the bluff. The lower layers of rock are shale; the cap rock is sandstone. Cross the small drainage.

41.9   You will see a large overhang above the trail. Many mature beech trees grow in this area.

43.0   The trail turns upstream along Big Creek. You can see a boat ramp
       across the creek. This is your last view of the Big South Fork River
       from the Sheltowee Trace. The trail goes uphill.

43.3   Notice the rapids in Big Creek as it descends steeply to the river. In 50
       yards the trail will enter the Daniel Boone National Forest. The trail
       narrows while going through a rhododendron thicket high above Big
       Creek.

43.5   Ford Big Creek and follow the rock steps up the opposite bank. The
       trail parallels the north bank of the creek.

43.6   The trail joins an old roadbed. Go right.

43.7   U.S. Forest Service boundary. The trail travels along a county road
       past a private residence. When the road forks, go uphill to the left. In
       100 yards, just before the road begins a steep uphill climb, steps lead
       off the road to the right. If you miss this portion of the trail, don't
       worry. The trail will rejoin the road in 0.3 mile.

44.0   The trail, back on the road, continues for about 30 yards before
       leaving the road again to climb the hillside. Watch carefully for this
       left turn. If you see two large culverts under the county road, you
       have missed the trail.

44.3   Ford the creek. The hillside and valley have recently been logged.

44.4   Ford the creek. In 70 yards, you will ford the creek again. You can
       see tall bluffs above the logged hillside.

44.5   Cross the small drainage.

44.6   Cross the north branch of Big Creek once again. Stone steps lead up
       the bank. The trail now keeps to the left (north) of this creek.

44.7   Pass under the small rock overhang and cross the branch. You'll
       cross another in 30 yards. The trail begins a very steep uphill climb.

44.8   Notice the large overhanging-ledge waterfall to the right of the trail.

44.83 The trail reaches the top of the steep incline, crosses the stream
       above the waterfall, and recrosses it in 80 yards. You can't see the
       trail now. Stay on the left side of the stream close to the boulders as
       you climb slightly uphill. You will see the trail beyond the boulders.

45.0   Cross the stream.

45.1   Cross another branch and go up the stone steps. There is an old mine opening at the back of the rock shelter to the left of the trail. *Do not enter it: Old mines are dangerous.* The trail starts up a steep-sided valley filled with hemlock, beech, and rhododendron. Large boulders lie scattered down the drainage branch.

46.2   Sandstone bluffs rise to the left of the trail. Shale eroding from beneath the sandstone-capped rock has left pillar formations.

46.3   At the head of the drainage, a waterfall pours over the semicircular bluff. The trail passes beneath the undercut bluff behind the waterfall. Large blocks of sandstone have fallen from the overhang as the shale beneath them eroded.

46.4   Climb up the rock steps at the far side of the waterfall.

46.5   The trail emerges on top of the bluff.

46.7   After passing beneath telephone lines, cross the county road and continue to follow the creek.

47.1   The trail joins a dirt road. Go right. When the road forks in 50 yards, stay left. In about 25 yards, the trail will leave the roadbed to the left.

47.2   Cross the dirt road beneath the power line.

47.4   There is a directional sign by the paved road. Go south along the paved road for 0.3 mile, passing private residences and crossing the railroad before reaching U.S. 27 at the community of Flat Rock, Kentucky.

47.7   Cross U.S. 27 at the Sheltowee Trace National Recreation Trail markers. Follow the gravel road in front of you. The road will curve to the right, passing by the Flat Rock Baptist Church. Continue along the gravel road.

48.0   The trail leaves the gravel road, entering the woods on the right.

48.8   The trail emerges at the trailhead parking area on U.S. 27, approximately 1 mile north of the Stearns Ranger Station. The sign at the trailhead indicates that it is 6 miles to Yahoo Falls, but we measured the distance as 6.9 miles. The distance to Cumberland Falls is given as 17 miles, but we found it to be 18.6 miles. The trail to Cumberland Falls leaves the trailhead to the southeast.

48.9   After going under the power line, the trail crosses an old logging road.

49.1   Recrossing beneath the power line, the trail follows an old logging road for about 225 feet, then leaves the road and turns sharply to the left.

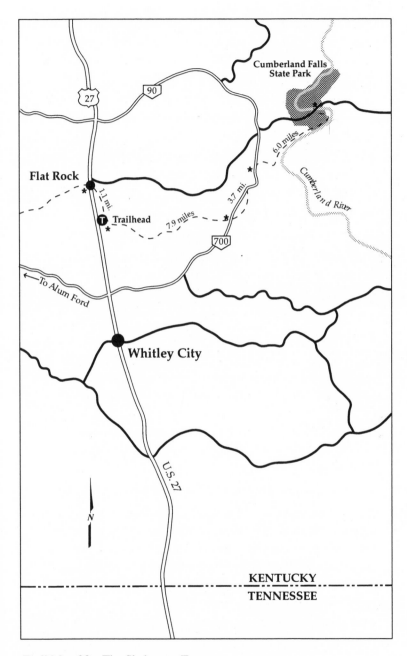

Trail Map 20e. The Sheltowee Trace:
Flat Rock, Kentucky, to Cumberland Falls State Park

49.2   Rounding the end of a small bluff, the trail gradually descends and re-crosses underneath the power line. The vegetation changes to hemlock as the trail follows the bluff line eastward toward Railroad Fork Creek.

48.4   The trail descends rock steps and crosses Railroad Fork Creek beneath the bluff at the small waterfall. The trail narrows, now traveling along the north side of the creek. Rhododendron and mountain laurel fill the drainage branches.

48.9   The trail crosses to the south side of Railroad Fork Creek and turns left, following the creek downstream. Although there are no real stepping-stones in the creek crossings, you can ford in low water. The trail follows the hillside and crosses several drainage branches.

49.2   The Stearns Coal and Lumber Company mined this area in the 1930s. The trail follows the route used by the railroad tram to haul out the coal. You can see the remains of an old concrete foundation across the branch. (Thorsen 1987)

49.6   The trail follows the small branch, crosses, and then turns back toward Railroad Fork Creek. The stone foundations to the left and right of the trail are the remains of an old trestle.

50.3   The floodplain along Railroad Fork Creek widens, opening up sufficiently for camping in dry weather.

50.5   The trail descends steps to the crossing at Railroad Fork Creek and continues along the north side of the branch.

51.0   The trail passes between the rock walls of the old railroad cut, turns left, and starts uphill.

51.3   The trail levels out again. The floodplain beside the creek widens, making it suitable for camping.

51.6   An old logging road joins the trail from your right.

51.7   After crossing to the south side of Railroad Fork Creek, you come to an intersection of four roads. The Sheltowee Trace follows the middle road straight ahead. As you climb the hill you will see a brown sign with a white arrow directing you to turn left.

52.0   Having crossed several small drainage branches, the trail now passes among jumbled boulders at the base of a large bluff.

52.3   While crossing the drainage, notice the water coming from a small, cave-like entrance that was once walled up. Used as a spring house

for an old home site, only a small section of the stonework remains.
(Thorsen 1987)

52.8   After crossing several more small drainages, the trail again follows the
        old railroad bed. When you come to the wooden signpost with the
        National Recreation Trail symbol, follow the roadbed to the right.

52.9   Follow the trail uphill and to the right. The trail turns to the left just
        before reaching the rock bluff. A white arrow is painted on a large
        rock in the road.

53.0   You pass a large rock shelter.

53.3   The trail crosses Pigeon Roost Branch.

53.4   An old road descends from the hill to the right of the trail. Continue
        straight ahead and around the curve of the trail to the left. The trail
        goes around some rocks and uphill. *Be careful: Here the trail is
        badly eroded and slants steeply.*

53.9   Pass underneath the rock overhang along the bluff line.

54.4   You can see Indian Creek with its sandy, rock-littered bottom. The
        trail descends into the rockhouse and continues along the bluff line
        beneath it.

55.0   Having made its way around several smaller drainage branches, the
        trail again passes beneath the rock ledge of the bluff line. This
        pattern is repeated.

55.4   For about 100 feet the trail enters a narrow space between rocks and
        the bluff line.

56.1   The Sheltowee Trace goes uphill to the right. Ignore the trail
        downhill to the left.

56.2   The trail joins an old roadbed. Turn left. There are National Forest
        Service arrows pointing in the direction of the trail. After the timber
        was harvested from this ridge, pines were planted in 1988. Near the
        ridgetop a Sheltowee Trace National Recreation Trail marker directs
        you to follow the roadbed to the left.

56.3   A brown-and-white arrow points to the right where you leave the old
        roadbed and follow the trail around the ridge. A few remaining trees
        blazed with a white diamond mark the trail.

56.5   The trail crosses an old logging road.

56.7   The trail crosses KY 700 and enters the woods. In about 100 feet the trail will turn left. Until merging with KY 700, the Sheltowee Trace parallels the road on its east side.

56.9   Cross at the head of the drainage branch just below KY 700.

57.3   Notice the small shelf waterfall in the branch.

57.8   Although you can now see the highway, the trail continues around the hillside.

58.1   The trail enters KY 700 and travels along the highway for the next 2.3 miles. You will pass private residences. *Always be careful when hiking along roadways.*

58.7   The road curves sharply right and continues downhill toward the bridge.

58.9   Cross the bridge over Indian Creek. Continue following KY 700 steadily uphill for 0.5 mile.

60.4   A Sheltowee Trace National Recreation Trail marker and arrow direct you to turn right at the gravel road.

60.6   At a farmhouse the trail leaves the gravel portion of the road and continues along the dirt road to the left.

61.3   You can begin to see the Cumberland River. The road descends by rock shelves.

61.47   The badly eroded road first makes a hard left and then cuts back sharply to the right.

61.55   Above the Cumberland River at McKee Bend, the trail leaves the road, goes down two stone steps to the left, and makes its way down to the river. Watch carefully, as you could easily miss this intersection.

61.8   A line of rapids stretches across the width of the Cumberland River. This is the first in a series of rapids known as Pitch Rapids. Follow the small path to the right down to the river's edge for a better view.

61.9   Cross Pitch Branch at the small rockhouse.

62.1   The trail descends to the rock shelf along the river's edge. Unfortunately, the river's beauty is spoiled by the trash and debris caught up by high water and deposited along the edge of the river. High water often covers portions of the Sheltowee Trace along the Cumberland River. After crossing the rock shelf for about 400 feet, you reenter the woods. Your trail works its way along the river, traveling up many small drainage branches for easier crossing.

63.6   Slick shoals. Shoals are shallow areas that cause the river to ripple.

63.9   The trail crosses private property at a cleared area. While the road going uphill leads up to KY 90, the trail continues straight ahead.

64.0   Red paint on the trees marks the U.S. Forest Service boundary. A trail leads off to the left, but the Sheltowee Trace follows the road along the edge of the river.

64.6   The trail jogs left approximately 50 feet and then turns back to the right.

64.8   In the Blue Bend area, the trail turns away from the river and goes uphill.

64.9   Climb the rock steps and hike along the bluff underneath the rock overhang.

65.0   The trail narrows between the bluff and a large rock.

65.1   The trail enters an old roadbed. Go right. (You can easily miss this blazed intersection if you are hiking in the opposite direction.) In 500 feet, near the bluff line, the trail crosses a small drainage branch.

65.4   The trail winds through a narrow passage where low rock retaining walls line the trail. Notice the tree roots reaching for soil around the large rock.

65.6   Rounding the end of a large boulder, the trail nears the river.

65.7   Climb the steps between the two large boulders.

65.8   Cumberland Falls State Park concrete boundary marker. You can see the shoals in the river.

65.9   The trail climbs 16 rock steps as it makes its way uphill nearer the bluff line.

66.1   The trail turns up the drainage branch. Within 100 feet you cross the branch and climb the long, steep flight of rock steps.

66.12   The trail winds its way between large rocks underneath the rock shelter. Within 250 feet a sign at the base of the sheer rock wall gives the mileage to Cumberland Falls as 0.5 mile. In another 50 feet the trail forks. A trail to the left leads up the base of the bluff, while your trail to the right continues on to the bridge.

66.24   The trail emerges at the bridge over the Cumberland River.

66.4   Cross the bridge on KY 90. The entrance to the parking area at Cumberland Falls is to your left. You'll find a snack bar and store at the far end of the parking lot near the falls. The road to the right will take you to the top of the hill and Dupont Lodge, where Kentucky State Park Rangers are on duty twenty-four hours a day.

Named after the Cumberland River, the falls is 125 feet wide and 68 feet high. In flood stage, its width increases to 300 feet and its height decreases to 45 feet. Cumberland Falls has the only moonbow in the Western Hemisphere. On a clear night with a full moon, a moonbow, or arch of white light, begins at the base of the falls and continues downstream. You can see colors in the moonbow during the fall and winter months. The only other moonbow in the world is at Victoria Falls on the Zambezi River in Africa (*Cumberland Falls State Park Program Guide:* 1).

For this guide our directions will end the Sheltowee Trace at Cumberland Falls, although the trail continues northward through Kentucky.

Appendix 1. Trail Chart

Trail	Rating	Distance	Page
Tennessee Trails			
1. Bandy Creek Campground Trailhead			
Just off Tn 297			
Bandy Creek Campground Loop hardwood forest, gravel path	easy	1.3 miles one way	27
Grand Gap Loop, Option 1 Fall Branch Falls, large rockhouse	moderate	10.2 miles round trip	27
Grand Loop, Option 2 Fall Branch Falls, large rockhouse	moderate	17 miles round trip	30
Grand Gap Loop, Option 3 Angel Falls Overlook	difficult	13.2 miles round trip	33
Grand Cap Loop , Option 4 Fall Branch, river trail, Leatherwood Ford	difficult	9.0 miles one way	33
John Litton /General Slaven Farm Loop Old John Litton Farm, Fall Branch	moderate	6.3 miles	34
Oscar Blevins Farm Loop Historic Homesite, Bandy Creek, bluff, waterfall	easy	3.6 miles	38
2. Jacks Ridge Trailhead			
Northwest of Bandy Creek Campground			
Laurel Fork Loop scenic views, creek fordings, Blevins Cemetery, Charit Creek	difficult	11.1 miles	46
3. West Entrance Trailhead			
On TN 297			
Bandy Creek Campground Bandy Creek, bluff, waterfall	easy	3.4 miles one way	52
Jacks Ridge via Laurel Fork creek fordings	difficult	4.7 miles one way	54

Trail	Rating	Distance	Page
4. Middle Creek Trailhead			
Western boundary, Fork Ridge Road			
Middle Creek Loop high cliffs, rock shelters	moderate	3.5 miles round trip	56
West Entrance, via Laurel Fork Indian Rock House, creek fordings	difficult	8.3 miles one way	59
5. Sawmill Trailhead			
Western boundary, Fork Ridge Road			
Slave Falls Loop Indian Rock House, Slave Falls	easy	3.7. miles	63
Charit Creek Lodge via Slave Falls Slave Falls, Needle Arch	difficult	4.8 miles one way	66
6. Twin Arches Trailhead			
Western boundary, 2.4 miles off Divide Road			
Twin Arches large natural arches	moderate	1.4 miles round trip	70
Twin Arches Loop bluffs, rock shelters, Jakes Place, Charit Creek Hostel	difficult	5.5 miles	73
7. Rock Creek Loop Trailhead			
Western Boundary, 2.9 miles off Divide Road			
Rock Creek Massey Branch, Rock Creek, rockhouse	difficult	7.1 miles	80
8. Leatherwood Ford Trailhead			
On TN 297 at the river			
O & W Bridge historic bridge, river trail	easy	4.6 miles round trip	87
Leatherwood Loop scenic overlook	moderate	3.3 miles	89
Angel Falls class IV rapids, river trail	easy	2 miles one way	91
Station Camp Crossing via Angel Falls and the John Smith mine site	moderate	8.3 miles one way	93

Trail	Rating	Distance	Page
John Smith Mine site, river trail to the reclaimed mine site only	moderate	6.8 miles round trip	
Angel Falls Overlook Fall Branch, rock shelter, scenic overlooks	difficult	2.9 miles one way	95

9. East Rim and Leatherwood Loop
Eastern Boundary, off TN 297

East Rim Overlook scenic overlook	easy	100 yards	98
Leatherwood Loop Overlook scenic overlook	easy	1.4 miles round trip	100
Sunset Overlook scenic overlook	easy	1.3 miles one way	101

10. Burnt Mill Bridge Trailhead
Southern boundary

Burnt Mill Bridge Loop river trail, branches, rock shelters waterfall	moderate	4.3 miles	102
John Muir Spur unfinished trail	moderate	3.6 miles one way	106

11. Honey Creek
Southern boundary

Honey Creek Loop streams, waterfalls, bluffs, rock shelters, creek fordings, scenic overlooks, rugged terrain	very difficult	5.63 miles round trip	107

12. Historic Rugby
Southern boundary, on TN 52

Gentlemens Swimming Hole historic trail	difficult	0.8 mile round trip	117
Meeting of the Waters river trail, steep bluffs, White Oak Creek	difficult	2.4 miles round trip	119

13. John Muir Trail

O & W Bridge to Pickett State Forest		48.2	123

Trail	Rating	Distance	Page

Kentucky Trails

14. Bear Creek Scenic Area
Northeastern boundary, off KY 742

Bear Creek Overlook scenic overlook	easy	0.5 mile round trip	146
Split Bow Arch Loop	moderate	0.64 mile round trip	147

15. Blue Heron
Northeastern boundary near Stearns, KY

Blue Heron Loop nearby campground, Blue Heron Tipple Devils Jump, Cracks-in-the-Rock	moderate	6.4 miles	149
Catawba Overlook scenic overlook	moderate	3.2 miles round trip	156
Big Spring Falls waterfalls	moderate	7.48 miles round trip	156

16. Yahoo Falls
Northeastern boundary, off KY 700

Yahoo Falls Scenic Area Yahoo Falls, scenic overlooks rock shelter, picnic area	moderate	about 3.5 miles for all trails	159

17. Yamacraw–Yahoo
Northeastern boundary, Yamacraw Bridge KY 92

Yamacraw–Yahoo Loop river trail, streams, waterfalls, bluffs, rock shelters, Yahoo Falls, Yahoo Arch	difficult	15.4 miles round trip	163

18. Kentucky Trail
*Peters Mountain Trailhead
to Yamacraw Bridge*

		27.2 miles	171

19. Kentucky–John Muir Connector
Linkage of two long distance trails

	difficult	1.4 miles	184

20. Sheltowee Trace
*Pickett State Park
to Cumberland Falls State Park*

		66.4 miles	186

Appendix 2. Backpacking Combinations

The Big South Fork offers many long distance hikes other than the John Muir Trail, the Kentucky Trail and the Sheltowee Trace. By combining trails and selecting different options along these routes, you can create backpacking trips of varying length and difficulty. (We would also like to point out that simply hiking to a destination and backtracking is also a good choice. Viewing features from a different perspective is just like hiking a new trail.) Suggested times allow for an average of 10 miles per day. The page number given refers to text that describes the trail and an (R) means that the trail description must be reversed. Reversing trail descriptions can be very tricky. Study the maps carefully.

Bandy Creek Campground Trailhead

1. John Muir Trail and Laurel Fork of Station Camp Creek: Combining beautiful boulder-filled creeks and small waterfalls with outstanding over-looks, this loop is one of the most popular back-country hikes.
   Suggested time: Three nights on the trail.

From	To	Blaze	Miles	Total Miles	See Page
Campground	Grand Gap Loop	Red arrowhead	5.1		29
(To the right)	Grand Gap Loop	Blue JMT	6.8	11.9	30
Grand Gap Loop	Duncan Hollow	"	4.4	16.3	126
Duncan Hollow	Laurel Fork (Bridge)	"	5.6	21.9	127
Laurel Fork	Junct. w/Jacks Ridge	Red arrowhead	4.0	25.9	(R) 49
Laurel Fork	Junct. w/West Entrance	"	2.6	28.5	(R) 55
Laurel Fork	To West Entrance	"	1.7	30.2	(R) 54
West Entrance	Bandy Creek	"	3.4	33.6	52

Alternative A. Eliminate 6.8-mile Grand Gap Loop.
Suggested time: Two nights on the trail.

From	To	Blaze	Miles	Total Miles	See Page
Campground	Grand Gap Loop	Red arrowhead	5.1		29
Grand Gap Loop	Duncan Hollow Bridge	Blue JMT	4.4	9.5	126
Duncan Hollow	Laurel Fork	Red arrowhead	5.6	15.1	127
Laurel Fork	To West Entrance	"	8.3	23.4	(R) 49 &55
West Entrance	Bandy Creek	"	3.4	26.8	52

Alternative B. Eliminate the Grand Gap Loop and exit at Jacks Ridge.
Suggested time: One night with two long days.

From	To	Blaze	Miles	Total Miles	See Page
Campground	Grand Gap Loop	Red arrowhead	5.1		29
JMT	Laurel Fork Bridge	Blue JMT	10.0	15.1	126
Laurel Fork	Junct. w/Jacks Ridge	Red arrowhead	4.0	19.1	49
Laurel Fork	Jacks Ridge Trailhead	Yellow horsehead	0.4	19.5	(R) 46
Jacks Ridge	Bandy Creek Road (left)		0.8	20.3	(R) 44
Bandy Creek Rd	Collier Ridge Bike Trail		0.3	20.6	(R) 45
Right on Bike Trail	Blevins Farm Loop	Post w/orange	0.1	20.7	—
Left on loop	Bandy Creek Trailhead	Red arrowhead	1.2	21.9	(R) 40

2. Laurel Fork Creek and the Twin Arches Loop: By adding a visit to the
Twin Arches to the Laurel Fork Loop, you can combine beautiful creeks and
intriguing geological features to create a difficult 20.2-mile overnighter. You
may opt for a more leisurely and enjoyable two-night trip.

From	To	Blaze	Miles	Total Miles	See Page
Bandy Creek	Jacks Ridge Trailhead	(see options)	@2.3		44
Jacks Ridge	Laurel Fork Creek	Yellow horsehead	0.4	2.7	46
Laurel Fork	Bridge near Station Camp	Red arrowhead	4.0	6.7	47
Station Camp	Charit Creek	Yellow horsehead	4.0	10.7	49
Twin Arches Loop	Charit Creek	Red arrowhead	4.1	14.8	77; 75
Charit Creek	Laurel Fork Creek	Red arrowhead & Yellow horsehead	2.7	17.5	50
Laurel Fork	Bandy Creek		@2.7	20.2	(R) 44

Leatherwood Ford Trailhead

Enjoy the Big South Fork River from two very different perspectives. First follow it along the floodplain to Station Camp, and then fording the river, climb to the ridgetop for awesome views of the river gorge. *Advance scouting and good judgment must precede any attempt at crossing the river.* (This is the reasoning behind putting the river crossing near the beginning of the trip.) You'll need at least two nights out for this one.

From	To	Blaze	Miles	Total Miles	See Page
Leatherwood	Rough Shoals	Red arrowhead	4.1		94
Rough Shoals	Station Camp Crossing	"	4.2	8.3	95
St. Camp Crossing	Laurel Fork Bridge	Blue JMT	@1.0	9.3	(R) 130
Laurel Fork	Duncan Hollow Bridge	"	5.6	14.9	(R) 129
Duncan Hollow	Grand Gap Loop	"	4.4	19.3	(R) 127
(left on GG Loop)	Junct. w/Angel Falls O.	"	5.5	24.8	(R) 32
Grand Gap Loop	Leatherwood Ford	"	2.7	27.5	(R) 97

West Entrance Trailhead

Upper Laurel Fork Creek, Slave Falls and Twin Arches: If you like creek crossings you will love the hike up Laurel Fork Creek to the Slave Falls Loop. A waterfall, arches and rockshelters keep the trail interesting as you descend to Charit Creek. Climb up and down Fork Ridge and you are back at Laurel Fork Creek for a wet, mild-weather recommended hike of 19.8 miles. Two short days on each end of a two-nighter allows time to really explore and enjoy the interesting features along this trail.

From	To	Blaze	Miles	Total Miles	See Page
West Entrance	Laurel Fork	"	1.7		(R) 62-60 (1.8)
Laurel Fork	Slave Falls Loop (left)	"	4.7	6.4	(R) 65 (0.85)
Fork Ridge Road	Twin Arches Junct.	"	3.5	9.9	67
T. Arches Junct.	(Left) Charit Creek	"	2.9	12.8	(R) 77
Charit Creek	Laurel Fork	Red arrowhead			
		Yellow horsehead	2.7	15.5	50
Up Laurel Fork	Junct. w/West Ent.	Red arrowhead	2.6	18.1	(R) 55
Laurel Fork	West Entrance	"	1.7	19.8	(R) 54

Middle Creek Trailhead

Rockshelters abound on this adventure. Was it a temporary shelter for the early Indian, or the location of a well-hidden moonshine still? The uses of these eroded sandstone creations were as varied as the shelters themselves. While camping at Jakes Place is no longer allowed, an overnight stay in that general vicinity will give you two full days of hiking and exploring.

From	To	Blaze	Miles	Total Miles	See Page
Middle Creek	Connector Trail	Red arrowhead	2.5		(R) 59
Connector	Slave Falls Loop	"	0.8	3.3	—
Right on Loop	Junct. w/trail to Falls	"	2.25	5.55	63
Slave Falls Spur		"	0.4	5.95	67
Slave Falls Loop	Needle Arch	"	0.1	6.05	67
Needle Arch	Junct. w/Twin Arches	"	2.45	8.5	68
Left on Loop	Twin Arches	"	2.0	10.5	(R) 77
Arches	Charit Creek	"	0.9	11.4	(R) 79
Charit Creek	Junct. w/Slave Falls Tr.	"	1.25	12.65	(R) 77
Slave Falls Trail	Middle Creek Connector		3.55	16.2	(R) 68
Connector	Junct. w/Middle Creek	"	0.8	17.0	—
Middle Creek	Trailhead	"	1.0	18.0	(R) 56

Peters Mountain Trailhead

Using the Kentucky Trail and the Kentucky-John Muir Connector to access the John Muir Trail, you can hike through history as you pass through the abandoned community of No Business. Imagine the logging and mining activity as you step on the old railroad ties along Massey Branch. When the John Muir Trail turns left, you'll turn right and begin to follow the Sheltowee Trace back to Peters Mountain Trailhead. While two nights and three long days can get you around this loop, the Daniel Boone National Forest has several side trails that would make this area a fun-filled week on Rock Creek. You may want to make the Great Meadows Campground your base camp and explore from there.

From	To	Blaze	Miles	Total Miles	See Page
Peters Mtn.	KY-JMT Connector	White diamond/			
		Red arrowhead	3.5		173
Connector	Big Island Option	Red arrowhead	1.4	4.9	184
South along river	Junct. w/ option	Blue JMT	2.1	7.0	(R) 134
JMT B.Island Opt.	No. Business Creek	"	1.9	8.9	134
No Business Creek	JMT Overlook	"	2.6	11.5	135
JMT Overlook	Divide Road	"	7.4	18.9	137
Divide Road	Massey Branch Bridge	"	0.5	19.4	138
Massey Branch	JMT/Sheltowee Junct.	White diamond	1.2	20.6	138
Sheltowee Trace	Great Meadows CG	"	3.6	24.2	190
Great Meadows	Hemlock Grove	"	2.0	26.2	192
Up Mark Branch	Peters Mtn. Trailhead	"	2.2	28.4	196

Blue Heron

In case you are lucky enough to have a week to spend backpacking, you will appreciate the variety that the combination of the Kentucky Trail and the Sheltowee Trace has to offer. Relive coal mining history at the Blue Heron ghost structures and then walk across the tipple bridge to begin your trip. Creeks and arches, waterfalls and overlooks make this hike a favorite of backpackers. (The future completion of a trail that now deadends because of private property or its relocation will allow for a nearly 10-mile shorter loop while still taking in the best features of both trails.)

From	To	Blaze	Miles	Total Miles	See Page
Blue Heron Tipple Br.					
north on KY Trail	Junct. w/STT	Red arrowhead	6.5		180
Sheltowee Trace	Koger Arch	White diamond	1.8	8.3	(R) 202
Koger Arch	Laurel Ridge Road	"	6.7	15.0	(R) 201
Laurel Ridge Road	Junct. w/KY Trail	"	3.9	18.9	(R) 198
KY Trail	Difficulty Creek	Red arrowhead	3.4	22.3	173
Difficulty Creek	Oil Well Branch	"	5.1	27.4	174
Oil Well Branch	Ledbetter Trailhead	"	2.3	29.7	176
Ledbetter Trailhead	Blue Heron	"	6.9	36.6	177

Appendix 3. Addresses and Telephone Numbers

Big South Fork National River and Recreation Area
Rt. 3, Box 401
Oneida, TN 37841
Bandy Creek Visitor Center (615) 879-3625
Park Headquarters (Admin. Offices) (615) 569-9778
Blue Heron (606) 376-3787
After hours emergency contact:
Fentress County Sheriff's Office, TN (615) 879-8142
Scott County Sheriff's Office, TN (615) 663-2245
McCreary County Sheriff's Office, KY (606) 376-2322

Cumberland Falls State Resort Park
Corbin, KY 40701
(606) 528-4121 or 1-800-325-0063

Historic Rugby
P. O. Box 8, Hwy. 52
Rugby, TN 37733
(615) 628-2441

KY Dept. of Fish and Wildlife Resources
Div. of Public Relations
#1 Game Farm Road
Frankfort, KY 40601
Information: (502) 564-4336
Violations: 1-800-25 ALERT

Pickett State Park
Rock Creek Route, Box 174
Jamestown, TN 38556
(615) 879-5821

Tennessee Wildlife Resource Agency, Region III
216 E. Penfield
Crossville, TN 38555
Information: (615) 484-9571 or 1-800-262-6704
Violations: 1-800-255-TWRA

U.S. Forest Service
Daniel Boone National Forest
Stearns Ranger District
P. O. Box 429
Whitley City, KY 42653
(606) 376-5302

Concessionaires:

Bandy Creek Stables P. O. Box 191 Huntsville, TN 37756 (615) 879-4013	Short term horse boarding, horse rentals with guided trips, tack shop
Big South Fork Scenic Railway P. O. Box 368 Stearns, KY 42647 (606) 376-5330 1-800-462-5664	Scenic trips to Blue Heron Coal Mining Community
Charit Creek Lodge 250 Lonesome Valley Road Sevierville, TN 37862 (615) 429-5704	Primitive lodging for groups and individuals with meals

Eastern National Park & Monument Association
c/o Big South Fork NRRA
Rt. 3, Box 401
Oneida, TN 37841   Books and crafts; sales
(615) 879-3625   at Bandy Creek & Blue Heron

Commercial Use Licensees

Backwoods Adventure   Canoe and raft rentals,
327 Industrial Lane   bicycle and equipment rentals,
P. O. Box 366   shuttle service
Oneida, TN 37841
(615) 569-9573

Carolina Wilderness   Guided raft and funyak trips
P. O. Box 488
Hot Springs, NC 28743
1-800-872-7437

Cumberland Rapid Transit   Canoe rental, guided raft trips,
Box 200, Rock Creek Route·   rock climbing instruction,
Jamestown, TN 38556   rappelling & single rope
(615) 879-4818   technique, wild cave tours,
                                 shuttle service

Sheltowee Trace Outfitters   Guided raft trips, canoe rental,
P. O. Box 1060   tube trips, shuttle service,
Whitley City, KY 42653   fishing and backpacking info
1-800-541-RAFT
(606) 679-5026

*Please note that any listing for Concession Operators and Commercial Use
Licensees is subject to change. New ones may be added and old ones might
not renew.

Appendix 4.
Checklist: Mammals of the Big South Fork

Species	Habitat
Virginia Opossum	All habitats
Masked Shrew	Woodlands
Southeastern Shrew	Woodlands
Water Shrew	Woodlands
Smoky Shrew	Woodlands
Short-tailed Shrew	Woodlands
Least Shrew	Woodlands
Hairy-tailed Mole	All habitats
Eastern Mole	All habitats
Little Brown Myotis	Out at dusk
Southeastern Myotis	Out at dusk
Gray Myotis	Out at dusk
Keen's Myotis	Out at dusk
Indiana Myotis	Out at dusk
Small-footed Myotis	Out at dusk
Silver-haired Myotis	Out at dusk
Eastern Pipistrelle	Out at dusk
Big Brown Bat	Out at dusk
Red Bat	Out at dusk
Hoary Bat	Out at dusk
Evening Bat	Out at dusk
Rafinesque's Big-eared Bat	Out at dusk
Eastern Cottontail	Open areas
New England Cottontail	Open areas
Eastern Chipmunk	Most wooded areas
Woodchuck	In and around openings
Gray Squirrel	Woodlands, mature timber beside openings
Fox Squirrel	Woodlands, mature timber beside openings
Southern Flying Squirrel	Woodlands, mature timber beside openings
Beaver	Main stem of river

Marsh Rice Rat	Stream bottoms
Eastern Harvest Mouse	Woodlands
Deer Mouse	Woodlands
White-footed Mouse	Woodlands
Cotton Mouse	Woodlands
Golden Mouse	Woodlands
Hispid Cotton Rat	Woodlands
Eastern Wood Rat	Woodlands
Meadow Vole	Woodlands near openings
Woodland Vole	Woodlands near openings
Muskrat	Pools on main stem of river
Black Rat	Near developed areas
House Mouse	Near developed areas
Meadow Jumping Mouse	Openings
Coyote	All habitats
Red Fox	Larger openings
Gray Fox	Woodlands
Raccoon	All habitats
Long-tailed Weasel	Old house sites, rock piles
Mink	River and streams
Eastern Spotted Skunk	Old house sites, edge of openings
Striped Skunk	Edge of openings
River Otter	Main stem of river
Bobcat	Dense thickets, rock bluffs, small openings
European Wild Boar	Thickets, rock bluffs, small drainages
White-tailed Deer	All habitats

Sources: List courtesy of the National Park Service; notes on habitats courtesy of Jack Collier.

Appendix 5.
Checklist: Birds of the Big South Fork

Species	Status
Pied-billed Grebe	Uncommon winter visitor
Great Blue Heron†	Uncommon migrant
Green-backed Heron	Rare summer visitor
Canada Goose†	Uncommon migrant
Mallard†	Uncommon migrant
Black Vulture	Rare summer resident
Turkey Vulture	Common permanent resident
Osprey	Rare spring and fall migrant
Sharp-shinned Hawk	Rare permanent resident
Cooper's Hawk	Rare winter resident
Red-shouldered Hawk	Uncommon permanent resident
Broad-winged Hawk	Uncommon summer resident
Red-tailed Hawk	Uncommon permanent resident
American Kestrel	Rare permanent resident
Merlin†	Rare migrant
Ruffed Grouse	Uncommon permanent resident
Wild Turkey	Uncommon permanent resident
Northern Bobwhite	Rare permanent resident
Killdeer	Rare summer resident
Spotted Sandpiper	Uncommon spring and fall migrant
Common Snipe†	Rare winter resident
American Woodcock	Rare permanent resident
Rock Dove†	Common resident
Mourning Dove	Uncommon permanent resident
Black-billed Cuckoo†	Uncommon summer resident
Yellow-billed Cuckoo	Fairly common summer resident
Eastern Screech-Owl	Uncommon permanent resident
Great Horned Owl	Uncommon permanent resident
Barred Owl	Uncommon permanent resident
Short-eared Owl†	Uncommon winter resident

Common Nighthawk†	Common summer resident
Whip-poor-will	Fairly common summer resident
Chimney Swift	Rare summer resident
Ruby-throated Hummingbird	Uncommon summer resident
Belted Kingfisher	Uncommon permanent resident
Red-headed Woodpecker†	Rare resident
Red-bellied Woodpecker	Uncommon permanent resident
Yellow-bellied Sapsucker	Uncommon winter resident
Downy Woodpecker	Common permanent resident
Hairy Woodpecker	Fairly common permanent resident
Northern Flicker	Uncommon permanent resident
Pileated Woodpecker	Fairly common permanent resident
Eastern Wood-Pewee	Common summer resident
Acadian Flycatcher	Common summer resident
Least Flycatcher†	Uncommon summer resident
Eastern Phoebe	Common summer, uncommon winter resident
Great Crested Flycatcher	Fairly common summer resident
Eastern Kingbird†	Common summer resident
Purple Martin	Rare summer resident
Tree Swallow†	Uncommon migrant
Northern Rough-winged Swallow	Uncommon summer resident
Bank Swallow†	Uncommon migrant
Barn Swallow	Uncommon summer resident
Blue Jay	Common permanent resident
American Crow	Common permanent resident
Carolina Chickadee	Common permanent resident
Tufted Titmouse	Common permanent resident
Red-breasted Nuthatch	Uncommon winter resident
White-breasted Nuthatch	Fairly common permanent resident
Brown Creeper	Uncommon winter resident
Carolina Wren	Fairly common permanent resident
House Wren†	Common resident
Winter Wren	Uncommon winter resident
Golden-crowned Kinglet	Common winter resident
Ruby-crowned Kinglet	Uncommon winter resident
Blue-gray Gnatcatcher	Common summer resident

Eastern Bluebird	Uncommon permanent resident
Veery†	Uncommon migrant
Gray-cheeked Thrush†	Uncommon migrant
Swainson's Thrush	Uncommon spring and fall migrant
Hermit Thrush	Uncommon winter resident
Wood Thrush	Common summer resident
American Robin	Uncommon summer, fairly common winter resident
Gray Catbird	Uncommon summer resident
Northern Mockingbird†	Fairly common resident
Brown Thrasher	Uncommon summer resident
Cedar Waxwing	Uncommon permanent resident
Loggerhead Shrike†	Uncommon resident
European Starling	Rare permanent resident
White-eyed Vireo	Fairly common summer resident
Solitary Vireo	Uncommon summer resident
Yellow-throated Vireo	Fairly common summer resident
Red-eyed Vireo	Abundant summer resident
Blue-winged Warbler	Uncommon spring and fall migrant
Golden-winged Warbler†	Rare migrant
Tennessee Warbler	Fairly common spring and fall migrant
Northern Parula Warbler	Fairly common summer resident
Yellow Warbler†	Uncommon summer resident
Chestnut-sided Warbler	Uncommon spring and fall migrant
Magnolia Warbler†	Uncommon migrant
Cape May Warbler†	Uncommon migrant
Black-throated Blue Warbler†	Uncommon migrant
Yellow-rumped Warbler	Fairly common winter resident
Black-throated Green Warbler	Common summer resident
Blackburnian Warbler†	Uncommon migrant
Yellow-throated Warbler	Common summer resident
Pine Warbler	Common summer resident
Prairie Warbler	Uncommon summer resident
Palm Warbler	Uncommon spring and fall migrant
Bay-breasted Warbler	Fairly common spring and fall migrant
Blackpoll Warbler	Fairly common spring migrant
Black-and-white Warbler	Common summer resident
American Redstart	Fairly common summer resident

Worm-eating Warbler	Fairly common summer resident
Swainson's Warbler	Uncommon summer resident
Ovenbird	Abundant summer resident
Northern Waterthrush†	Uncommon migrant
Louisiana Waterthrush	Fairly common summer resident
Kentucky Warbler	Common summer resident
Common Yellowthroat	Uncommon summer resident
Hooded Warbler	Common summer resident
Yellow-breasted Chat	Uncommon summer resident
Summer Tanager	Uncommon summer resident
Scarlet Tanager	Common summer resident
Northern Cardinal	Common permanent resident
Rose-breasted Grosbeak	Fairly common spring and fall migrant
Blue Grosbeak†	Uncommon migrant
Indigo Bunting	Abundant summer resident
Painted Bunting†	Rare summer resident
Rufous-sided Towhee	Fairly common summer resident
Chipping Sparrow	Uncommon summer resident
Field Sparrow	Uncommon permanent resident
Vesper Sparrow†	Uncommon migrant
Savannah Sparrow†	Uncommon migrant
Song Sparrow	Uncommon permanent resident
Swamp Sparrow†	Rare winter resident
White-throated Sparrow	Common winter resident
White-crowned Sparrow†	Uncommon migrant
Dark-eyed Junco	Common winter resident
Bobolink†	Uncommon migrant
Red-winged Blackbird	Rare permanent resident
Eastern Meadowlark	Rare permanent resident
Common Grackle	Uncommon permanent resident
Brown-headed Cowbird	Fairly common summer resident
Orchard Oriole	Uncommon summer resident
Northern Oriole†	Uncommon summer resident
Purple Finch	Fairly common winter resident
House Finch†	Fairly common resident
Red Crossbill	Rare winter visitor
American Goldfinch	Uncommon permanent resident
Pine Siskin	Uncommon winter resident

Evening Grosbeak   Uncommon winter resident
House Sparrow†   Common resident

Sources: Base list courtesy of Charles P. Nicholson, Jr.;
additional sightings (†) courtesy of Dan and Myra Bickford.

Appendix 6.
Checklist: Wildflowers of the Big South Fork

Early Spring – March

Bloodroot
Coltsfoot (alien)
Dandelion (alien)
Early Saxifrage
Harbinger-of-Spring

Hepatica
Purple Cress
Purslane Speedwell
Rue-Anemone
Spring Beauty

Star Chickweed
Trout Lily
Twinleaf

Mid-Spring – April

Blue Phlox
Bluets
Buttercup sp.
Common Cinquefoil
Cut-leaved Toothwort
Dwarf Iris
Dwarf Larkspur
Dutchman's Breeches

Fire Pink
Foamflower
Golden Ragwort
Little Brown Jug
Mountain Spurge
Pennywort
Periwinkle
Pussy Toes

Slender Toothwort
Spiderwort
Spring Cress
Squirrel Corn
Stone Crop
Trillium

Late Spring – May

Bindweed
Chickweed
Chrysogonum
Coreopsis
Dwarf Gineng
Horse-Nettle
Indian Cucumber Root
Jack-in-the-Pulpit
Lady's Slipper
Large-Flowered Bellwort

May Apple
Mountain Laurel
Queen Anne's Lace
Showy Orchi
Sweet Cicely
Trailing Arbutus
Vetch sp. (alien)
Violet sp.
Violet Wood-Sorrel
Virginia Bluebells

White Baneberry
Wild Columbine
Wild Geranium
Wild Ginger
Wild Sweet-William
Wild Yam
Yellow Lady's Slipper
Yellowroot

Early Summer – June

Beard-Tongue	Hop Clover	Spotted Wintergreen
Black Cohosh	Indian-Pipe	St. Johnswort
Butterfly-Weed	Lamb's Quarters	Teaberry
Common Milkweed	Orange Hawkweed	Venus Looking Glass
Common Mullein (alien)	Ox-Eye Daisy	Viper's Bugloss
Common Skullcap	Ragwort	Waterleaf
Day-Lily (alien)	Rosebay Rhododendron	Yellow Wood-Sorrel
Evening Primrose	Ruellia	
Flame Azalea	Sneezewood	

Mid-Summer – July

Bedstraw	Nodding Wild Onion	Sensitive Brier
Black-Eyed Susan	Partridgeberry	Smartweed
Cardinal Flower	Pipsisiwa	Spotted Joe-Pye-Weed
Chickory	Poke Weed	Tick-Trefoil
Dodder	Purple Coneflower	Virginia Dayflower
Flowering Spurge	Rattlesnake-Plantain	White Snakeroot
Hoary Mountain Mint	Rose Pink	
Jewelweed	Rosebud Orchis	

Late Summer – August

Beggar-Ticks	Great Lobella	Sweet Everlasting
Bee-Balm	Harebell	Tickseed
Bergamot	Hog-Peanut	Turtlehead
Blazing Star	Horse-Balm	White Lettuce
Common Thistle	Jerusalem Artichoke	Wood Sunflower
False Foxglove	New England Aster	
Goldern-Aster	New York Ironweed	

Autumn – September - October

Autumn Sneezeweed	Goldenrod (sp)	Purple Gerardia
Calico Aster	Lion's-Foot	White Snakeroot
Gall-of-the-Earth	Mistflower	White Wood Aster

Source: List courtesy of the National Park Service, compiled by Ranger Sue Duncan.

References

Literature Cited

American National Red Cross. 1976. *Whitewater in an Open Canoe.* ARC 2173.

Bickford, Myra. Letter to authors, July 9, 1988.

Blevins, Laccie W., and Ray F. 1982. *Jonathan Blevins, Sr. of Virginia and His Descendants.* Johnson City, Tenn: Overmountain Press.

Bowater Trails: Special Maps and Information. N.d. N.p.

Brandt, Robert S. Letter to authors, March 24, 1988.

Collins, Robert F. 1975. *A History of the Daniel Boone National Forest 1770–1970.* Winchester, Ky.

Corgan, James X., and John T. Parks. 1979. *Natural Bridges of Tennessee.* Tennessee Division of Geology Bulletin 80.

Cumberland Falls State Park Program Guide. N.d. Corbin, Ky.

Gable, Dorothy. 1981. *James Litton: "The Wayfaring Stranger."* Oneida, Tenn.: Litton Historical Society.

Historic Rugby: English Village in the Tennessee Cumberlands. N.d. Rugby, Tenn.: Historic Rugby, Inc.

Howell, Benita J. 1981. *A Survey of Folklife along the Big South Fork of the Cumberland River.* Knoxville: University of Tennessee Department of Anthropology Report on Investigations no. 30.

Jones, DeWitt, and T. H. Watkins. 1976. *John Muir's America.* New York: Crown Publishers.

Muir, John. [1916] 1981. *A Thousand-Mile Walk To the Gulf.* Ed. William Frederic Badè, with foreword by Peter Jenkins. Boston: Houghton Mifflin.

Nicholson, Charles P., Jr, Letter to authors, June 21, 1988.

The Rugbeian. July 16, 1881.

Sanderson, Esther Sharp. 1974. *Scott County: Gem of the Cumberlands.* Huntsville, Tenn.: Esther Sharp Sanderson.

Smith, David Neal, "John Hawk Colorful Character in Early Big South Fork Era." *Scott County News*, December 15, 1988.

Smith, H. Clay. 1985. *Dusty Bits of the Forgotten Past.* Oneida, Tenn.: Scott County Historical Society.

U.S. Army Corps of Engineers. Nashville District. 1976. *Big South Fork National River and Recreation Area: Final Environmental Impact Study.*

_____. 1982. *Inventory and Evaluation of Architectural and Engineering Resources of the Big South Fork National River and Recreation Area, Tennessee and Kentucky.* Prepared by Environmental Consultants, Inc. Contract no. DACW62-81-C-0013.

_____. 1985. *A Wildlife Management Plan for the Big South Fork National River and Recreation Area.* Prepared by James R. Clark. Contract no. DACW62-82-C-0061.

_____. 1986. *Structural Treatment Plan for National Register Eligible Architectural Structures of the Big South Fork National River and Recreation Area.*

U.S. Department of Agriculture. Forest Service Southern Region. N.d. *Sheltowee Trace National Recreation Trail.*

U.S. Department of the Interior. National Park Service. 1992. *Some Is Better Getters.* Anne Malanka, ed. Unpublished manuscript, Headquarters, Big South Fork National River and Recreation Area, Oneida, Tenn.

U.S. Department of the Interior. National Park Service. 1981. *The History of the No Business and Station Camp Communities.* Prepared by Steve E. Humphrey. Photocopy of rough draft, Park Library, Headquarters, Big South Fork National River and Recreation Area, Oneida, Tenn.

_____. 1986. *Interpretive Content for the Blue Heron Area of the Big South Fork National River and Recreation Area.* Prepared by Demartin Marona Cranston Downes. Photocopy, Park Library, Headquarters, Big South Fork National River and Recreation Area, Oneida, Tenn.

Interviews

Bickford, Dan. August 1986–June 1988. Big South Fork National River and Recreation Area, Tenn.

Blevins, Conley. July, August 1992. Big South Fork National River and Recreation Area, Ky.

Blevins, Oscar and Ermon. May, June 1987. Allardt, Tenn.

Brandt, Robert. By telephone. August 1986-June 1988. Nashville, Tenn.

Brumm, Bill. August 1992. U.S. Forest Service, Stearns District Office, Ky.

Cannon, John. August 1991. Big South Fork National River and Recreation Area, Tenn.

Carroll, Bill. August 1986. Big South Fork National River and Recreation Area, Tenn.

Clark, Floyd. By telephone. October 1986. Oneida, Tenn.

Collier, Jack. August 1986–June 1988. Big South Fork National River and Recreation Area, Tenn.

Collins, Lisa. July, August 1992. Big South Fork National River and Recreation Area, Ky.

Cornelius, Ron. March 1987. Big South Fork National River and Recreation Area, Tenn.

Des Jean, Tom. November 1986. July–September 1992. Big South Fork National River and Recreation Area, Tenn.

Dickinson, Bill. August 1992. Big South Fork National River and Recreation Area, Tenn.

Duncan, Howard Ray. August 1986–June 1988. June–September 1992. Big South Fork National River and Recreation Area, Tenn.

Duncan, Sue. August 1992. Big South Fork National River and Recreation Area, Tenn.

Linder, Wally. June, July, August 1992. Big South Fork National River and Recreation Area, Tenn.

Lipp, Ann. August 1992. Big South Fork National River and Recreation Area, Ky.

Malanka, Anne. July, August 1992. Big South Fork National River and Recreation Area, Tenn.

Mason, John. By telephone. July 1987. Whitley City, Ky.

Murphy, Janice. August 1992. Big South Fork National River and Recreation Area, Ky.

Seven, Steve. August 1986 - June 1988. Big South Fork National River and Recreation Area, Tenn.

Smith, Herbert. By telephone. July 1987. Oneida, Tenn.

Smith, Steve. August 1986–June 1988. Big South Fork National River and Recreation Area, Tenn.

Spradlin, Etta. August 1992. Big South Fork National River and Recreation Area, Tenn.

Thorsen, Jim. October 1986–March 1988. Stearns Ranger District, Ky

Vial, Charlie. August 1986. Big South Fork National River and Recreation Area, Tenn.

Wiggins, Jim. August 1992. Big South Fork National River and Recreation Area, Tenn.

Wilson, Ron. August 1992. Big South Fork National River and Recreation Area, Tenn.

Maps

A Guide to the Gentlemens Swimming Hole Trail at Historic Rugby, Big South Fork National River and Recreation Area. 1991. National Park Service.

Big South Fork National River and Recreation Area. 1986. Tennessee Valley Authority Mapping Service Branch.

Bowater Trails: Special Maps and Information. N.d. N.p.

Cumberland River Basin, Big South Fork National River and Recreation Area, Kentucky and Tennessee. N.d. U.S. Army Engineer District, Nashville.

Yahoo Falls Scenic Area, Big South Fork National River and Recreation Area. N.d. N.p.

Index

accommodations, 13–14
Alf Dump, 96
Alum Ford Campground, 13, 167, 203
archeological sites, 21
arches, 3
—Buffalo Arch, 191
—Gobblers Arch, 194
—Koger Arch, 201
—Needle Arch, 67–68
—Split Bow Arch, 148
—Twin Arches, 3, 69, 70–75,
—Yahoo Arch, 169

Bandy Creek, 25, 42, 52–53
Bandy Creek Campground and Visitor
    Center, 11–13, 25
bears, 6, 7
Beaty, Martin, 151, 176
Betty Branch, 135
bicycle trails, 17
Big Branch, 132, 134
Big Creek, 205
Big Island, 133
Big South Fork National River and
    Recreation Area, 9, 11–12, 51
Big South Fork River, 1, 11, 167
Big South Fork Scenic Railway, 13, 25,
    145, 149
Big Tide of '29, 89
Bill Branch, 94
Black House Branch, 51
Blevins, Clara Sue, 44–45
Blevins, Conley, 154

Blevins, Ermon, 40
Blevins, George, 44
Blevins, Jack, 78
Blevins, Jacob, 41, 45
Blevins, Jake, 45, 76
Blevins, Rev. John, 40
Blevins, Jonathan, 40, 45, 49
Blevins, Katie, 45
Blevins, Lora, 44
Blevins, Maynard, 154
Blevins, Oscar, 40–41
Blevins, Viannah, 45, 76
Blue Heron Campground and Visitor
    Complex, 12–13, 149, 153
Blue Heron Coal Tipple (trestle) 153, 180
Boone, Daniel, 186
Bowater Company, 108–9
Boy Scout camp, 154
Burke, Hudson, 133
Burke, Jonathan, 132
Burkes Branch, 134
Burkes Knob, 135
Burnt Mill Bridge, 102

camping, 13–14, 20–21
canoeing, 14, 92, 102
cemeteries, 21
—Blevins (Station Camp Creek), 49
—Hattie Blevins, 80
—Katie Blevins, 40, 44
—King, 177
—Laurel Dale, 118
—Waters, 179

Charit Creek, 50, 77–78
Charit Creek Lodge, 14, 50, 77–78
Chief Blackfish, 186
Chief Doublehead, 159
chimney rocks, 123, 135
Civil War, 8, 77, 132, 133
Civilian Conservation Corps (CCC), 143, 189
Clara Sue Blevins Farm, 40, 44–45
Clear Fork River, 1, 102–4, 117–19
Cotton Patch Shelter, 166, 203
Cracks-in-the-Rock, 149, 152
Cumberland Falls State Park, 14, 211–12
Cumberland River, 210–12

Daniel Boone National Forest, 13, 145, 191–92, 205
Devils Creek, 151, 181
Difficulty Creek, 174
Divide Road, 123, 138, 191
Dry Creek, 134
Duncan Hollow, 127

East Rim Road, 98

the Falls. *See* rapids: Angel Falls
Fall Branch, 29–30, 33, 37, 96–97, 125
farming, 5, 7–8, 36, 41–42
fishing, 15–16, 89, 94
ford. *See* Big Island, Leatherwood Ford, Station Camp Crossing
forest, 3–4, 42

geology, 2–3
Gragg, G. W., 85
Grassy Fork Creek, 182–83, 201–2
Great Meadows Campground, 13, 192
Gregory, Hiram, 159

Harrow Road Cafe, 14
Harvey Branch, 131
Hemlock Grove Picnic Area, 13, 192, 195
hiking trails, 17–18; *see also* Kentucky Trails; Tennessee Trails
Historic Rugby, 14, 25, 117
Honey Creek, 112–15
horse trails, 16
Hughes, Thomas, 117
hunting, 5, 19; regulations, 15–16; *see also* longhunters; *see also* trapping

Indian Creek, 209, 210
Indian trails, 7, 85, 133
Indians
—Cherokee, 7, 159
—Paleo-Indians, 7, 85
—Shawnee, 186
—Yamacraw, 163

Jakes Place, 69, 76
John Litton Cabin, 130–31
John Litton/General Slaven Farm, 36–37
the Jumps. *See* rapids: Devils Jump

Kentucky Dept. of Fish and Wildlife Resources, 15
Kentucky Trails, 145–46
—Bear Creek Overlook, 146
—Blue Heron Loop, 149–56
—Catawba Overlook and Big Spring Falls, 156–58
—Gobblers Arch, 194–95
—Kentucky-John Muir Connector, 134, 174, 184–85
—Kentucky Trail, 145, 171–83, 184, 202
—Mark Branch Loop, 195–96
—Sheltowee Trace, 17, 145–46, 161, 163, 173, 186–212

—Split Bow Arch, 147–48
—Yahoo Falls, 159–61
—Yamacraw-Yahoo Loop, 145, 163–70,
   203

Lake Cumberland, 1, 161, 167
Laurel Branch, 155
Laurel Crossing Branch, 177
Laurel Fork Creek, 46–49, 51, 54–55,
   60–62, 129
Leatherwood Ford, 85
Leatherwood Ford Bridge (TN 297), 85
Leatherwood Ford Bridge (wooden), 34,
   96, 125
Lick Creek, 165, 170, 203
Litton, Elvira Doss, 36, 45
Litton, James, 36
Litton, John, 36, 45, 130
logging, 4, 8–9, 30, 87–89, 96
Lone Cliff Branch, 175
longhunters, 7, 78

M. I. Thompson Lumber Company, 142
Mark Branch, 192–94, 195–96
Massey Branch, 80–82, 138, 191
mining, 4, 8–9, 89, 92, 94, 154–55, 179,
   180; see also niter mining
—Anderson mine, 92
—Blue Heron Coal Tipple, 153
—Blue Heron Mine, 152–53
—John Smith Mine Site, 94
mountain biking, 17
Muir, John, 121

National Park Service, 11, 12, 14, 191–
   92
Negro Creek, 166, 169–70, 203
New River, 1
New River Bridge, 102

niter mining, 75, 133
No Business Community, 133–34
No Business Creek, 134
North Fall Branch, 37
North White Oak Creek, 89, 98, 101

O & W Railroad, 89, 121, 123, 124
O & W Railroad Bridge (trestle), 89,
   121, 123
Oil Well Branch, 176
Oscar Blevins Farm, 39–42
overlooks
—Angel Falls Overlook, 31, 93, 97
—Bear Creek Overlook, 147
—Blue Heron Tipple Overlook, 152
—Catawba Overlook, 156, 157
—Devils Jump Overlook, 150–51
—East Rim Overlook, 98
—Honey Creek Overlook, 109, 111, 115
—John Muir Overlook, 137
—Leatherwood Loop Overlook, 90, 100
—Sunset Overlook, 101
—Split Bow Arch Overlook, 147, 148
—Thompson Overlook, 143, 189
—Yahoo Falls, overlooks, 161

Parch Corn Creek, 130, 131
Parch Corn Creek Hunting Camp, 78; see
   also Charit Creek Lodge
Payne, Poley, 52
Pickett State Forest, 9, 144, 194
Pickett State Park, 9, 14, 140–44, 187
Pigeon Roost Branch, 209
Pitch Branch, 210
Princess Cornblossom, 159, 161
Puncheon Camp Branch, 197

rafting. See canoeing
Railroad Fork Branch, 208

rapids, 1, 8, 14, 111
—Angel Fall, 91, 92–93
—Bandy Creek-Echo Rock, 87, 90, 124
—Devils Jump, 11, 93, 150–52, 154, 157
—Double Falls, 14
—the Ell, 14
—Honey Creek, 111
—O & W, 89
—Pitch, 210
—Slick Shoals, 211
—Washing Machine, 14
Reed, J. R., 87
Roaring Paunch Creek, 181
Roaring Rock Cataract, 161, 168
Rock Creek, 82–84, 139–40, 141–42, 173, 182–83, 190–92, 202
rockhouse, 3, 29, 37, 57–59
—Indian Rockhouse (Honey Creek), 113
—Indian Rock House (Slave Falls Loop), 60, 65
—Muleshoe Rockshelter, 42
—Yahoo Falls, 159–61
Rough Shoals Branch, 95
Rugby. See Historic Rugby
rules and regulations (backcountry camping), 20–21

safety, 18–20
safety zones, 16, 19
Sand Branch, 87, 124
sawmills, 63, 96
Scott State Forest, 34–35
shoals. See rapids
Simpson, Joe, 77, 78
Slaven, Dewey, 136
Slaven, Elisha, 136
Slaven, General, 34, 37
Smith, Alfred, 31
Smith, Archie, 31

Smith, Elva, 31
Smith, Herbert, 31
Smith, John, 93–95
Southern Railroad, 8, 89, 124
Spring Branch, 199
Station Camp Community, 48, 95, 130
Station Camp Creek, 49–50, 78, 129
Station Camp Crossing (low-water ford), 95, 123, 129–30
Station Camp Road, 123
Stearns Coal and Lumber Company, 8–9, 41, 92, 145, 208
Stearns logging railroad, 82, 140, 190
Stearns Ranger District (U.S. Forest Service), 177, 195
swimming, 13, 19, 85, 119

Tackett boys, 77
Tackett Creek, 136
Tennessee Stave and Lumber Company, 92
Tennessee Trails, 25
—Angel Falls, 91–93
—Angel Falls Overlook, 31, 33, 95–97, 126
—Bandy Creek Campground (West Entrance), 52–54
—Bandy Creek Campground Loop, 27
—Big Island Option, 133–34, 184
—Oscar Blevins Farm Loop, 39–43, 53–54
—Burnt Mill Bridge Loop, 102–5, 106
—Charit Creek Lodge (trailhead on Fork Ridge Road), 74, 50–51
—Charit Creek Lodge via Slave Falls, 66–69
—East Rim Overlook, 98
—Gentlemens Swimming Hole, 117–18
—Grand Gap Loop, 27–34, 97, 125–28

—Hidden Passage, 140, 143–44, 187, 188
—Honey Creek Loop, 107–15
—Jacks Ridge via Laurel Fork Creek, 54–55
—John Litton/General Slaven Farm Loop, 34–38
—John Muir Spur, 106
—John Muir Trail, 17, 30–32, 82–83, 87–89, 96–97, 106, 121–44, 184, 190–91
—Laurel Fork Loop, 46–51
—Leatherwood Loop, 90–91, 100
—Leatherwood Loop Overlook, 100
—Meeting of the Waters, 117–19
—Middle Creek Loop, 56–62
—O & W Bridge, 87–89
—Rock Creek Loop, 80–84, 138–40
—Rock Creek (Pickett State Forest), 138–40, 190
—Slave Falls Loop, 63–66
—Station Camp Crossing, 93–95
—Sunset Overlook, 101
—Twin Arches, 70–72
—Twin Arches Loop, 68–69, 73–79
—West Entrance Trailhead via Laurel Fork Creek, 59–62
Tennessee Wildlife Resource Agency, 15
Thompson Creek, 142–44, 190
trailheads, 23
—Bandy Creek Campground, 25, 27, 34, 38, 44
—Bear Creek Scenic Area, 145, 146
—Blue Heron Loop, 149
—Burnt Mill Bridge, 102
—Charit Creek Lodge Hiking, 14, 50, 51
—East Rim Overlook, 98
—Flat Rock, 187, 206
—Gentlemens Swimming Hole, 117, 118
—Honey Creek Loop, 107, 115

—Jacks Ridge, 40, 46, 55
—Leatherwood Ford, 85, 90, 125
—Leatherwood Loop, 98, 100
—Ledbetter, 171, 173, 177
—Middle Creek, 56, 59
—O & W Bridge, 121, 123
—Peters Mountain, 171, 173, 196–97
—Rock Creek Loop, 80
—Sawmill, 63, 66
—Twin Arches, 70, 74
—West Entrance, 52, 54, 62
—Yahoo Falls Scenic Area, 159
—Yamacraw-Yahoo, 163, 203
trapping, 52
Tree Top Rock, 114, 115
Troublesome Creek, 175–76
Troxell, Big Jake, 159
Troxell, Little Jake, 161

U. S. Army Corps of Engineers, 11, 85
U. S. Forest Service, 13, 191–92

waterfalls, 1, 67
—Big Spring Falls, 156, 157, 179
—Boulder House Falls, 114
—Crystal Falls, 144, 187
—Cumberland Falls, 212
—Dick Gap Falls, 156, 157, 180
—Double Falls, 143, 189
—Fall Branch Falls, 29, 37
—Hide-Out Falls, 111, 112
—Honey Creek Falls, 115
—Ice Castle Falls, 114
—Lick Creek Falls, 165,
—Mark Branch Falls, 196,
—Moonshine Falls, 110
—Princess Falls, 165, 203
—Slave Falls, 66, 67, 68
—Yahoo Falls, 168, 203

Watson Branch, 175
White Oak Creek, 119
wildlife, 5–6, 20, 225–31
Wilson Ridge, 173, 201
Work Progress Administration (WPA),
  85

Yahoo Creek, 161, 168, 203
Yahoo Falls Picnic Area, 161, 167, 168,
  203
Yamacraw Bridge (KY 92), 163, 183, 202
Yamacraw Bridge (trestle), 183, 202
York, Alvin C., 25, 144